PRESTON'S BOOK-KEEPING.

DISTRICT SCHOOL BOOK-KEEPING. Quarto stitched. An excellent work for beginners........ 31

SINGLE ENTRY BOOK-KEEPING. 8vo........ 63

BOOK-KEEPING, BY SINGLE AND DOUBLE ENTRY. A complete system, with many valuable Business Forms, and a Treatise on Equation of Payments. 8vo........ $1 13

These works are by LYMAN PRESTON, for many years a teacher of the science, as well as a practical book-keeper. They are particularly valuable for the clearness and simplicity of the lessons, and can be readily understood without the aid of a teacher.

COFFIN'S CONIC SECTIONS.

ELEMENTS OF CONIC SECTIONS AND ANALYTICAL GEOMETRY. By PROF. COFFIN, of Lafayette College, Pa. 8vo........ 1 00

KEY TO COFFIN'S ANALYTICAL GEOMETRY........ 50

This treatise is introduced into the first colleges of the country, and is approved by our leading Professors, as Loomis, Everhart, Fouché, Stevens, A. W. Smith, &c.

DAY'S MATHEMATICS.

A COURSE OF MATHEMATICS, containing the principles of Plane Trigonometry, Mensuration, Navigation, and Surveying. By President DAY, of Yale College. 8vo........ 2 00

PHILOSOPHY AND ASTRONOMY.

OLMSTED'S RUDIMENTS OF NATURAL PHILOSOPHY AND ASTRONOMY. This work is intended to be used in District and Common Schools, where merely the elements of the sciences are taught, and also as a preparatory class-book for the younger scholars in Academies; for these purposes it is admirably adapted. 18mo. Illustrated by numerous engravings........ 56

OLMSTED'S SCHOOL ASTRONOMY. A compendium of Astronomy for the use of pupils in the higher classes of Common Schools and in Academies. Revised edition. 12mo........ 75

OLMSTED'S COLLEGE ASTRONOMY. 8vo., sheep........ 2 00

OLMSTED'S COLLEGE PHILOSOPHY. 8vo., sheep........ 3 00

These works were prepared by Prof. Olmsted for the use of his classes in Yale College, and are acknowledged to be the best works on the subject yet before the public; the author's name is, in itself, a sufficient guaranty of their excellence.

MASON'S PRACTICAL ASTRONOMY. 8vo........ 1 25

This work, by the late E. P. Mason, is regarded by competent judges as the best work extant on the subject of Practical Astronomy.

COFFIN'S ECLIPSES.

SOLAR AND LUNAR ECLIPSES, familiarly illustrated and explained, with the method of calculating them, as taught in the New England Colleges. By JAMES H. COFFIN, A.M. 8vo........ 1 25

INQUIRIES

CONCERNING

THE INTELLECTUAL POWERS,

AND

THE INVESTIGATION OF TRUTH.

BY JOHN ABERCROMBIE, M.D. F.R.S.

Fellow of the Royal College of Physicians in Edinburgh, &c., and First Physician to His Majesty in Scotland.

WITH ADDITIONS AND EXPLANATIONS TO ADAPT THE WORK TO THE USE OF SCHOOLS AND ACADEMIES,

BY JACOB ABBOTT.

REVISED EDITION.

NEW YORK:
COLLINS & BROTHER,
NO. 82 WARREN STREET.
1859.

PREFACE.

The text of the following work, strictly speaking, is Dr. Abercrombie's treatise on the Human Mind, entire. In connection with this treatise, however, the original edition has two articles attached to it by the author, for the sole benefit of the class whom he was addressing, viz. a class of medical students. The first to which we refer is a history of the science of Intellectual Philosophy, prefixed to the work ; the second, an admirable set of directions, to guide medical students in their professional inquiries. These treatises do not of necessity constitute a part of a treatise on the Philosophy of Mind. They are accordingly omitted in this edition. What, in the editor's opinion, constitutes the treatise itself, is published entire, without alterations or omissions, the editor holding his author's language sacred. The additions which have been made are intended, not to supply any supposed deficiencies in the original, but simply to adapt it to a purpose for which the book is, in the main, admirably suited : they are intended as nearly as was possible to be such additional explanations as the editor conceived the author would himself have made, if he had had in view, whilst preparing the book, the purpose to which it is now applied.

The practice of studying such a work as this by formal questions, the answer to which pupils commit to memory cannot be too severely censured. There seemed, however to be something necessary as a guide to the contents of the page, both for the pupil in reviewing the lesson, and for the teacher at the recitation. That minute and familiar acquaintance, not only with the doctrines taught in the lesson, but with the particular contents of every page and paragraph, so essential in enabling the teacher to ask his questions with fluency, very few teachers have the time to secure. The editor has accordingly added an analysis of the page in the margin. This analysis is given sometimes in questions, and sometimes in topics or titles, which can easily be put by the teacher into the form of questions if he pleases; or, what will perhaps be better, they can, at the recitation, be given to the pupil as topics, on which he is to state in substance the sentiments of the author.

In regard to the value of Dr. Abercrombie's treatise, there is, and there can be, but one opinion. Its useful tendency is most decided, both in making the pupil acquainted with his powers, and in guiding him to the most efficient and successful use of them. The effect of a proper study of this work must be highly salutary upon every mind brought under its influence; and it is a kind of effect which is exactly suited to guard against the peculiar dangers of the age.

Boston, September, 1833.

CONTENTS.

PART I.

OF THE NATURE AND EXTENT OF OUR KNOWLEDGE OF MIND.

2*

PART II.

OF THE ORIGIN OF OUR KNOWLEDGE OF FACTS RELATING BOTH TO MATTER AND MIND.

SECTION I.

SENSATION AND PERCEPTION.

SECTION II.

CONSCIOUSNESS AND REFLECTION.

SECTION III.

TESTIMONY.

PART III.

OF THE INTELLECTUAL OPERATIONS.

SECTION I.

MEMORY.

SECTION II.

ABSTRACTION.

SECTION III.

IMAGINATION.

SECTION IV.

REASON OR JUDGMENT.

§ I.—OF THE USE OF REASON IN THE INVESTIGATION OF TRUTH.

---

§ II.—OF THE USE OF REASON IN CORRECTING THE IMPRESSIONS OF THE MIND IN REGARD TO EXTERNAL THINGS.

PART IV.

VIEW OF THE QUALITIES AND ACQUIREMENTS WHICH CONSTITUTE A WELL REGULATED MIND.

INTRODUCTION.

METHOD OF USING THE BOOK.

TO BE CAREFULLY STUDIED BY THE PUPILS AS THEIR FIRST LESSON

THE design of the study of Intellectual Philosophy is not merely, as in the case of most other studies, the acquisition of *knowledge*. Something far more important, and far more difficult to attain, is in view. In the study of Chemistry, History, Geography, and other similar sciences, the main object is to obtain information—to become acquainted with facts. But although the science of Mind does indeed present to view a most valuable and interesting class of facts, it is not merely with reference to these that the study is pursued. This science aims at a higher object. It is intended to introduce the pupil to a new range of thought, and to bring out into action, and consequently into more full development, the mental faculties. It is its aim to exercise and strengthen the thinking and reasoning powers,—to enable the mind to grasp abstruse and perplexing subjects,—to think clearly and to reason correctly, in regard to truths that lie in those depths which the senses cannot explore.

Design of the study, what? Compared with other studies. What is its chief aim?

Of course, the study of Intellectual Philosophy is not and cannot be an easy one. Its very difficulty is one source of the benefit to be derived from it; for it is by encountering and overcoming this difficulty, that intellectual strength is acquired. In Gymnastics, the exertion necessary to perform the feats is the very means by which the advantage is secured, and it is to require this exertion that the whole apparatus is contrived. Now mathematical and metaphysical studies are intended as a sort of intellectual gymnastics, in which the tasks ought indeed to be brought fairly within the powers of the pupil, but they ought nearly to equal those powers, so as to call them into active and vigorous exercise, or the end will be lost. If, therefore, the writer of a treatise on such a subject comes down so completely to the level of the young as to make the study mere light reading, he fails entirely of accomplishing what ought to be his highest aim. He destroys the difficulty and the advantage together. It is indeed true that a very useful book may be written for children, with the design of merely *giving them information* on some subjects connected with the structure of their minds. It might be entertaining, and to a considerable degree instructive, but it would answer few of the important purposes which ought to be in view, in the introduction of such a study into literary institutions. It would not develop the reasoning or thinking powers. It would awaken no new intellectual effort.

Such being the nature of this study, it is plain that it ought not to be commenced by any pupil without a proper understanding of its object and design. Such an understanding is essential. That it may come more distinctly and definitely before the mind, I propose to enumerate the qualifications which each individual should see that he possesses, before he commences the study of this work.

The study difficult. Why? Gymnastics. Difference between reading and study in this subject.

1. *Ability to understand the language of the work.* It is not a child's book. It was written by a man, and was intended to be read by men. The editor has made no effort to alter it in this respect, so that the book stands on a level, as to its style and language, with the great mass of books intended to influence and interest the mature. It ought to be so; for to be able to understand such writing is necessary for all, and if the pupil is far enough advanced in his education to study metaphysics, it is high time for him to be habituated to it. Let no pupil therefore, after he is fairly engaged in the study, complain that he cannot understand the lessons. This is a point which ought to be settled before he begins.

Take for instance the following passage, which may perhaps be considered as a fair specimen. Let the pupil read it attentively, and see whether or not he can fully understand it.

"There is a class of intellectual habits directly the reverse of those now referred to; namely, habits of inattention, by which the mind, long unaccustomed to have the attention steadily directed to any important object, becomes frivolous and absent, or lost amid its own waking dreams. A mind in this condition becomes incapable of following a train of reasoning, and even of observing facts with accuracy and tracing their relations. Hence nothing is more opposed to the cultivation of intellectual character; and when such a person attempts to reason, or to follow out a course of investigation, he falls into slight and partial views, unsound deductions, and frivolous arguments. This state of mind, therefore, ought to be carefully guarded against in the young, as, when it is once established, it can be removed only by a long and laborious effort, and after a certain period of life is probably irremediable.

"In rude and savage life remarkable examples occur of the effect of habits of minute attention to those circumstances to which the mind is intensely directed by their relation to the safety or advantage of the observer. The American

---

First qualification—what? Language of the book. Mode of ascertaining the pupil's ability to understand it. Substance of the passage quoted—what?

hunter finds his way in the trackless forests by attention to minute appearances in the trees, which indicate to him the points of the compass. He traces the progress of his enemies or his friends by the marks of their footsteps; and judges of their numbers, their haltings, their employments, by circumstances which would entirely escape the observation of persons unaccustomed to a mode of life requiring such exercises of attention. Numerous examples of this kind are mentioned by travellers, particularly among the original natives of America."

The pupil may read as attentively as he pleases. He may make use of a dictionary, or any other similar help. He may make occasional inquiries of a friend; but if he cannot, with such assistance, really understand the train of thought presented in such a passage, and give a tolerable account of it to his teacher, he had better for the present postpone the study of Intellectual Philosophy: his mind is too immature.

II. *Mental cultivation enough to be interested in the subject of the work.* The subjects discussed, and the views presented, are of such a nature, that the undisciplined can take no interest in them. They cannot appreciate them. Unless the mind has made considerable progress in its development, and in its attainments in other branches, and unless it has, in some degree, formed habits of patient attention, it must fail in the attempt to penetrate such a subject as this. The pupil, in such a case, after going a little way, will say the book is dull and dry. He will attribute to the study, or to the mode in which it is treated. a failure, which really results from his own deficiency. He ought to reflect when tempted to make this charge, that it cannot be possible that the study is, in itself, uninteresting. This treatise of Dr. Abercrombie's has been bought and read with avidity by tens of thousands in Great Britain and America, who could have been led to it by no motive

---

Second qualification. Consequences of commencing the study without it. The stud really interesting: how proved to be so.

whatever, but the strong interest which the subject inspires. They, therefore, who are not interested in it, after making faithful efforts, fail of being so because their minds are not yet prepared to appreciate what they read; and by complaining of the dryness or dullness of the book, they are really exposing their own incompetency to enter into the spirit of it. The teacher ought to take care that his pupils do not commence the work, until they are capable of feeling the interest which it is calculated to awaken.

III. *A willingness to give to the subject the severe, patient, and persevering study which it demands.* Some will wish to take up such a branch merely for the sake of having something new. Others because their vanity is flattered by the idea that they are studying Philosophy. Others still, because they wish for the honor of being in a class with certain individuals known as good scholars. Beginning with such ideas and motives, will only lead to disappointment and failure. The pupil ought to approach this subject with a distinct understanding that though it is full of interest, it will be full of difficulty; that it will try, to the utmost, his powers; and that the pleasure which he is to seek in the pursuit of it, is the enjoyment of high intellectual effort,—the interest of encountering and overcoming difficulties,—and opening to himself a new field of knowledge, and a new scope for the exercise of his powers.

I come now to describe a method of studying and reciting the lessons in such a work as this. I say *a* method, because it is only meant to be proposed for adoption in cases where another or a better one is not at hand. Experienced and skilful teachers have their own modes of conducting such studies, and the recitations connected with them, with which there ought to

---

Complaints of its dullness show what? Third qualification. Wrong motives for commencing the study. Proper views of it. Method of studying—why proposed.

be no interference. The plan about to be proposed may, however, be of use in assisting teachers who are, for the first time, introducing this study to their schools; and the principles on which it is based are well worthy the attention of every pupil who is about to commence this study.

1. When you sit down to the study of a lesson in this work, be careful to be free from interruption, and to have such a period of time before you, to be occupied in the work, as will give you the opportunity really to enter into it. Then banish other thoughts entirely from the mind, and remove yourself as far as possible from other objects of interest or sources of interruption. The habit into which many young persons allow themselves to fall, of studying lessons in fragments of time, having the book, perhaps, for some time before them, but allowing their attention to be continually diverted from their pursuit, will only lead to superficial and utterly useless attainments. It is destructive to all those habits of mind necessary for success in any important intellectual pursuit. It is especially injurious in such a study as this. Intellectual Philosophy is emphatically the *science of thought*, and nothing effectual can be done in it without patient, continued, and solitary study.

2. Ascertain before you commence any lesson what place it occupies in the general plan of the book, with which, at the outset, you should become very thoroughly acquainted. Nothing promotes so much the formation of logical and systematic habits of mind, and nothing so effectually assists the memory, in regard to what any particular work contains, as the keeping constantly in view the *general plan* of the book; looking at it as a *whole*, and understanding distinctly, not merely each truth, or system of truths brought to view, but the place which it occupies in the general design.

First direction. A common but faulty mode of studying described. Its effects—what? Second direction. Effects of this practice.

3. This preparation being made, you are prepared to read the lesson, which should be done, the first time, with great attention and care, and with especial effort to understand the connection between each sentence and paragraph, and those which precede and follow it. It should always be borne in mind, that treatises on such subjects as these, present trains of thought and reasoning, not mere detached ideas and sentences. Every remark, therefore, should be examined, not by itself, but in its connections. This should be especially observed in regard to the anecdotes and illustrations, with which the work abounds. The *bearing* of each one on the subject should be very carefully studied. They are all intended to prove some point, or to illustrate some position. After reading such narratives, then, you should not only take care to understand it as a story, but should ask yourself such questions as these: "Why is the story introduced here? What does the author mean to prove by it? What principle does it illustrate?"

There is, for example, in the section on Memory, a story of the author's seeing the wife of one of his patients, but he could not think who it was, until he accidentally passed a cottage where he had attended the patient, when all the circumstances came to his mind. This is a very simple story to read and remember, *merely as a story*. But to do that alone is only light reading; it is not *study* at all, far less the study of the Philosophy of Mind. But if you inquire what the narrative is designed to illustrate, by looking back a paragraph or two, you will see that the subject is Memory, as affected by Local Association, and that this incident is intended to show how events were recalled to the memory of the author, by his coming in sight of a cottage *with which they were strongly associated*, although all his direct efforts failed to bring them to mind.

Third direction. Connections of the passage. Anecdotes and illustrations, how to be studied? Example. Mode of studying it? Difference between reading and study.

Thus it illustrates a principle; and careful effort to discover and clearly to understand the principles thus illustrated, is what constitutes the difference between merely reading a story book, and studying the Philosophy of Mind.

The pupil, too, should avail himself of collateral helps in understanding the lesson. Every geographical, or historical, or personal allusion should be examined with the help of the proper books. If a distinguished individual is mentioned, find the account of his life in a biographical dictionary. If a place is named, seek it on the map. There is one other direction which I am sorry to say it is absolutely necessary to mention. Look out all the words, whose meaning you do not distinctly and fully understand, in a dictionary. Strange as it may seem, in nine cases out of ten, a pupil in school will find in his lesson a sentence containing words he does not understand, and, perplexing himself some minutes with it in vain, he will go to his recitation in ignorance of its meaning, as if he never had heard of such a contrivance as a dictionary. Now the habit of seeking from other books explanations and assistance in regard to your studies is of incalculable value. It will cause you some additional trouble, but it will multiply, many fold, your interest and success.

4. After having thus read, with minute and critical attention, the portion assigned, the pupil should next take a cursory review of it, by glancing the eye over the paragraphs, noticing the heads, and the questions or topics in the margin, for the purpose of taking in, as it were, a view of the passage as a whole. The order of discussion which the author adopts, and the regular manner in which the several steps of an argument, or the several applications of a principle, succeed one another, should be carefully observed. There are the same reasons for doing this, in regard to any particular chapter, as in regard to the whole work. The connec-

---

Collateral helps. Examples of this. Use of dictionary. Fourth direction. Review of the lesson.

tion, too, between the passage which constitutes the lesson, and the rest of the book, i. e. the place which it occupies in the plan of the author, should be brought to mind again. You thus classify and arrange, in your own mind, what is learned, and not only fix it more firmly, but you are acquiring logical habits of mind, which will be of lasting and incalculable value.

5. You will thus have acquired a thorough knowledge of the lesson, but this is by no means all that is necessary. You must learn to recite it. That is, you must learn to express, in your own language, the ideas you have thus acquired. This is a distinct and an important point. Nothing is more common than for pupils to say, when they attempt to recite in such a study as this, "I know the answer, but I cannot express it;" as if the power to express was not as important as the ability to understand.

The pupil then must make special preparation for this part of his duty, that is, for expressing in his own language the thoughts and principles of the author. The best way, perhaps, of making this preparation, is to go over the lesson, looking only at the topics in the margin, and repeating aloud, or in a whisper, or in thought, the substance of what is stated under each. Be careful that what you say makes complete and perfect sense of itself, that it is expressed in clear and natural language, and that it is a full exposition of the author's meaning.

Such a study as this ought not to be recited by mere question and answer. Whenever the subject will allow, it is better for the teacher to give out a subject or topic, on which the pupil may express the sentiments of the writer. This is altogether the pleasantest, as well as the most useful mode of recitation. Those unaccustomed to it will, of course, find a little difficulty at first. But the very effort to surmount this difficulty will be as useful in developing and strengthening the intellectual powers, as any other effort which the study requires.

Connections of the lesson. Fifth direction. Learning to recite. What implied in this. Common excuse. Preparation—how to be made. Mode of questioning

You should go over the lesson, then, for the purpose of reciting it by yourself as it were, by looking at the marginal titles, one by one, and distinctly stating to yourself the substance of the author's views upon each. If this preparation is made, and if the recitation is conducted on the same principles, the pupils will soon find themselves making very perceptible and rapid progress in that most important art, viz. expressing their sentiments with fluency, distinctness, and promptitude.

It will be evident, from what is said above, that the pupil ought not to commit to memory the language of the author. This practice may indeed be useful in strengthening the memory, and in some other ways, but very far higher objects ought to be in view in studying such a work as this, which will be far better attained by the pupils depending entirely on themselves for the language in which they express their ideas. To illustrate distinctly the mode of recitation intended, I will give a specimen. The following passage will serve as text.

"Memory is very much influenced by ATTENTION, or a full and distinct perception of the fact or object, with a view to its being remembered; and by the perception being kept before the mind, in this distinct manner, for a certain time. The distinct recollection of the fact, in such cases, is generally in proportion to the intensity with which it has been contemplated; and this is also very much strengthened by its being repeatedly brought before the mind. Most people, accordingly, have experienced that a statement is more strongly impressed upon the memory by being several times repeated to others. It is on the same principle that memory is greatly assisted by writing down the object of our knowledge, especially if this be done in a distinct and systematic manner. A subject also is more distinctly conceived, and more correctly remembered, after we have instructed another person in it. Such exercises are not strictly to be considered as helps to the memory, but as excitements to attention; and as thus leading to that clear and full com-

Advantage of this mode. Committing to memory.

prehension of the subject which is required for the distinct remembrance of it.

"It is familiar to every one that there are great differences in memory, both in respect to the facility of acquirement and the power of retention. In the former, there appear to be original differences, but a great deal also depends upon habit. In the power of retention much depends, as we shall afterwards see, upon the habit of correct association; but, besides this, there are facts which seem to show a singular connection with the manner in which the acquisition was made. The following fact was communicated to me by an able and intelligent friend, who heard it from the individual to whom it relates. A distinguished theatrical performer, in consequence of the sudden illness of another actor, had occasion to prepare himself, on very short notice, for a part which was entirely new to him; and the part was long and rather difficult. He acquired it in a very short time, and went through it with perfect accuracy, but immediately after the performance forgot every word of it."

The titles or topics in the margin, attached to this passage, are the following: *Attention—Means of securing it—Differences in memory—Illustration.* Now in hearing a recitation from it, the teacher will ordinarily be guided by, but not confined to them, as you will see exemplified in the following dialogue. The pupil, too, will use his own language, which will vary very considerably from that of the author, as will be perceived by a comparison.

Teacher. The first topic is attention.

First Pupil. The author says that it consists in keeping the object distinctly before the mind, for a certain time, so that it may make a strong impression. It assists very much in enabling us to remember it afterwards.

Teacher. The best means of confining the attention to any object?

The marginal titles how to be used? Language of the pupil in recitation.

Second Pupil. There are several modes; one is by repeating the thing several times to other persons; another is, by writing an account of it, especially if it is done systematically; a third, endeavoring to *explain* it to others.

Teacher. How is it these methods produce the effect?

Second Pupil. They help us to obtain clear and distinct ideas, and they fix the attention for some time on the subject.

Teacher. What does he say of differences in memory?

Third Pupil. There is a great difference in different individuals; in some cases it is natural, and in others acquired.

Teacher. A story is told here to illustrate this subject.

Fourth Pupil. An actor was obliged to learn a part once at a very short notice, and by making a great effort he succeeded, and went through it once, but he forgot it immediately afterwards.

Teacher. What is the precise point which this fact is intended to illustrate?

Fourth Pupil. I did not clearly understand.

6. After the class has, in this thorough manner, gone through with one of the divisions of the book, they should pause, to review it; and the best, as well as the pleasantest mode of conducting a review, is to assign to the class some written exercises on the portion to be thus re-examined. These exercises may be of various kinds; I shall, however, mention only two.

(1.) An abstract of the chapter to be reviewed; that is, a brief exposition, in writing, of the plan of the chapter, with the substance of the writer's views on each head. Such an abstract, though it will require some labor at first, will be, with a little practice, a pleasant

* Sixth direction. Review—how to be conducted. First method—what? Its uses.

exercise; and perhaps there is nothing which so effectually assists in digesting the knowledge which the pupil has obtained, and in fixing it indelibly upon the mind, and nothing is so conducive to accurate logical habits of thought, as this writing an analysis of a scientific work. It may be very brief, and elliptical in its style; its logical accuracy is the main point to be secured. By devoting a single exercise at the end of each section to such an exercise, a class can go on regularly through the book, and, with very little delay, make an abstract of the whole.

(2.) Writing additional illustrations of the principles brought to view,—illustrations furnished either by the experience or observation of the pupil, or by what he has read in books. For example, in the chapter on dreaming, the author enumerates four or five sources of the ideas which come to the mind in dreams. Now the teacher might, after finishing that chapter, require each one of the class, for the next exercise, to write an account of a dream, and to state at the end of it to which of the classes it is to be referred. Nothing could more effectually familiarize the mind of the pupil with the principles which the chapter contains than such an exercise. In many cases, perhaps in nearly all, the dreams would be complex, and must be analyzed, and the several parts separately assigned. The effect of such an effort is obvious.

There are multitudes of other subjects discussed in the work, equally suitable for this purpose. Wherever anecdotes are told, illustrating the laws of the human mind, the pupil can add others; for these laws are the same in all minds, and are constantly in operation. Writing these additional illustrations, especially if they are derived from your own experience, will have another most powerful effect. They will turn your attention within, and accustom you to watch the operations, and

---

Style and manner. Second mode. Example. Advantages of it. Common misunderstanding in regard to the nature of this study

study the laws of your own minds. Many pupils do not seem to understand that it is the powers and movements of the immaterial principle within their own bosoms, which are the objects of investigation in such a science. Because illustrations are drawn from the histories of men with strange names, who lived in other countries, and a half a century ago, they seem insensibly to imbibe the idea, that it is the philosophy of *these men's* minds which they are studying, not their own. Now the fact is, that appeals are made to the history and experience of these individuals, simply because they are more accessible to the writers of books. A perfect system of Intellectual Philosophy might be written, with all its illustrations drawn from the thoughts and feelings of any single pupil in the class. The mind is in its essential laws everywhere the same; and of course you can find the evidence of the existence and operation of all these laws in your own breasts, if you will look there. What you cannot, by proper research, find confirmed by your own experience, or your observations upon those around you, is not a law of mind.

Such is substantially the course which is recommended to those who shall commence the study of this work. It will be perceived that the object of it is to make the study of it, if possible, not what it too often is, the mere mechanical repetition of answers marked and committed to memory, but an intellectual and thorough investigation of a science. If the book is studied in this way, it must have a most powerful influence in cultivating accurate and discriminating habits, in developing intellectual power, and in storing the mind with facts of the most direct and practical importance, in all the connections of society, and in all the business of life.

Its true design. General object of this introduction.

INQUIRIES

CONCERNING

THE INTELLECTUAL POWERS, ETC.

PART I.

OF THE NATURE AND EXTENT OF OUR KNOWLEDGE OF MIND.

THE mind is that part of our being which thinks and wills, remembers and reasons: we know nothing of it except from these functions. By means of the corporeal senses it holds intercourse with the things of the external world, and receives impressions from them. But of this connection also we know nothing but the facts; when we attempt to speculate upon its nature and cause, we wander at once from the path of philosophical inquiry into conjectures which are as far beyond the proper sphere as they are beyond the reach of the human faculties. The object of true science on such a subject, therefore, is simply to investigate the facts, or the relations of phenomena, respecting the operations of mind itself, and the intercourse which it carries on with the things of the external world.

This important rule in the philosophy of mind has been fully recognised in very modern times only, so that the science, as a faithful interpretation of nature, may be considered as of recent origin. Before the period now referred to, the investigation was encumbered by the most fruitless speculations respecting the essence of mind, and other discussions which led to no discovery of truth. It was contended, for example, that the mind cannot act where it is

---

The mind—what? Its connection with the material world? Object of true science? In what sense is the science recent? Nature of former speculations.

not present, and that consequently it cannot be said to perceive external objects themselves, but only their images, forms, or sensible species, which were said to be conveyed through the senses, and represented to the mind in the same manner in which images are formed in a camera obscura. By the internal functions of mind these sensible species were then supposed to be refined into phantasms, the objects of memory and imagination; and these, after undergoing a further process, became intelligible species, the objects of pure intellect. By a very natural application of this doctrine, it was maintained by bishop Berkeley and the philosophers of his school, that as the mind can perceive nothing but its own impressions or images, we can derive no evidence from our senses of the existence of the external world; and Mr. Hume carried the argument a little further, by maintaining that we have as little proof of the existence of mind, and that nothing exists in the universe except impressions and ideas. Of another sect of philosophers who arose out of the same system, each individual professed to believe his own existence, but would not admit the existence of any other being; hence they received the appropriate name of Egotists.

The various eminent individuals by whom the fallacy of these speculations was exposed, combated them upon the principle that the doctrine of ideas is entirely a fiction of philosophers; and that a confidence in the information conveyed to us by our senses must be considered as a first truth, or a fundamental law of our nature, susceptible of no explanation, and admitting of no other evidence than that which is derived from the universal conviction of mankind. Nor does it, to common minds, appear a slight indication of the validity of this mode of reasoning, that the philosophers who supported this theory do not appear to have acted upon their own system; but in every thing which concerned their personal accommodation or personal safety, showed the same confidence in the evidence of their senses as other men.

The deductions made from the ideal theory by Berkeley and Hume seem to have been applications of it which its for-

Supposed process by which we become acquainted with external objects. Errors resulting. Berkeley's opinion? Hume's opinion? How refuted. Did these philosophers really believe their own system?

mer advocates had not contemplated. But it is a singular fact, as stated by Dr. Reid, that nearly all philosophers, from Plato to Mr. Hume, agree in maintaining that the mind does not perceive external things themselves, but only their ideas, images, or species. This doctrine was founded upon the maxim that mind cannot act where it is not present; and we find one writer only, who, admitting the maxim, called in question the application of it so far as to maintain that the mind, in perceiving external things, leaves the body, and comes into contact with the objects of its perception.

Such speculations ought to be entirely banished from the science of mind, as not only useless and unprofitable, but as referring to things entirely beyond the reach of the human faculties, and therefore contrary to the first principles of philosophical investigation. To the same class we are to refer all speculations in regard to the essence of mind, the manner in which thought is produced, and the means by which the intercourse is carried on between the mind and external objects. These remarkable functions were at one time explained by an imaginary essence called the animal spirits, which were supposed to be in constant motion, performing the office of messengers between the brain and the organs of sense. By another class of philosophers, of no very ancient date, thinking was ascribed to vibrations in the particles of the brain. The communication of perceptions from the senses to the mind has been accounted for in the same manner by the motions of the nervous fluid, by vibrations of the nerves, or by a subtile essence, resembling electricity or galvanism. The mind, again, has been compared to a camera obscura, to a mirror, and to a storehouse. In opposition, however, to all such hypotheses, which are equally incapable either of proof or of refutation, our duty is to keep steadily in view, that the objects of true science are facts alone, and the relations of these facts to each other. The mind can be compared to nothing in nature; it has been endowed by its Creator with a power of perceiving external things; but the manner in which it does so is entirely beyond our comprehension. All attempts, therefore,

Dr Reid's statement? Foundation of this doctrine. Author's opinion of such speculations? Theory of animal spirits. Theory of vibrations. Various other theories to explain or illustrate its operations by a reference to any thing else, can be considered only as vain and futile. They are endeavors to establish a resemblance where there is not a vestige of an analogy; and consequently they can lead to no useful result. It is only by a rigid adherence to this course of investigation that we can expect to make any progress in true knowledge, or to impart to our inquiries in any department of science the characters either of truth or utility.

The ideal theory, with all the doctrines founded upon it, may now be considered as gone by. But certain speculations are still occasionally brought out by writers of a particular order, which are referable to the same class, namely, hypotheses which are to be treated, not merely as unsound, but as being, by their very nature, directly opposed to the first principles of philosophical inquiry. Among these, the most prominent is the doctrine of materialism, of which it may be advisable to take a slight view in the commencement of this essay. On the principles which have been referred to, the following considerations may be submitted as bearing upon the subject.

The term matter is a name which we apply to a certain combination of properties, or to certain substances which are solid, extended, and divisible, and which are known to us only by these properties. The term mind, in the same manner, is a name which we apply to a certain combination of functions, or to a certain power which we feel within, which thinks, and wills, and reasons; and is known to us only by these functions. The former we know only by our senses, the latter only by our consciousness. In regard to their essence or occult qualities, we know quite as little about matter as we do about mind; and in as far as our utmost conception of them extends, we have no ground for believing that they have any thing in common.

It is highly important that the pupil should entertain clear ideas of the distinction between the *essence* and the *properties* of bodies. Take, for an example to illustrate this, an orange. It has a peculiar color. This color is one of its *properties*. Imagine this to be taken away. It has taste, which is another property. Remove this also.

Proper view of the nature of mind? Doctrine of materialism. Reason for alluding to it. Proper applications of the terms matter and mind? Distinction between essence and properties? Illustration.

It has solidity; that is, it can be *felt*. Imagine, though it is difficult to do so, this property to be removed, so that the hand would pass through it without meeting with any resistance, as if it were a shadow, or an optical deception. Suppose that, in the same way, all other properties are removed, viz. *form, smell weight*, &c. What would at last be left? Is there an unknown something, around which all these properties cluster? To this something, the term *essence* is applied. Now all of which we have, or can have any real knowledge, is the *properties*, both in the case of matter and mind.

The true object of philosophy is simply to investigate the facts in regard to both; and materialism is not to be viewed only as unsound reasoning, but as a logical absurdity, and a total misconception of the first principles of philosophical inquiry. Does the materialist tell us that the principle which thinks is material, or the result of organization, we have only to ask him what light he expects to throw upon the subject by such an assertion? For the principle which thinks is known to us only by thinking; and the substances which are solid and extended are known to us only by their solidity and extension. When we say of the former that it is immaterial, we simply express the fact that it is known to us by properties altogether distinct from the properties to which we have given the name of matter, and, as far as we know, has nothing in common with them. Beyond these properties, we know as little about matter as we do about mind; so that materialism is scarcely less extravagant than would be the attempt to explain any phenomenon by referring it to some other altogether distinct and dissimilar; to say, for example, that color is a modification of sound, or gravity a species of fermentation. The assertion, indeed, would be fully as plausible, and calculated to throw as much light upon the subject, were a person anxious to explain the nature of matter, to tell us that it is the result of a particular manifestation of mind. Something analogous to this, in fact, seems to be the foundation of the theory of Boscovich, who conceives all bodies to consist of unextended atoms or mathematical points endowed with a certain power of repulsion, and consequently makes the essence of matter to consist merely in the property of resistance. We have, in truth, the same kind of evidence for

---

True philosophy—what? Its principles violated by materialists—how? Theory of Boscovich. Nature of the evidence of the existence both of matter and mind.

the existence of mind that we have for the existence of matter, namely, from its properties; and of the two, the former appears to be the least liable to deception. "Of all the truths we know," says Mr. Stewart, "the existence of mind is the most certain. Even the system of Berkeley concerning the non-existence of matter is far more conceivable than that nothing but matter exists in the universe."

A similar mode of reasoning may be applied to the modification of materialism more prevalent in modern times, by which mind is considered as a result of organization, or, in other words, a function of the brain; and upon which has been founded the conclusion, that, like our bodily senses, it will cease to be when the bodily frame is dissolved. The brain, it is true, is the centre of that influence on which depend sensation and motion. There is a remarkable connection between this organ and the manifestations of mind; and by various diseases of the brain these manifestations are often modified, impaired, or suspended. We shall afterward see that these results are very far from being uniform; but even if they were uniform, the facts would warrant no such conclusion respecting the nature of mind; for they accord equally with the supposition that the brain is the organ of communication between the mind and the external world. When the materialist advances a single step beyond this, he plunges at once into conclusions which are entirely gratuitous and unwarranted. We rest nothing more upon this argument than that these conclusions are unwarranted; but we might go further than this, and contend that the presumption is clearly on the other side, when we consider the broad and obvious distinction which exists between the peculiar phenomena of mind and those functions which are exercised through the means of bodily organization. They do not admit of being brought into comparison, and have nothing in common. The most exquisite of our bodily senses are entirely dependent for their exercise upon impressions from external things. We see not without the presence both of light and a body reflecting it; and if we could suppose light to be annihilated, though the eye were to retain its perfect condition, sight would be ex-

---

Modern materialism? Connection of the mind with the brain. Dependence of the senses on external objects.

tinguished. But mind owns no such dependence on external things, except in the origin of its knowledge in regard to them. When this knowledge has once been acquired it is retained and recalled at pleasure; and mind exercises its various functions without any dependence upon impressions from the external world. That which has long ceased to exist is still distinctly before it, or is recalled after having been long forgotten, in a manner even still more wonderful; and scenes, deeds, or beings, which never existed, are called up in long and harmonious succession, invested with all the characters of truth, and all the vividness of present existence. The mind remembers, conceives, combines, and reasons; it loves, and fears, and hopes, in the total absence of any impression from without that can influence in the smallest degree these emotions; and we have the fullest conviction that it would continue to exercise the same functions in undiminished activity, though all material things were at once annihilated.

This argument, indeed, may be considered as only negative, but this is all that the subject admits of. For when we endeavor to speculate directly on the essence of mind, we are immediately lost in perplexity, in consequence of our total ignorance of the subject, and the use of terms borrowed from analogies with material things. Hence the unsatisfactory nature of every physiological or metaphysical argument respecting the essence of mind, arising entirely from the attempt to reason on the subject in a manner of which it is not susceptible. It admits not of any ordinary process of logic, for the facts on which it rests are the objects of consciousness only; and the argument must consist in an appeal to the consciousness of every man, that he feels a power within totally distinct from any function of the body. What other conception than this can he form of that power by which he recalls the past, and provides for the future; by which he ranges uncontrolled from world to world, and from system to system; surveys the works of all-creating power, and rises to the contemplation of the eternal Cause? To what function of matter shall he liken that principle by which he loves and fears, and joys and sor

Independence of the mind. Examples. Inference from this. Essence of mind. Worth of reasoning about it. Real foundation of our belief that the soul is distinct from the body?

rows; by which he is elevated with hope, excited by enthusiasm, or sunk into the horrors of despair? These changes also he feels, in many instances, to be equally independent of impressions from without, and of the condition of his bodily frame. In the most peaceful state of every corporeal function, passion, remorse, or anguish may rage within; and while the body is racked by the most frightful diseases, the mind may repose in tranquillity and hope. He is taught by physiology that every part of his body is in a constant state of change, and that within a certain period every particle of it is renewed. But, amid these changes, he feels that the being whom he calls himself, remains essentially the same. In particular, his remembrance of the occurrences of his early days he feels to be totally inconsistent with the idea of an impression made upon a material organ, unless he has recourse to the absurdity of supposing that one series of particles, as they departed, transferred the picture to those which came to occupy their room.

If the being, then, which we call mind or soul be, to the utmost extent of our knowledge, thus dissimilar to, and distinct from, any thing that we know to be a result of bodily organization, what reason have we to believe that it should be affected by any change in the arrangement of material organs, except in so far as relates to its intercourse with this external world? The effects of that change which we call the death of an animal body are nothing more than a change in the arrangement of its constituent elements; for it can be demonstrated, on the strictest principles of chemistry, that not one particle of these elements ceases to exist. We have, in fact, no conception of annihilation; and our whole experience is opposed to the belief that one atom which ever existed has ceased to exist. There is, therefore, as Dr. Brown has well remarked, in the very decay of the body, an analogy which would seem to indicate the continued existence of the thinking principle, since that which we term decay is itself only another name for continued existence. To conceive, then, that any thing mental ceases to exist after death, when we know that every thing corporeal continues to exist, is a gratuitous assump-

---

Evidence of consciousness. The feelings of the mind in many cases independent of bodily changes. Effect of death on the soul? Dr. Brown's remark.

tion, contrary to every rule of philosophical inquiry, and in direct opposition, not only to all the facts relating to mind itself, but even to the analogy which is furnished by the dissolution of the bodily frame.

To this mode of reasoning it has been objected, that it would go to establish an immaterial principle in the lower animals, which in them exhibits many of the phenomena of mind. I have only to answer, be it so. There are in the lower animals many of the phenomena of mind; and, with regard to these, we also contend, that they are entirely distinct from any thing we know as the properties of matter,—which is all that we mean, or can mean, by being immaterial. There are other principles superadded to material things, of the nature of which we are equally ignorant; such, for example, as the principle of vegetable life, and that of animal life. To say that these are properties of matter is merely arguing about a term; for what we mean by matter is something which is solid, extended, and divisible. That these properties are, in certain individuals, combined with simple or vegetable life,—in others, with animal life, that is, life and the powers of sensation and motion,—and in others with animal life, and certain of those properties which we call mind,—are all facts equally beyond our comprehension. For any thing we know, they may all be immortal principles; and for any thing we know, matter itself may be immortal. The simple truth is, that we know nothing on the subject; and while, on the one hand, we have no title to assume an essence to be mortal because it possesses only the properties of matter; neither, on the other hand, have we any right to infer an essence to be immortal, because it possesses properties different from those of matter. We talk, indeed, about matter, and we talk about mind; we speculate concerning materiality and immateriality, until we argue ourselves into a kind of belief that we really understand something of the subject. The truth is that we understand nothing. Matter and mind are known to us by certain properties; these properties are quite distinct from each other; but in regard to both, it is entirely out of the reach of our faculties to advance a single step beyond the facts which are before us. Whether

Objection to this reasoning? Answer? Mental phenomena in the lower animals. Other principles. Our knowledge limited to what?

in their substratum or ultimate essence they are the same, or whether they are different, we know not, and never can know in our present state of being. Let us, then, be satisfied with the facts, when our utmost faculties can carry us no farther; let us cease to push our feeble speculations, when our duty is only to wonder and adore.

These considerations, while they are directly opposed to the crude conclusions of the materialist, also serve to show us how much the subject is removed beyond our limited faculties; and it is not on such speculations, therefore, that we rest the evidence for a future state of being. We know nothing of the nature or the essence of mind; but whatever may be its essence, and whatever may be the nature and extent of that mysterious connection which the Deity has established between it and our bodily organization, these points have no reference whatever to the great question of its future existence. This is a principle which seems to have been too much lost sight of in the discussion of this subject, namely, that our speculations respecting the immateriality of the rational human soul have no influence on our belief of its immortality. This momentous truth rests on a species of evidence altogether different, which addresses itself to the moral constitution of man. It is found in those principles of his nature by which he feels upon his spirit the awe of a God, and looks forward to the future with anxiety or with hope;—by which he knows to distinguish truth from falsehood, and evil from good, and has forced upon him the conviction that he is a moral and responsible being. This is the power of conscience, that monitor within which raises its voice in the breast of every man, a witness for his Creator. He who resigns himself to its guidance, and he who repels its warnings, are both compelled to acknowledge its power; and, whether the good man rejoices in the prospect of immortality, or the victim of remorse withers beneath an influence unseen by human eye, and shrinks from the anticipation of a reckoning to come, each has forced upon him a conviction, such as argument never gave, that the being which is essentially himself is distinct from any function of the body, and will survive in

---

Immortality of the soul. Real evidence of it—what? Conscience. Irresistible conviction on this subject.

undiminished vigor when the body shall have fallen into decay.

When, indeed, we take into the inquiry the high principles of moral obligation, and the moral government of the Deity, this important truth is entirely independent of all our feeble speculations on the essence of mind. For though we were to suppose, with the materialist, that the rational soul of man is a mere chemical combination, which, by the dissolution of its elements, is dissipated to the four winds of heaven, where is the improbability that the Power which framed the wondrous compound may collect these elements again, and combine them anew, for the great purposes of his moral administration? In our speculations on such a momentous subject, we are too apt to be influenced by our conceptions of the powers and properties of physical things; but there is a point where this principle must be abandoned, and where the soundest philosophy requires that we take along with us a full recognisance of the power of God.

There is thus, in the consciousness of every man, a deep impression of continued existence. The casuist may reason against it till he bewilder himself in his own sophistries; but a voice within gives the lie to his vain speculations, and pleads with authority for a life which is to come. The sincere and humble inquirer cherishes the impression, while he seeks for farther light on a subject so momentous; and he thus receives, with absolute conviction, the truth which beams upon him from the revelation of God,—that the mysterious part of his being, which thinks, and wills and reasons, shall indeed survive the wreck of its mortal tenement, and is destined for immortality.

Does materialism, if admitted disprove immortality? How illustrated. Concluding remarks.

PART II

OF THE ORIGIN OF OUR KNOWLEDGE OF FACTS RELATING BOTH TO MIND AND MATTER.

AMONG writers on the science of mind, there was formerly much controversy in regard to the origin of our ideas. Some maintained that they are derived entirely from perception, that is, through the external senses; others considered them as arising partly from perception and partly from consciousness, or reflection; and some added a third class, which they called innate ideas, and which were supposed to exist in the mind itself, independently of and prior to the exercise either of perception or reflection. This phraseology had its origin in the ancient theory of ideas, according to which something was supposed to exist distinct both from the mind and the external object of its perception. This, as we have formerly seen, was what philosophers meant by an idea. It was believed to be the immediate object of the mind's perception, but to be only a kind of image or representative of the object perceived. This hypothesis, which kept its place in the science of mind till a very recent period, is now generally admitted to have been a fiction of philosophers; and the phraseology respecting ideas is abandoned by the best practical writers; because, though the ancient doctrine be exploded, and the term may be used only in a figurative sense, it still seems to imply something existing in the mind distinct from the mind itself. The impressions derived from external things are therefore to be considered as the occasions on which the various powers of the mind are brought into action. These powers themselves then become the objects of consciousness or reflection, and by their further exercise we acquire certain notions which arise out of the mental operations. This doctrine gives no encouragement to the scheme of materialism, for it is clear that we cannot remember till we are furnish-

Different opinions. Ancient theory of ideas—what? Present opinion of this theory Modern view—what?

ed with some fact to be remembered; but this can never be supposed to affect our belief in the existence of the power of memory before the fact was so furnished. If we could suppose the case of a man who had lived all his life in the dark, he certainly could not see, but we should not say that the admission of light imparted to him the power of vision; it only furnished the circumstances which gave occasion to the exercise of sight. It has accordingly been shown by Mr. Stewart, that though we may not be conscious of our mental powers till they are called into action, yet this may arise from the most simple sensation,—such as affords no evidence of the properties, or even of the existence of the material world.

Through the senses, then, we acquire a knowledge of the facts relating to external things. The mental processes thus brought into action then become the subjects of consciousness, and we acquire a knowledge of the facts relating to them. By a further exercise of these powers on various facts referring to both matter and mind, we acquire certain notions arising out of our reflection upon the relations of these facts, such as our notions of time, motion, number, cause and effect, and personal identity; and we acquire, further, the impression of certain fundamental laws of belief, which are not referable to any process of reasoning, but are to be considered as a part of our constitution, or a spontaneous and instinctive exercise of reason in every sound mind.

The origin of our knowledge then is referable, in a philosophical point of view, to perception and reflection. But, in point of fact, the knowledge which is acquired by an individual through his own perception and reflection is but a small part of what he possesses; much of the knowledge possessed by every one is acquired through the perceptions of other men. In an essay, therefore, which is intended to be entirely practical, I shall include this last department under the head of Testimony. The division of this part of the subject will therefore be,

1. Sensation and Perception.
2. Consciousness and Reflection.
3. Testimony.

Illustration. Knowledge of external things—how acquired? Of their relations? Two sources? Additional source. Summary.

SECTION I.

OF SENSATION AND PERCEPTION.

We know nothing of perception except the fact that certain impressions made upon the organs of sense convey to the mind a knowledge of the properties of external things. Some of the older speculations on this subject have already been referred to. In these the mind was compared to a camera obscura, and the transmission of the forms or images of things to it from the organs of sense was explained by the motion of the animal spirits, or the nervous fluid, or by vibrations in the substance of the nerves. All such speculations are now dismissed from the investigation, being considered as attempts to penetrate into mysteries which are beyond the reach of the human faculties, and consequently not the legitimate objects of a philosophical inquiry.

Our first knowledge of the existence and properties of the material world is evidently of a complex nature. It seems to arise from the combined action of several senses, conveying to us the general notion of certain essences which are solid and extended, or possessed of those properties which characterize material things. Without this general knowledge previously acquired, our various senses acting individually could convey to us no definite notion of the properties of external things. A smell, that is, a mere odor, for example, might be perceived by us, but would convey nothing more than the sensation simply. It could not communicate the impression of this being a property of an external body, until we had previously acquired a knowledge of the existence of that body, and had come by observation to associate the sensation with the body from which it proceeds. The same holds true of the other senses; and we are thus led at the very first step of our inquiry to a complicated process of mind without which our mere sensations could convey to us no definite knowledge.

Having thus acquired a knowledge of the existence and

Former theories. How now considered? First knowledge—how obtained? Succeeding steps—what?

general properties of material things, we next derive from our various senses a knowledge of their more minute characters. These are generally divided into primary and secondary. The primary qualities of material things are such as are essential, and must at all times belong to matter; such as solidity and extension. These properties necessarily convey to us a conviction of something existing out of the mind, and distinct from its own sensations. The secondary qualities, again, are color, temperature, smell, taste, &c. These are not essential properties of matter, but qualities producing sensations in a sentient being; they may or they may not belong to any particular body, or they may be attached to it at one time and not at another. Hence they convey to us primarily no definite notion in regard to the existence or properties of external things, except, as Mr. Stewart expresses it, "as the unknown cause of a known sensation." One of the quibbles or paradoxes of the scholastic philosophy was, denying the real existence of these secondary qualities of matter. Every one is familiar with the humorous account given in the "Guardian" of the attainments of a youth from college, and his display of them when on a visit to lady Lizard, his mother. "When the girls were sorting a set of knots he would demonstrate to them that all the ribands were of the same color, or rather of no color at all. My lady Lizard herself, though she was not a little pleased with her son's improvement, was one day almost angry with him; for, having accidentally burnt her fingers as she was lighting the lamp for her teapot, in the midst of her anguish Jack laid hold of the opportunity to instruct her that there is no such thing as heat in the fire." Such speculations, which were at one time common in the schools of philosophy, had their origin wholly in an abuse of terms. The term heat, for example, has two meanings, which are quite distinct from each other. It means a sensation produced in a sentient being, and in this sense it may be said with truth that there is no heat in fire; but it means also a quality in material substances capable of producing this sensation, and it is in this sense that we speak of heat as a property of matter.

Classification of qualities. Definitions. Extract given in the Guardian.

Notwithstanding this explanation of the different senses in which the word heat is used, many persons find it difficult to understand that there is any sense in which it can be said with truth that there is no heat in fire. But a little reflection will make it plain.

If a man puts his hand among coals he feels a *burning, painful* sensation, which we call heat. Now when it is said there is no heat in fire, the meaning is that there is no such *burning, painful sensation.* And certainly no one can suppose that there is. There cannot be *suffering* in the fire, or even any feeling of warmth, or sensation of any kind; and it is in this sense alone that the word is used, when the existence of heat in the fire is denied. So with all the other secondary qualities. Smells, tastes, sounds, &c. are all *feelings* in us. The external objects themselves cannot have these feelings, or any other. They have some peculiarity or property which excites these feelings in us, but not the feelings or sensations themselves.

The process by which we acquire a knowledge of external things is usually divided into two stages, namely, sensation and perception; the former implying the corporeal, the latter the mental part of it. Others apply the term perception to both; and, according to Dr. Brown, sensation is the simple impression made upon the organs of sense; perception is an association formed between this impression and an external substance which we have ascertained to be concerned in producing it. Our senses, by which this knowledge is acquired, are generally reckoned five,—viz: sight, hearing, taste, smell, and touch. Dr. Brown proposes to add our muscular frame, and apparently with good reason; for there seems ground for believing that it is by resistance to muscular action that we acquire the notion of solidity, and that this could not be acquired by touch alone

Our first impression of the existence and solidity of material objects, then, seems to be derived from touch combined with muscular resistance; and at the same time we acquire the knowledge of temperature, roughness or smoothness, &c. There has been some difference of opinion in regard to the manner in which we acquire the notion of extension, including figure and magnitude. It is evident that it cannot be acquired from touch alone; but it may be acquired from touch combined with muscular motion, as when we move the hand over the surface of a body. This, however, includes also the idea of time,—for our notion of the extent of a surface when the hand moves over it is very

---

Explanation. Secondary qualities; their nature? Distinction between sensation and perception. Number of the senses. First notions—how obtained?

much influenced by the velocity with which the motion is made. Hence time has been supposed by some to be one of our very earliest impressions, and antecedent even to the notion of extension or space. It is probable, however, that the notion of extension may also be acquired in a more simple manner from the combined operation of touch and vision. If this opinion be correct, it will follow that our first knowledge of the existence and essential properties of material things is derived from the combined operation of sight, touch, and muscular action.

With regard to all our senses, however, the truth seems to be, that the first notions conveyed by them are of a very limited and imperfect kind; and that our real knowledge is acquired only after considerable observation and experience, in the course of which the impressions of one sense are corrected and assisted by those of others, and by a process of mind acting upon the whole. The primary objects of vision, for example, seem to be simply light or color and expansion. But the judgments which we are in the daily habit of forming upon vision are of a much more extensive kind, embracing also distance, magnitude, and what has been called tangible figure, such as the figure of a cube or a sphere. This last, it is evident, cannot be considered as a primary object of vision but as entirely the result of experience derived from the sense of touch; for we never could have formed any conception of the figure of a cube or a sphere by vision alone. Distance and magnitude, also. are evidently not the primary objects of vision; for persons who have been suddenly cured of congenital blindness, by the operation for cataract, have no conception of the distance or magnitude of objects; they perceive only simple expansion of surface with color. Our judgment of distance and magnitude by vision, therefore, is an acquired habit. founded upon the knowledge which we have received by other means of the properties of the objects. Accordingly, it is familiar to every one, that we have no idea of the distance of an object, except we have some notion of its magnitude; nor, on the other hand, of its magnitude, except we have some knowledge of its distance. The application of

---

First notions derived from the senses. Primary objects of vision? Ideas of distance and magnitude—how obtained? Connection of these ideas

this principle is also familiar in perspective drawing, in which the diminished size of known objects is made to convey the notion of distance. On the same principle, known objects seen through a telescope do not appear to be magnified, but to be brought nearer. In the same manner with regard to sounds; we have no idea of their intensity, except we have some notion of their distance, and *vice versa.* A given degree of sound, for example, if we believed it to have been produced in the next room, we might conclude to proceed from the fall of some trifling body; but if we supposed it to be at the distance of several miles, we should immediately conclude that it proceeded from a tremendous explosion.

In regard to certain small distances, however, there is a power of judging by sight alone; and it appears to arise out of the degree of inclination which is given to the axis of vision in directing the two eyes to the object. Thus, in snuffing a candle, or carrying the finger to a small object within arm's length, it will be found that we are very apt to miss it if we look with one eye only, but can touch it with unerring certainty when both eyes are directed to it.

This experiment may be easily tried. Hold some small object, a lead pencil for instance, with the point upwards at the distance of about a foot from the eye. Then, with one eye closed, endeavor to bring the end of the finger down exactly upon the point of the pencil. It will be found quite difficult to do it exactly, though with both eyes open it will be easy.

It appears to be on the same principle that we enjoy in a greater degree the deception produced by a painting, when we look at it with one eye, especially if we also look through a tube. By the former we cut off the means of correcting the illusion by the direction of the axis of vision; and by the latter we remove the influence of all neighboring objects. It is impossible to determine the precise distance to which we can extend this power of judging of distance by the inclination of the axis of vision, but it does not appear to be great; and in regard to all greater distances, the judgment by vision is evidently an acquired habit, arising out of such a mental exercise as has now been referred to.

Intensity and distance of sounds Small distances judged of by sight alone. Experiment with paintings.

There are some other circumstances, also, the result of experience, by which we are greatly influenced in all such cases, particularly the degree of illumination of the objects, and the degree of distinctness of their outline and minute parts. Thus, in a picture, distant objects are represented as faintly illuminated, and with indistinctness of outline and minute parts; and *vice versa.* On this principle, objects seen through a fog, or in obscure light, are apt to appear much larger than they really are; because, in the mental process which takes place in regard to them, we first assume them to be distant, from their imperfect outline and faint illumination, and then, judging from this assumed distance, we conclude them to be of great size. On the other hand, objects seen in an unusually clear state of the atmosphere appear nearer than they really are, from the greater distinctness of their outline. In our judgment of distance by sight, we are also greatly influenced by the eye resting on intermediate objects; and hence the difficulty of judging of distances at sea. A striking illustration of the same principle is furnished by captain Parry, in regard to objects seen across a uniform surface of snow. "We had frequent occasion, in our walks on shore, to remark the deception which takes place in estimating the distance and magnitude of objects, when viewed over an unvaried surface of snow. It was not uncommon for us to direct our steps towards what we took to be a large mass of stone, at the distance of half a mile from us, but which we were able to take up in our hands after one minute's walk. This was more particularly the case when ascending the brow of a hill." Captain Parry adds, that this deception did not become less on account of the frequency with which its effects were experienced; and a late writer has used this as an objection to the doctrine lately referred to, respecting the influence of experience on our judgment of distance by vision. But this is evidently founded on a misconception of the effect of experience in such cases. Captain Parry could mean only, that he did not acquire the power of judging of the distance or magnitude of unknown objects. Had he been approaching an object by which he had once been de-

Effects of distance—what? Illustration from Parry's Journal. The deception not diminished by experience. Reason

ceived, knowing it to be the same, he would not have been deceived a second time; but, judging from its known magnitude, would have inferred its distance. Thus the result of experience is to enable us to judge of the distance of an object of known magnitude, or of the magnitude of an object at a known distance; but, in regard to objects of which both the distance and magnitude are unknown, it teaches us only not to trust the indications of vision.

In our judgment of vision by the magnitude of objects again, we are much influenced by comparison with other objects, the magnitude of which is supposed to be known. I remember once having occasion to pass along Ludgate Hill, when the great door of St. Paul's was open, and several persons were standing in it. They appeared to be very little children; but, on coming up to them, were found to be full-grown persons. In the mental process which here took place, the door had been assumed as a known magnitude, and the other objects judged of by it. Had I attended to the door being much larger than any door that one is in the habit of seeing, the mind would have made allowance for the apparent size of the persons; and, on the other hand, had these been known to be full-grown persons, a judgment would have been formed of the size of the door. On the same principle, travellers visiting the pyramids of Egypt have repeatedly remarked, how greatly the notion of their magnitude is increased by a number of large animals, as camels, being assembled at their base.

There is something exceedingly remarkable in the manner in which loss or diminution of one sense is followed by increase of the intensity of others, or rather, perhaps, by an increased attention to the indications of other senses. Blind persons acquire a wonderful delicacy of touch; in some cases, it is said, to the extent of distinguishing colors. Mr. Saunderson, the blind mathematician, could distinguish by his hand, in a series of Roman medals, the true from the counterfeit, with a more unerring discrimination than the eye of a professed virtuoso; and, when he was present at

---

What is really gained by experience. Influence of comparison in judgment by vision. Illustration. Explanation. Illustration from the pyramids. Effect of the loss or diminution of a sense. Examples. Saunderson.

the astronomical observations in the garden of his college, he was accustomed to perceive every cloud which passed over the sun. This remarkable power, which has sometimes been referred to an increased intensity of particular senses, in many cases evidently resolves itself into an increased habit of attention to the indications of all those senses which the individual retains. Two instances have been related to me of blind men who were much esteemed as judges of horses. One of these, in giving his opinion of a horse, declared him to be blind, though this had escaped the observation of several persons who had the use of their eyes, and who were with some difficulty convinced of it. Being asked to give an account of the principle on which he had decided, he said it was by the sound of the horse's step in walking, which implied a peculiar and unusual caution in his manner of putting down his feet. The other individual, in similar circumstances, pronounced a horse to be blind of one eye, though this had also escaped the observation of those concerned. When he was asked to explain the facts on which he founded his judgment, he said he felt the one eye to be colder than the other. It is related of the late Dr. Moyse, the well-known blind philosopher, that he could distinguish a black dress on his friends by its smell: and there seems to be good evidence that blind persons have acquired the power of distinguishing colors by the touch. In a case of this kind, mentioned by Mr. Boyle, the individual stated that black imparted to his sense of touch the greatest degree of asperity, and blue the least. Dr. Rush relates of two blind young men, brothers, of the city of Philadelphia, that they knew when they approached a post in walking across a street, by a peculiar sound which the ground under their feet emitted in the neighborhood of the post; and that they could tell the names of a number of tame pigeons, with which they amused themselves in a little garden, by only hearing them fly over their heads. I have known several instances of persons affected with that extreme degree of deafness which occurs in the deaf and dumb, who had a peculiar susceptibility to particular kinds

---

Two blind men. Dr. Moyse. Instances adduced by Dr. Rush. Certain sounds perceived by the deaf.

of sounds, depending apparently upon an impression communicated to their organs of touch or simple sensation. They could tell, for instance, the approach of a carriage in the street, without seeing it, before it was taken notice of by persons who had the use of all their senses. An analogous fact is observed in the habit acquired by the deaf and dumb, of understanding what is said to them by watching the motion of the lips of the speaker. Examples still more wonderful are on record, but certainly require confirmation. A story, for instance, has lately been mentioned in some of the medical journals, of a gentleman in France who lost every sense, except the feeling of one side of his face; yet it is said that his family acquired a method of holding communication with him, by tracing characters upon the part which retained its sensation.

Much ingenuity has been bestowed upon attempts to explain how, with two eyes, we see only one object, and why that object is seen erect, when we know that the image on the retina is inverted. All that need be said upon the subject, and all that can properly be said, appears to be, that such is the constitution of our nervous system. It is on the same principle, that by the sense of touch, in which may be concerned a thousand or ten thousand distinct points of contact, we receive the impression of only one body; or, what perhaps may appear a more strictly analogous case, we receive the impression of but one body, though we grasp the substance with two hands, or with ten distinct fingers. For the healthy perception in both these cases, however, a certain arrangement is required, which we may call the natural harmony of the nervous system; and when this harmony is disturbed, the result is remarkably altered. Thus, squinting produces the vision of a double image,* because the images fall upon what we may call unharmonizing points of the retina; and the same principle may be illustrated in a very curious manner by a simple experiment with the

* This effect may easily be produced by pressing one of the eyes a little out of its natural position by means of the finger at the corner of it, while looking at a single object. It will be made to appear double.

Extraordinary case of a gentleman in France. Difficulty of explaining why the object appears single and erect Analogous case. Effect of squinting, what?

sense of touch. If a small round body, such as a pea, be laid upon the palm of the one hand, and rolled about between the first and second fingers of the other, in their natural position, one pea only is felt; but, if the fingers are crossed, so that the pea is rolled between the opposite surfaces of the two fingers, a most distinct impression of two peas is conveyed.

Of the whole of the remarkable process of sensation and perception, we know nothing but the facts, that certain impressions made upon the organs of sense are followed by certain perceptions in the mind; and that this takes place, in some way, through the medium of the brain and nervous system. We are in the habit of saying, that the impressions are conveyed to the brain; but, even in this, we probably advance a step beyond what is warranted. We know that the nerves derive their influence from their connection with the brain, or as forming along with it one great medium of sensation; but we do not know whether impressions made upon the nervous fabric connected with the organs of sense are conveyed to the brain; or whether the mind perceives them directly, as they are made upon the organs of sense. The whole subject is one of those mysteries which are placed above our reach, and in which we cannot advance a single step beyond the knowledge of the facts. Any attempt to speculate upon it is therefore to be considered as contrary to the first principles of philosophical inquiry. We must simply receive the facts as of that class which we cannot account for in the smallest degree; and the evidence which we derive from our senses, of the existence and properties of the things of the material world, is to be recognised as one of those fundamental laws of belief which admit of no other proof than that which is found in the universal conviction of mankind.

Before concluding the subject of perception, it remains to be noticed that a certain voluntary effort is required for the full exercise of it; or, at least, for that degree of perception which leaves an impression capable of being retained. It is familiar to every one, that when the mind is closely occupied, numerous objects may pass before our eyes, and cir-

---

Experiment with the touch. Extent of our knowledge of sensation. The brain Difficulty of the subject. Voluntary effort necessary. Evidence of it.

cumstances may be talked of in our hearing, of which we do not retain the slightest recollection; and this is often in such a degree as implies, not a want of memory only, but an actual want of the perception of the objects. We cannot doubt, however, that there was the sensation of them; that is, the usual impression made upon the eye in the one case, and the ear in the other. What is wanting, is a certain effort of the mind itself, without which sensation is not necessarily followed by perception;—this is what we call *Attention.* It is a state or act of the mind which is exercised by different individuals in very different degrees. It is much influenced by habit; and though it may not often be wanting in such a degree as to prevent the perception of objects, it is often deficient in a manner which prevents the recollection of them, and consequently has an extensive influence upon the intellectual character.

The effect of attention is illustrated by various mental phenomena of daily occurrence. If we are placed in such a situation that the eye commands an extensive landscape, presenting a great variety of objects, or the wall of an apartment covered with pictures, we have the power of fixing the mind upon one object in such a manner that all the rest become to us nearly as if they did not exist. Yet we know that they are actually seen, as far as the mere sense of vision is concerned; that is, images of all of them are formed upon the retina; but they are not objects of attention, or of that peculiar voluntary effort of mind which is necessary for the full perception of them. In the same manner, a practised musician can, in the midst of a musical performance, direct his attention to one part, such as the bass,—can continue this for such a time as he pleases, and then again enjoy the general harmony of the whole. On the same principle, the mind may be so intensely fixed upon something within itself, as an object of conception or memory, or a process of reasoning, as to have no full perception of present external impressions. We shall afterward have occasion to refer to a state of mind in which this exists in such a degree, that objects of conception or memory are believed to have a real and present existence; and in which this erro-

Name of this? Effect of attention illustrated In the sense of sight. Of hearing

neous impression is not corrected by impressions from external things:—this occurs in insanity.

Attention is very much influenced by habit; and connected with this subject there are some facts of great interest. There is a remarkable law of the system, by which actions at first requiring much attention are after frequent repetition performed with a much less degree of it, or without the mind being conscious of any effort. This is exemplified in various processes of daily occurrence, as reading and writing, but most remarkably in music. Musical performance at first requires the closest attention, but the effort becomes constantly less, until it is often not perceived at all; and a lady may be seen running over a piece of music on a piano, and at the same time talking on another subject. A young lady, mentioned by Dr. Darwin, executed a long and very difficult piece of music with the utmost precision, under the eye of her master; but seemed agitated during the execution of it, and when she had concluded, burst into tears. It turned out that her attention had, during the whole time, been intensely occupied with the agonies of a favorite canary-bird, which at last dropped dead in its cage. We see the same principle exemplified in the rapidity with which an expert arithmetician can run up a long column of figures, without being conscious of the individual combinations. It is illustrated in another manner by the feats of jugglers, the deception produced by which depends upon their performing a certain number of motions with such rapidity that the attention of the spectators does not follow all the combinations.

In teaching such arts as music or arithmetic, this principle is also illustrated; for the most expert arithmetician or musical performer is not necessarily, and perhaps not generally, the best teacher of the art; but he who, with a competent knowledge of it, directs his attention to the individual minute combinations through which it is necessary for the learner to advance.

In processes more purely intellectual, we find the influence of habit brought under our view in a similar manner

Influence of habits of attention. Illustrations. Anecdote of the young lady. Other illustrations. Illustration of this principle from the art of teaching. Influence of habit in facilitating intellectual processes particularly in following the steps of a process of reasoning. A person little accustomed to such a process advances step by step, with minute attention to each as he proceeds; while another perceives at once the result, with little consciousness of the steps by which he arrived at it. For this reason, also, it frequently happens that in certain departments of science the profound philosopher makes a bad teacher. He proceeds too rapidly for his audience, and without sufficient attention to the intermediate steps by which it is necessary for them to advance; and they may derive much more instruction from an inferior man, whose mental process on the subject approaches more nearly to that which, in the first instance, must be theirs. We remark the same difference in public speaking and in writing; and we talk of a speaker or a writer who is easily followed, and another who is followed with difficulty. The former retards the series of his thoughts, so as to bring distinctly before his hearers or his readers every step in the mental process. The latter advances without sufficient attention to this, and consequently can be followed by those only who are sufficiently acquainted with the subject to fill up the intermediate steps, or not to require them.

There is a class of intellectual habits directly the reverse of those now referred to; namely, habits of inattention, by which the mind, long unaccustomed to have the attention steadily directed to any important object, becomes frivolous and absent, or lost amid its own waking dreams. A mind in this condition becomes incapable of following a train of reasoning, and even of observing facts with accuracy and tracing their relations. Hence nothing is more opposed to the cultivation of intellectual character; and when such a person attempts to reason, or to follow out a course of investigation, he falls into slight and partial views, unsound deductions, and frivolous arguments. This state of mind, therefore, ought to be carefully guarded against in the young; as, when it is once established, it can be removed only by a long and laborious effort, and after a certain period of life is probably irremediable.

In rude and savage life remarkable examples occur of

Bad teaching. Public speaking. Habits of inattention. Consequences? Habits of attention in savage life the effect of habits of minute attention to those circumstances to which the mind is intensely directed by their relation to the safety or advantage of the observer. The American hunter finds his way in the trackless forests by attention to minute appearances in the trees, which indicate to him the points of the compass. He traces the progress of his enemies or his friends by the marks of their footsteps; and judges of their numbers, their haltings, their employments, by circumstances which would entirely escape the observation of persons unaccustomed to a mode of life requiring such exercises of attention. Numerous examples of this kind are mentioned by travellers, particularly among the aboriginal natives of America.

OF FALSE PERCEPTIONS.

Before leaving this subject, it is necessary to refer to some remarkable facts respecting perceptions taking place, without the presence of any external body corresponding with them. These are called false perceptions, and they are usually referred to two classes; namely, those arising in the organs of sense, in which the mind does not participate; and those which are connected with hallucination of mind, or a belief of the real existence of the object The former only belong to this part of the subject. The latter will be referred to in another part of our inquiry, as they do not consist of false impressions on the senses, but depend upon the mind mistaking its own conceptions for real and present existences.

Of false perceptions, properly so called, the most familiar are the *muscæ volitantes* floating before the eyes, and sounds in the ears resembling the ringing of bells, or the noise of a waterfall. Changes are also met with in the organs of sense giving rise to remarkable varieties of perception. Dr. Falconer mentions a gentleman who had such a morbid state of sensation that cold bodies felt to him as if they were intensely hot. A gentleman mentioned by Dr. Conolly, when recovering from measles, saw objects dimi-

Examples? False perceptions—what? How classified? Common examples

nished to the smallest imiginable size; and a patient mentioned by Baron Darry, on recovering from amaurosis, saw men as giants, and all objects magnified in a most remarkable manner: it is not mentioned how long these peculiarities continued. This last peculiarity of perception occurred also to a particular friend of mine in recovering from typhus fever. His own body appeared to him to be about ten feet high. His bed seemed to be seven or eight feet from the floor, so that he felt the greatest dread in attempting to get out of it; and the opening of the chimney of his apartment appeared as large as the arch of a bridge. A singular peculiarity of this case however was, that the persons about him with whom he was familiar did not appear above their natural size. But the most interesting phenomena connected with affections of this kind are furnished by the various modifications of spectral illusions. These are referable to three classes.

I. Impressions of visible objects remaining for some time after the eye is shut, or has been withdrawn from them generally accompanied by some remarkable change in the color of the objects. Various interesting experiments of this kind are related by Dr. Darwin; one of the most striking is the following:—"I covered a paper about four inches square with yellow, and with a pen filled with a blue color wrote upon the middle of it the word BANKS in capitals; and sitting with my back to the sun, fixed my eyes for a minute exactly on the centre of the letter N in the word. After shutting my eyes, and shading them somewhat with my hand, the word was distinctly seen in the spectrum, in yellow colors on a blue ground; and then on opening my eyes on a yellowish wall at twenty feet distance, the magnified name of BANKS appeared on the wall written in golden characters."

With a very little ingenuity, this kind of spectral illusions can be easily produced in great variety. Take a common red wafer, and lay it upon a sheet of white paper. Bring the eye down to within six or eight inches of it, and gaze very steadily and intently upon it for the space of twenty or thirty seconds. On moving the eyes away, a beau-

---

False perception of magnitude. Examples of this. Spectral illusions; how many classes? First class? Darwin's experiments? Easy mode of producing these illusions

tiful light blue spot, of the size and shape of the wafer, will be seen on the sheet, and will follow the eyes as they move from side to side. By cutting the wafer in two, or notching its surface, or varying its form in any way, a corresponding variety in the form of the blue spot wi. be produced. The effect may be varied also by using wafers of different color, or even by bright pictures of various colors combined. The stronger the light, the more striking will be the effect. It ought to be added, that persons of weak eyes should be very cautious in trying these experiments.

A friend of mine had been one day looking intensely at a small print of the Virgin and Child, and had sat bending over it for some time. On raising his head he was startled by perceiving, at the farther end of the apartment, a female figure, the size of life, with a child in her arms. The first feeling of surprise having subsided, he instantly traced the source of the illusion, and remarked that the figure corresponded exactly with that which he had contemplated in the print, being what painters call a kit-cat figure, in which the lower parts of the body are not represented. The illusion continued distinct for about two minutes. Similar illusions of hearing are met with, though less frequently than those of vision. A gentleman recently recovered from an affection of the head, in which he had been much reduced by bleeding, had occasion to go into a large town a few miles from his residence. His attention was there attracted by the bugle of a regiment of horse, sounding a particular measure which is used at changing guard in the evening. He assured me that this sound was from that time never out of his ears for about nine months. During all this period he continued in a very precarious state of health; and it was only as his health became more confirmed that the sound of the bugle gradually left him. In regard to ocular spectra, another fact of a very singular nature appears to have been first observed by Sir Isaac Newton,—namely, that when he produced a spectrum of the sun by looking at it with the right eye, the left being covered, upon uncovering the left, and looking upon a white ground, a spectrum of the sun was seen with it also. He likewise acquired the power of recalling the spectra, after they had ceased, when he went into the dark, and directed his mind intensely,

---

Modes of varying the experiments. Caution. Illusion produced by looking at a print? Illusions of hearing. Newton's experiments?

"as when a man looks earnestly to see a thing which is difficult to be seen." By repeating these experiments frequently, such an effect was produced upon his eyes, "that for some months after," he says, "the spectrum of the sun began to return as often as I began to meditate upon the phenomena, even though I lay in bed at midnight with my curtains drawn."

II. Impressions of objects recently seen returning after a considerable interval. Various interesting examples of this kind are on record. Dr. Ferriar mentions of himself, that when about the age of fourteen, if he had been viewing any interesting object in the course of the day, as a romantic ruin, a fine seat, or a review of troops, so soon as evening came, if he had occasion to go into a dark room, the whole scene was brought before him with a brilliancy equal to what it possessed in daylight, and remained visible for some minutes.

III. False perceptions arising in the course of some bodily disorder, generally fever. A lady whom I attended some years ago, in a slight feverish disorder, saw distinctly a party of ladies and gentlemen sitting round her bedchamber, and a servant handing something to them on a tray. The scene continued in a greater or less degree for several days, and was varied by spectacles of castles and churches of a very brilliant appearance, as if they had been built of finely cut crystal. The whole was in this case entirely a visual phantasm, for there was no hallucination of mind. On the contrary, the patient had from the first a full impression that it was a morbid affection of vision, connected with the fever, and amused herself and her attendants by watching and describing the changes in the scenery. A gentleman who was also a patient of mine, of an irritable habit, and liable to a variety of uneasy sensations in his head, was sitting alone in his dining-room in the twilight, the door of the room being a little open. He saw distinctly a female figure enter, wrapped in a mantle, and the face concealed by a large black bonnet. She seemed to advance

---

Second class? Examples. Third class? Example; the sick lady. The mind in what state, in this case? Second example?

a few steps towards him and then stop. He had a full conviction that the figure was an illusion of vision, and amused himself for some time by watching it, at the same time observing that he could see through the figure, so as to perceive the lock of the door and other objects behind it. At length, when he moved his body a little forward, it disappeared. The appearances in these two cases were entirely visual illusions, and probably consisted of the renewal of real scenes or figures, in a manner somewhat analogous to those in Dr. Ferriar's case, though the renewal took place after a longer interval. When there is any degree of hallucination of mind, so that the phantasm is believed to have a real existence, the affection is entirely of a different nature, as will be more particularly mentioned under another part of our subject.

False perceptions may be corrected by one of three methods;—by the exercise of other senses—by a comparison with the perceptions of other persons—and by an exercise of judgment. If I suspect that my eye deceives me, I apply the hand, with the perfect conviction of the improbability that the two senses should be deceived at once. If this cannot be done, I appeal to the impressions of some other persons, with an equally strong conviction that the same sense will not be deceived in the same manner in several persons at once. Or I may do it in another way, by a reference to some known and fixed object. Suppose, for example, I see two objects where I imagine there should be but one, and suspect a visual deception; I turn my eyes to some object which I know to be single—such as the sun. If I see the sun double, I know that there is a delusion of vision; if I see the sun single, I conclude the original perception to be correct. These processes imply a certain exercise of judgment; and there are other cases in which the same conviction may arise from an exercise of judgment, without any process of this kind. In one of the cases now referred to, for example, the correction took place instantly, from observing that the lock of the door was seen as if through the figure.

Explanations. Correcting false impressions, in what ways? First method? Second method?

SECTION II.

OF CONSCIOUSNESS AND REFLECTION.

Consciousness appears to mean, simply, the act of attending to what is passing in the mind at the time. That more extensive operation to which we ought to give the name of reflection, as distinguished from simple consciousness, seems to be connected with a power of remembering past perceptions and past mental processes,—of comparing them with present feelings, so as to trace between them a relation, as belonging to the same sentient being,—and, further, of tracing the laws by which the mental processes themselves are regulated. It is employed also in tracing the relations and sequences of external things, and thus proves the source of certain notions expressive of these relations. It is therefore a compound operation of mind, including various mental processes, especially consciousness, memory, and the act of comparison or judgment. The knowledge which we derive from this source, whether we call it consciousness or reflection, is referable to three heads.

I. A knowledge of the mental processes, and the laws and relations by which they are regulated; a knowledge, for example, of the laws and facts relating to memory, conception, imagination, and judgment. These will be more particularly referred to in a subsequent part of our inquiry. In the same manner we acquire our knowledge of those which have been called the active and moral powers, as love, hope, fear, joy, gratitude, &c.

II. Certain notions arising out of the exercise of the mental processes, in reference to the succession and relations of things; our notion, for example, of time, arising out of memory and consciousness,—our notion of cause—of mo-

Definition of consciousness? Distinction between it and reflection? Its nature? How many kinds of knowledge derived from it? First head; mental processes? Second head; certain abstract ideas?

tion—number—duration—extension or space. From simple perception we seem to acquire a knowledge of external things as existing only at the moment; and from simple consciousness a knowledge of a mental impression as existing only at the moment. Our notions of the succession of things, as implying time and motion, require the exercise of consciousness and memory; and our notions of cause, and the various other relations of things to each other, require both memory and comparison. To the same head, in reference to another department of these faculties, belong our notions of truth and falsehood—right and wrong. These result from a certain exercise of mind, aided by that remarkable principle in our constitution which commonly receives the name of conscience.

III. With this exercise of the mental functions there spring up in the mind certain convictions, or intuitive and instinctive principles of belief. They are the immediate result of a certain exercise of the understanding, but are not referable to any process of induction or chain of reasoning, and can be considered only as an original and fundamental part of our constitution. This is a subject of great and extensive importance, and the articles of belief which are referable to it are chiefly the following:

(1.) A conviction of our own existence as sentient and thinking beings, and of mind as something distinct from the functions of the body.

(2.) A confidence in the evidence of our senses in regard to the existence and properties of external things; or a conviction that they have a real existence independent of our sensations.

(3.) A confidence in our own mental processes—that facts, for example, which are suggested to us by our memory, really occurred.

(4.) A belief in our personal identity, derived from the combined operations of consciousness and memory; or a remembrance of past mental feelings and a comparison of them with present mental feelings, as belonging to the same sentient being.

Third head; intuitive convictions? Examples?

(5.) A conviction that every event must have a cause, and a cause adequate to the effect.

(6.) A confidence in the uniformity of the operations of nature; or that the same cause, acting in the same circumstances, will always be followed by the same effect.

These first or instinctive principles of belief will be referred to in a more particular manner when we come to speak of the use of reason in the investigation of truth. They are usually called First Truths, and will be seen to occupy a most important place as the foundation of all reasoning. Many ingenious but fallacious arguments were at one time wasted in attempts to establish them by processes of reasoning. These again were assailed by sophistical and skeptical writers, who easily succeeded in showing the fallacy of these arguments, and thus assumed the credit of undermining the authority of the truths themselves. All this species of sophistical warfare is now gone by; and the most important era in the modern science of reasoning was, when it was distinctly shown that these first truths admit of no other evidence than the conviction which forces itself upon the understanding of all classes of men. Since that period it has been generally allowed that they admit of no proof by processes of reasoning; and, on the other hand, that they are entirely unaffected by the arguments by which all such reasoning was shown to be fallacious.

SECTION III.

OF TESTIMONY.

A VERY small portion of our knowledge of externa things is obtained through our own senses; by far the greater part is procured through other men, and this is received by us on the evidence of testimony. But, in receiving facts in this manner, we usually proceed with more

---

Controversies respecting First Truths. Proper view of these controversies? Evidence of testimony, why necessary?

caution than when they come to us by our personal observation. We are much influenced, in the first place, by our confidence in the veracity of the narrator, and our knowledge of the opportunities which he has had of ascertaining the facts he professes to relate. Thus, if he be a person on whose testimony we have formerly received important statements, which have turned out to be correct, we are the more ready to receive his testimony again; if he be a stranger to us, we receive it with greater caution; if he has formerly misled us, we view it with suspicion, or reject it altogether.

But there is another principle of very extensive application in such cases, and which is independent in a great measure of the character of the narrator. In receiving facts upon testimony, we are much influenced by their accordance with facts with which we are already acquainted. This is what, in common language, we call their probability; and statements which are probable, that is, in accordance with facts which we already know, are received upon a lower degree of evidence than those which are not in such accordance, or which, in other words, appear to us in the present state of our knowledge to be improbable. Now this is a sound and salutary caution, but we should beware of allowing it to influence us beyond its proper sphere. It should lead us to examine carefully the evidence upon which we receive facts not in accordance with those which we have already acquired; but we should beware of allowing it to engender skepticism. For, while an unbounded credulity is the part of a weak mind, which never thinks or reasons at all, an unlimited skepticism is the part of a contracted mind, which reasons upon imperfect data, or makes its own knowledge and extent of observation the standard and test of probability. An ignorant peasant may reject the testimony of a philosopher in regard to the size of the moon, because he thinks he has the evidence of his senses that it is only a foot in diameter; and a person, holding a respectable rank in society, is said to have received with contempt the doctrine of the revolution

---

Conditions of confidence in testimony? What is meant by probability? Its influence? Caution in regard to its influence Examples: reasoning in regard to the moon? In regard to the revolution of the earth?

of the earth on its axis, because he was perfectly satisfied that his house was never known to turn with its front to the north. When the king of Siam was told by a Dutch traveller that in Holland, at certain seasons of the year, water becomes so solid that an elephant might walk over it, he replied, "I have believed many extraordinary things which you have told me, because I took you for a man of truth and veracity, but now I am convinced that you lie." This confidence in one's own experience, as the test of probability, characterizes a mind which is confined in its views and limited in its acquirements; and the tendency of it would be the rejection of all knowledge for which we have not the evidence of our senses. Had the king of Siam once seen water in a frozen state, he would not only have been put right in regard to this fact, but his confidence would have been shaken in his own experience as the test of probability in other things; and he would have been more disposed for the further reception of truth upon the evidence of testimony.

Thus, progress in knowledge is not confined in its results to the mere facts which we acquire, but has also an extensive influence in enlarging the mind for the further reception of truth, and setting it free from many of those prejudices which influence men who are limited by a narrow field of observation. There may even be cases in which, without any regard to the veracity of the narrator, a cultivated mind perceives the elements of truth in a statement which is rejected by inferior minds as altogether incredible. An ingenious writer supposes a traveller of rather doubtful veracity bringing into the country of Archimedes an account of the steam-engine. His statement is rejected by his countrymen as altogether incredible. It is entirely at variance with their experience, and they think it much more probable that the traveller should lie, than that such a thing should be. But when he describes to Archimedes the arrangement of the machine, the philosopher perceives the result and, without any consideration of the veracity of the narrator, decides, upon the evidence derived from the relation of the facts themselves, and their accordance

---

Reasoning of the king of Siam? Influence of general knowledge on the belief of testimony? Example, supposition in regard to Archimedes? Ground of Archimedes' belief—what?

with principles which are known to him, that the statement is unquestionably true.

This illustration leads to a principle of the utmost practical importance. In judging of the credibility of a statement, we are not to be influenced simply by our actual experience of similar events; for this would limit our reception of new facts to their accordance with those which we already know. We must extend our views much farther than this, and proceed upon the knowledge which we have derived from other sources, of the powers and properties of the agent to which the event is ascribed. It is on this principle that the account of the steam-engine would have appeared probable to Archimedes, while it was rejected by his countrymen as absolutely incredible; because he would have judged, not according to his experience of similar machinery, but according to his knowledge of the powers and properties of steam. In the same manner, when the king of Siam rejected, as an incredible falsehood, the account of the freezing of water, if there had been at his court a philosopher who had attended to the properties of heat, he would have judged in a different manner, though the actual fact of the freezing of water might have been as new to him as it was to the king. He would have recollected that he had seen various solid bodies rendered fluid by the application of heat; and that, on the abstraction of the additional heat, they again became solid He would thus have argued the possibility, that, by a further abstraction of heat, bodies might become solid which are fluid in the ordinary temperature of the atmosphere. In this manner, the fact, which was rejected by the king, judging from his own experience, might have been received by the philosopher, judging from his knowledge of the powers and properties of heat—though he had acquired this knowledge from events apparently far removed from that to which he now applied it.

The principle here referred to is independent altogether of the direct reliance which we have on testimony, in regard to things which are at variance with our experience, when we are satisfied that the testimony has the characters

---

Important principle. How illustrated by the preceding anecdotes? How should the king of Siam have reasoned?

of credibility; but, even on these grounds, we may perceive the fallacy of that application of the doctrine of probability which has been employed by some writers, in opposition to the truths of revealed religion, and to the means by which they were promulgated—particularly the miracles of the sacred writings. Miracles, they contend, are deviations from the established course of nature, and are, consequently, contrary to our uniform experience. It accords with our experience that men should lie, and even that several men might concur in propagating the same lie; and, therefore, it is more probable that the narrators lied, than that the statement respecting miracles is true. Mr. Hume even went so far as to maintain, that a miracle is so contrary to what is founded upon firm and unalterable experience, that it cannot be established by any human testimony.

Hume's celebrated argument against the resurrection of Christ, and of course against the Christian religion, stated a little more fully is this: "Twelve witnesses," he says, though not exactly in these words, "I admit, agree in testifying that a man rose from the dead. I am consequently compelled to believe one of two things, either that twelve men agreed to tell a lie, or that a man rose from the dead. Either of these suppositions is, I confess, very extraordinary, but as one or the other must be true, I must admit the one that is least extraordinary. Now it seems to me more probable that men should lie, than that one who had been several days dead should return to life again; for it is a very common thing in this world for men to testify falsely; but it is 'contrary to all experience' that a man should rise from the dead."

To this Christian writers reply, in substance, as follows: "We admit the alternative, viz. that we must believe that twelve men have testified falsely, or that one man rose from the dead; and we also admit that we must believe the least improbable of the two. But we deny that the former is the least improbable. For it is not *very* improbable that the Creator should wish to make a communication to mankind; and if so, restoring to life the messenger who brought it, would be a very suitable and a very probable mode of authenticating it. But it *is* contrary to all experience, and all probability, that twelve men, without motive, should conspire to fabricate and disseminate a lie. In regard to the mode by which the Creator would authenticate a message to men, we have no experience; and there is certainly no presumption against the one in question. In regard to men's falsifying their word,

---

Hume's argument, what? Extent to which he carried his reasonings? Mr. Hume's argument stated more fully? The alternative he offers? His choice? In reply, what do Christian writers admit? What do they deny?

in the cause of virtue, and against their own interests, we have a great deal of experience, and it is all against it."

This brief view of the question will assist the pupil to understand more clearly the bearing of the reasoning which follows.

The fallacy of Mr. Hume's argument may probably be maintained from the principles which have been stated. It is, in fact, the same mode of reasoning which induced the king of Siam to reject the statement of water becoming solid. This was entirely contradicted by his "firm and unalterable experience," and, therefore, could not be received, even upon the evidence of a man whom he had already recognised as a witness of unquestionable veracity, and upon whose single testimony he had received as truth "many extraordinary things." He thought it much more probable that even this man lied, than that such a statement could be true. Strictly speaking, indeed, the objection of Mr. Hume may be considered as little better than a play upon words. For what renders an occurrence miraculous is precisely the fact of its being opposed to uniform experience. To say therefore that miracles are incredible because they are contrary to experience, is merely to say that they are incredible because they are miracles.

They who are imposed upon by such a sophism as this, do not, in the first place, attend to the fact, that the term experience, if so much is to be founded upon it, must be limited to the personal observation of every individual; that is, it can apply, in each particular case, only to the last fifty or sixty years at most, and to events which have happened during that period, at the spot where the individual was present. Whatever he knows of events which took place beyond this spot, or before that period, he knows, not from experience, but entirely from testimony: and a great part of our knowledge, of what we call the established course of nature, has been required in this manner. In the reception of new knowledge, then, an individual must either receive facts upon testimony, or believe nothing but that for which he has the evidence of his senses. It is unnecessary to state how much the latter supposition is at va-

---

Its fallacy, how shown? Hume's reasoning compared with that of the king of Siam? Experience, how limited? Necessity of placing confidence in testimony?

riance with the daily practice of every man; and how much information we are in the constant habit of receiving upon testimony, even in regard to things which are very much at variance with our personal observation. How many facts do we receive in this manner, with unsuspecting confidence, on the testimony of the historian, in regard to the occurrences of ancient times; and on the testimony of the naturalist and the traveller, respecting the natural and civil history of foreign countries. How few persons have verified, by their personal observation, the wonders which we receive on the testimony of the astronomer; and, even of the great phenomena of nature on the surface of our globe, how much do we receive upon testimony in regard to things which are widely at variance with our own experience. I need only mention the boiling springs of Iceland, and the phenomena of earthquakes and volcanoes. But, on the principles of Mr. Hume, these could not be believed. On the contrary, if one of our intelligent Highlanders were hearing described to him the devastations of a volcano, he would point to his heath-covered mountain, as the basis of his "firm and unalterable experience," and declare it to be more probable that travellers should lie than that such a statement could be true.

The reception of facts upon the evidence of testimony must therefore be considered as a fundamental principle of our nature, to be acted upon whenever we are satisfied that the testimony possesses certain characters of credibility. These are chiefly referable to three heads: that the individual has had sufficient opportunity of ascertaining the facts; that we have confidence in his power of judging of their accuracy; and that we have no suspicion of his being influenced by passion or prejudice in his testimony,—or, in other words, that we believe him to be an honest witness. Our confidence is further strengthened by several witnesses concurring in the same testimony, each of whom has had the same opportunities of ascertaining the facts, and presents the same characters of truth and honesty. On such testimony we are in the constant habit of receiving statements which

---

Extent of confidence universally placed in it. Examples. Supposed reasoning of Highlanders on Hume's principle? Proper views of confidence in testimony. Of what three conditions? Corroborating circumstances?

are much beyond the sphere of our personal observation, and widely at variance with our experience. These are the statements which, for the sake of a name, we may call marvellous. In regard to such, the foundation of incredulity, as we have seen, is generally ignorance; and it is interesting to trace the principles by which a man of cultivated mind is influenced in receiving upon testimony, statements which are rejected by the vulgar as totally incredible.

1. He is influenced by the recollection that many things at one time appeared to him marvellous which he now knows to be true: and he thence concludes that there may still be in nature many phenomena and many principles with which he is entirely unacquainted. In other words, he has learned from experience not to make his own knowledge his test of probability.

2. He is greatly influenced by perceiving in the statement some element of probability, or any kind of sequence or relation by which the alleged fact may be connected with principles which are known to him. It is in this manner that the freezing of water, which was rejected by the king of Siam as an incredible falsehood, might have appeared credible to a philosopher who had attended to the properties of heat, because he would have perceived in the statement a chain of relations connecting it with facts which he knew to be true.

3. He is much guided by his power of discriminating the credibility of testimony, or of distinguishing that species and that amount of it which he feels to be unworthy of absolute credit from that on which he relies with as implicit confidence as on the uniformity of the course of nature. The vulgar mind is often unable to make the necessary discrimination in this respect, and therefore is apt to fall into one of the extremes of credulity and scepticism. Mr. Hume, indeed, himself admits that there is a certain amount of testimony on which he would receive a statement widely at variance with his own uniform experience, as in the hypothetical case which he proposes,—the account of a total darkness over the whole earth, continuing for eight days, two

Belief of marvellous accounts? Considerations which influence cultivated minds in receiving testimony? First? Second? Example. Third?

hundred years ago. The evidence which he requires for it is simply the concurrence of testimonies,—namely, that all authors in all languages describe the event; and that travellers bring accounts from all quarters of traditions of the occurrence being still strong and lively among the people. On such evidence he admits that philosophers ought to receive it as certain.

These principles may be considered as the elements of our belief in regard to statements which are new to us; and it is interesting to remark how they balance and compensate each other. Thus, a statement which appears probable, or can be readily referred to known relations, is received upon a lower degree of testimony, as in the illustration respecting Archimedes and the steam-engine. Others, which we find greater difficulty in referring to any known principle, we may receive upon a certain amount of testimony which we feel to be worthy of absolute confidence. But there may be others of so very extraordinary a kind, and so far removed from, or even opposed to, every known principle, that we may hesitate in receiving them upon any kind of testimony; unless we can discover in relation to them something on which the mind can fix as an element of moral probability.

This leads us to a very obvious distinction of extraordinary events,—into those which are only marvellous, and those which are to be considered miraculous. A marvellous event is one which differs in all its elements from any thing that we previously knew, without being opposed to any known principle. But a miraculous event implies much more than this, being directly opposed to what every man knows to be the established and uniform course of nature It is further required that such an event shall be of so obvious and palpable a kind that every man is qualified to juge of its miraculous character, or is convinced it could not happen from the operation of any ordinary natural cause.

In receiving a statement respecting such an event we require the highest species of testimony, or that on which we rely with the same confidence as on the uniformity of

---

Application of these principles. Distinction of extraordinary events; what two kinds? Degree of testimony necessary to establish a miraculous event?

the course of nature herself. But even with this amount of testimony a doubt may still remain. For we have two amounts of probability which are equally balanced against each other; namely, the probability that such testimony should not deceive us, and the probability that there should be no deviation from the course of nature. The concurring evidence of numerous credible witnesses, indeed, gives a decided preponderance to the testimony; and upon a certain amount of testimony we might receive any statement, however improbable—as in the case admitted by Mr. Hume of a universal darkness. But, though in such a case we might receive the statement as a fact which we could not dispute, the mind would be left in a state of absolute suspense and uncertainty in regard to any judgment which we could form respecting it. Something more appears to be necessary for fixing the distinct belief of a miraculous interposition; and this is an impression of moral probability. This consists of two parts. (1.) A distinct reference of the event to a power which we feel to be capable of producing it; namely, a direct interposition of the Deity. (2.) The perception of an adequate object, or a conviction of high moral probability that an interposition of Divine power might be exerted in such circumstances, or for the accomplishment of such an object. Such are the miracles of the sacred writings. As events opposed to the common course of nature, they are, by the supposition, physically improbable in the highest degree. Were they not so, were they in the lowest degree probable, according to our conceptions of the course of nature, they could not be miracles, and consequently could not answer the purpose for which they are intended. But notwithstanding this species of improbability, they carry with them all the elements of absolute credibility; namely, the highest species of testimony, supported by a moral probability which bears directly upon every element of the statement. This may be briefly referred to the following heads:—

1. The human mind had wandered far from truth respecting God; and on the great question of his character and will, a future state, and the mode of acceptance in his

What necessary besides? Grounds of moral probability? Classification of the grounds of it, in this case. State of the human race?

sight, the light furnished by reason among the wisest of men was faint and feeble. On points of such importance there was the highest moral probability that the Deity would not leave mankind in this state of darkness, but would communicate to them some distinct knowledge.

2. It is further probable, that if such a communication were made to man, it would be accompanied by prodigies or miraculous events, calculated to show beyond a doubt the immediate agency of God, and thus to establish the divine authority of the record.

3. There is no improbability that the power of the Deity should produce deviations from the usual course of nature capable of answering such a purpose. For what we call the course of nature is nothing more than an order of events which he has established; and there is no improbability that for an adequate end he might produce a deviation from this order.

4. An important branch of the moral probability of the whole statement of the sacred writings arises from the characters of the truths themselves, challenging the assent and approbation of every uncontaminated mind. This part of the subject resolves itself into three parts; namely, the truths relating to the character and perfections of the Deity; the high and refined morality of the gospel; and the adaptation of the whole provisions of Christianity to the actual condition of man as a moral being. The former carry a conviction of their truth to the mind of every candid inquirer; the two latter fix themselves upon the conscience or moral feelings of all classes of men with an impression which is irresistible.

This mode of reasoning is not chargeable with that kind of fallacy which has sometimes been ascribed to it,—that it professes first to prove the doctrine by the miracle, and then to try the miracle by the doctrine. The tendency of it is only to deduce from the various elements which really enter into the argument, a kind of compound evidence, the strongest certainly which on such a subject the human mind is capable of receiving. It is composed of the character of the truths—the moral probability of a revelation of clear

Necessity of evidence of a revelation? Power sufficient. Internal evidence? Charge of fallacy? Reply.

knowledge on subjects of such infinite importance—and the highest species of testimony for the miraculous evidence by which the revelation was accompanied. There are principles in our nature calculated to perceive the manner in which the different parts of such an argument harmonize with each other; and, upon every principle of the human mind, it is impossible to conceive any thing more highly calculated to challenge the serious attention and absolute conviction of every sound understanding.

This imperfect view of a deeply interesting subject will be sufficient to show the fallacy of the objection which has been urged against the credibility of miracles,—that they are contrary to our unalterable experience of the established course of nature. There might have been some degree of plausibility in the argument, if these events had been alleged to have taken place in ordinary circumstances; but the case is essentially altered, and this kind of improbability is altogether removed, when in the alleged deviation a new agent is introduced entirely capable of producing it. Such, as we have seen, are the miracles of the sacred writings; and the question in regard to their probability is, not whether they are probable according to the usual course of nature, but whether they are probable in the circumstances in which they are alleged to have taken place; namely, in the case of a direct interposition of the Deity for certain great and adequate purposes. In such a case, our estimate of probability must be founded, according to the principles already stated, not upon our experience of similar events, but on the knowledge which we derive from other sources of the power of the agent to whom the event is ascribed. Now the agent to whom miracles are ascribed is the Supreme Being, the Creator of all things, the stupendous monuments of whose omnipotent power are before us, and within us, and around us. What we call the established course of nature is merely an order of events which he has appointed; and the question of probability is, whether it is probable that for certain adequate purposes he should produce a deviation from this order. For such a statement, indeed, we require strong, numerous, credible, and concur-

---

General view of the question? The real question in regard to the probability of miracles?

ring testimonies; but it comes to be simply a question of evidence: and there is no real improbability that in these circumstances such events should take place.

In this manner, then, there is entirely removed from the statement the improbability which is founded upon the uniformity of the ordinary course of nature; because it is not in the ordinary course of nature that the events are alleged to have taken place, but in circumstances altogether new and peculiar. The subsequent inquiry becomes, therefore simply a question of evidence; this evidence is derived from testimony; and we are thus led to take a slight view of the grounds on which we estimate the credibility of testimony.

Testimony, we are told, is fallacious, and is liable to deceive us. But so are our senses;—they also may deceive, and perhaps have deceived us, as in the case of ocular spectra; but we do not on that account discredit the evidence of our eyes; we only take means, in certain cases, for correcting their indications by other senses, as by touching the object, or by a comparison with the visual impressions of other men; and, whatever probability there is that the eyes of one man may be deceived in any one instance, the probability is as nothing that both his sight and touch should be deceived at once; or that the senses of ten men should be deceived in the same manner at the same time. It is the same with regard to testimony. It may have deceived us in particular instances; but this applies to one species of testimony only; there is another species which never deceived us. We learn by experience to separate distinctly the one from the other, and fix upon a species of testimony on which we rely with the same confidence as on the uniformity of the course of nature. Thus, if we find a man who in other respects shows every indication of a sound mind, relating an event which happened under his own inspection, and in such circumstances that he could not possibly be deceived; if his statement be such as contributes in no respect to his credit or advantage, but, on the contrary, exposes him to ridicule, contempt, and persecution, if, notwithstanding, he steadily perseveres in it, under

---

Form which the question assumes when the presumption against the fact is removed? Evidence of testimony and of the senses compared? Example Case in which confidence in testimony must be implicit?

every species of persecution, and even to the suffering of death; to suppose such a testimony intended to deceive, would be to assume a deviation from the established course of human character, as remarkable as any event which it could possibly convey to us. This might be maintained in regard to one such testimony; but if we find numerous witnesses agreeing in the same testimony, all equally informed of the facts, all showing the same characters of credibility, and without the possibility of concert or connivance, the evidence becomes, not convincing only, but incontrovertible.

The grounds on which we receive with confidence the evidence of testimony, may, therefore, be briefly stated in the following manner:—

1. That the statement refers to a matter of fact,—that the fact was such as could be easily ascertained by the person who relates it,—and that he had sufficient opportunity of ascertaining it. When the statement includes a point of opinion, the case comes under another principle; and we require, in the first instance, to separate what is opinion from what is fact.

2. That we have no reason to suspect the witness to be influenced by interest or passion in his evidence; or that he has any purpose to answer by it, calculated to promote his own advantage.

3. That various individuals, without suspicion of connivance, have concurred in the same statement. This is a point of the utmost importance; and in cases in which we are satisfied that there could be no connivance, a degree of evidence is derived from the concurrence of testimonies, which may be often independent even of the credibility of the individual witnesses. For, though it were probable that each of them singly might lie, the chances that they should all happen to agree in the same lie, may be found to amount to an impossibility. On this subject there is also a further principle of the greatest interest, which has been well illustrated by Laplace, namely, that the more improbable a statement is in which such witnesses agree, the greater is the probability of its truth. Thus we may have two men whom

---

Grounds of confidence in testimony? The subject? Freedom from bias. Concurrence of witnesses? Laplace's illustration?

we know to be so addicted to lying that we would not attach the smallest credit to their single testimony on any subject. If we find these concurring in a statement respecting an event which was highly probable, or very likely to have occurred at the time which they mention, we may still have a suspicion that they are lying, and that they may have happened to concur in the same lie, even though there should be no supposition of connivance. But if the statement was in the highest degree improbable, such as that of a man rising from the dead, we may feel it to be impossible that they could accidentally have agreed in such a statement; and, if we are satisfied that there could be no connivance, we may receive a conviction from its very improbability that it must be true. In cases of concurring testimonies, we expect that the witnesses shall agree in all essential and important particulars; and, on the other hand, evidence of the authenticity of testimony is sometimes derived from the various witnesses differing in trifling circumstances in such a manner as, without weakening the main statement, tends to remove the suspicion of collusion or connivance.

4. In all matters of testimony, we are greatly influenced by our confidence in a certain uniformity of human character. We attach much importance, for example, to our previous knowledge of the narrator's character for veracity; and a man may have acquired such a character in this respect, that we confide in his veracity in every instance in which his testimony is concerned, with a confidence equal to that with which we rely on the uniformity of the course of nature. In such a case, indeed, we proceed upon a uniformity which applies only to a particular order, namely, those whom we consider as men of veracity. But there is also a principle of uniformity which applies to the whole species; and in which we confide as regulating every man of sane mind. Thus, if the statement of a narrator contain circumstances calculated to promote his own advantage, we calculate on the probability of fabrication, and reject his evidence, except we had previously acquired absolute confidence in his veracity. But if, on the contrary, his statement operates against himself, conveying an imputation

---

Examples. Character? Views of interest.

against his own character, or exposing him to contempt, ridicule, or personal injury; without any previous knowledge of his veracity, we are satisfied that nothing could make him adhere to such a testimony, but an honest conviction of its truth.

5. A very important circumstance is the absence of any contradictory or conflicting testimony. This applies, in a striking manner, to the miraculous statements of the sacred writings; for, even on the part of those who were most interested in opposing them, there is no testimony which professes to show, that at the time when the miracles are said to have taken place, they did not take place. It is, indeed, a remarkable circumstance, that the earliest writers against Christianity ascribe the miraculous events to the power of sorcery or magic, but never attempt to call them in question as matters of fact.

6. Much corroboration of testimony may often be obtained from our knowledge of facts of such a nature as, without directly bearing upon the statements to which the testimony refers, cannot be accounted for on any other supposition than the conviction of these statements being true. This principle applies, in a remarkable manner, to the miraculous histories of the sacred writings. We know, as an historical fact, the rapid manner in which the Christian faith was propagated in the early ages, against the most formidable opposition, and by means of the feeblest human instruments. We are told, that this was owing to the conviction produced by miraculous displays of Divine power; we feel that the known effect corresponds with the alleged cause; and that it cannot be accounted for on any other principle.

It does not belong to our present inquiry to allude more particularly to the direct evidence by which the miracles of the sacred writings are supported; we merely refer, in this general manner, to the principles on which the evidence is to be estimated. A very interesting branch of the subject will come under our view when we speak of memory and arbitrary association. We shall then see the irresistible importance of the commemorative rites of Christianity, by which the memory of these events has been transmitted

---

Absence of opposing testimony? Corroborating circumstances? Illustration? Remarks upon the direct evidence of Christianity?

from age to age, or rather from year to year; and by which our minds are carried backward, in one unbroken series, to the time when the events occurred, and to the individuals who witnessed them. In this manner, also, is entirely removed any feeling of uncertainty which may attach to testimony, as we recede from the period at which the events took place, and as the individuals are multiplied. Upon the whole, therefore, the evidence becomes so clear and conclusive, that we may say of those who reject it what the great Author of Christianity said on another occasion,—"If they hear not these, neither will they be persuaded though one rose from the dead."

Evidence in proof of Christianity.

PART III.

OF THE INTELLECTUAL OPERATIONS.

THROUGH the various sources referred to in the preceding observations, we acquire the knowledge of a certain number of facts, relating either to the mind itself, or to things external to it. The next part of our inquiry refers to the operations (to use a figurative expression) which the mind performs upon the facts thus acquired. The term functions, or powers of mind, has often been applied to these operations; but, as we are not entitled to assume that they are not in fact separate functions in the usual acceptation of that expression, it is perhaps more correct, and accords better with our limited knowledge of mind, to speak simply of the operations which it is capable of performing upon a given series of facts. These seem to be chiefly referable to the following heads.

I. We remember the facts; and we can also recall them into the mind at pleasure. The former is MEMORY; the latter is that modification of it which we call RECOLLECTION. But, besides this simple recollection of facts, we can recall a perception; that is, the impression of an actual scene which has been witnessed, or a person who has been seen, so as to place them, as it were, before the mind, with all the vividness of the original perception. This process is called CONCEPTION. It is often described as a distinct power, or a distinct operation of the mind; but it seems to be so nearly allied to memory that it may be considered as a modification of it. It is the memory of a perception.

II. We separate facts from the relation in which they

Subject. Classification? Memory. Conception. **Abstraction.**

were originally presented to us, and contemplate some of them apart from the rest;—considering, for example, certain properties of bodies apart from their other properties. Among a variety of objects, we thus fix upon qualities which are common to a certain number of them, and so arrange them into genera and species. This process is usually called ABSTRACTION.

III. We separate scenes or classes of facts into their constituent elements, and form these elements into new combinations, so as to represent to ourselves scenes, or combinations of events, which have no real existence. This is IMAGINATION.

IV. We compare facts with each other,—observe their relations and connections,—and trace the results which follow particular combinations of them. We also observe their general characters, so as to deduce from the whole general facts or general principles. This is REASON or JUDGMENT.

In this arrangement, it will be observed, I confine myself entirely to facts. I do not say that the mind possesses distinct faculties, which we call memory, abstraction, imagination, and judgment,—for this at once leads into hypothesis; but simply, that, in point of fact, the mind remembers, abstracts, imagines, and judges. These processes appear to constitute distinct mental acts, which every one is conscious of who attends to the phenomena of his own mind. But beyond the simple facts we know nothing, and no human ingenuity can lead us one step farther. Some of the followers of Dr. Reid appear to have erred in this respect, by ascribing to the mind distinct faculties or functions, somewhat in the manner in which we ascribe to the body distinct senses. Dr. Brown, on the other hand, has shown much ingenuity in his attempts to simplify the arrangement of the mental processes, by referring them all to his two principles of simple and relative suggestion. But, without inquiring what has been gained to the science by this new phraseology, and avoiding entirely any system which seems to

---

Imagination. Judgment. Theories on this subject? Dr. Reid's? Dr. Brown's?

suppose distinct *functions* of mind, I confine myself to facts respecting the actual mental *operations;* and it appears to answer best the purpose of practical utility to speak of these operations in the arrangement, and by the names, which are commonly used by the generality of mankind.

SECTION I.

MEMORY.

By Memory we retain the impression of facts or events, and by Recollection we recall them into the mind by a voluntary effort. By Conception we recall perceptions, or the impression of actual scenes, persons, or transactions: thus a skilful painter can delineate from conception a landscape a considerable time after he has seen it, or the countenance of a friend who is dead or absent. These appear to be the leading phenomena which are referable to the head of memory.

There seem to be original differences in the power of memory, some individuals being remarkable for retentive memory, though not otherwise distinguished by their intellectual endowments. Thus, persons have been known to repeat a long discourse after once hearing it, or even a series of things without connection, as a long column of figures, or a number of words without meaning. There is on record the account of a man who could repeat the whole contents of a newspaper; and of another who could retain words that were dictated to him, without any connection, to the amount of six thousand. A man mentioned by Seneca, after hearing a poet read a new poem, claimed it as his own; and, in proof of his claim, repeated the poem from beginning to end, which the author could not do. A similar anecdote is told of an Englishman, whom the king of Prussia placed behind a screen when Voltaire came to read to him a new poem of considerable length. It has been alleged, that this kind of memory is generally connected

---

Author's remarks? Definitions? Original differences? Examples?

with inferiority of the other intellectual powers: but there appears to be no foundation for this. For, though the mere memory of words may be met with in a high degree in persons of defective understanding, it is also true that men of high endowments have been remarkable for memory. It is said that Themistocles could name all the citizens of Athens, amounting to twenty thousand; and that Cyrus knew the name of every soldier in his army.

The late Dr. Leyden was remarkable for his memory. I am informed, through a gentleman who was intimately acquainted with him, that he could repeat correctly a long act of parliament, or any similar document, after having once read it. When he was, on one occasion, congratulated by a friend on his remarkable power in this respect, he replied that instead of an advantage, it was often a source of great inconvenience. This he explained by saying, that when he wished to recollect a particular point in any thing which he had read, he could do it only by repeating to himself the whole from the commencement till he reached the point which he wished to recall.

We may find a mere local memory combined with very little judgment; that is, the power of remembering facts in the order in which they occurred, or words in the order in which they were addressed to the individual; but that kind of memory which is founded, not upon local or incidental relations, but on real analogies, must be considered as an important feature of a cultivated mind, and as holding an important place in the formation of intellectual character. The former kind of memory, however, is often the more ready, and is that which generally makes the greater show, both on account of its readiness, and likewise because the kind of facts with which it is chiefly conversant are usually those most in request in common conversation.

The facts now referred to are matters of curiosity only. The points of real interest and practical importance, in regard to memory, respect the manner in which it is influenced by the intellectual habits of individuals, and the principles on which it may be improved. These are referable

---

Influence on the other powers? Dr. Leyden's memory. Inconvenience resulting from it? Different kinds of memory? Two important points?

chiefly to two heads, namely, ATTENTION and ASSOCIATION.

Memory is very much influenced by ATTENTION, or a full and distinct perception of the fact or object with a view to its being remembered; and by the perception being kept before the mind, in this distinct manner, for a certain time. The distinct recollection of the fact, in such cases, is generally in proportion to the intensity with which it has been contemplated; and this is also very much strengthened by its being repeatedly brought before the mind. Most people, accordingly, have experienced that a statement is more strongly impressed upon the memory by being several times repeated to others. It is on the same principle, that memory is greatly assisted by writing down the object of our knowledge, especially if this be done in a distinct and systematic manner. A subject also is more distinctly conceived, and more correctly remembered, after we have instructed another person in it. Such exercises are not strictly to be considered as helps to the memory, but as excitements to attention; and as thus leading to that clear and full comprehension of the subject which is required for the distinct remembrance of it.

It is familiar to every one that there are great differences in memory, both in respect to the facility of acquirement and the power of retention. In the former there appear to be original differences, but a great deal also depends upon habit. In the power of retention much depends, as we shall afterwards see, upon the habit of correct association; but, besides this, there are facts which seem to show a singular connection with the manner in which the acquisition was made. The following fact was communicated to me by an able and intelligent friend, who heard it from the individual to whom it relates. A distinguished theatrical performer, in consequence of the sudden illness of another actor, had occasion to prepare himself, on very short notice, for a part which was entirely new to him; and the part was long and rather difficult. He acquired it in a very short time, and went through it with perfect accuracy, but immediately after the performance forgot every word of it. Characters

---

Attention. Means of securing it? Differences in memory. Illustration. Story o the actor?

which he had acquired in a more deliberate manner he never forgets, but can perform them at any time without a moment's preparation; but in regard to the character now mentioned, there was the farther and very singular fact, that though he has repeatedly performed it since that time, he has been obliged each time to prepare it anew, and has never acquired in regard to it that facility which is familiar to him in other instances. When questioned respecting the mental process which he employed the first time he performed this part, he says, that he ost sight entirely of the audience, and seemed to have nothing before him but the pages of the book from which he had learned it; and that if any thing had occurred to interrupt this illusion, he should have stopped instantly.

That degree of attention which is required for the full remembrance of a subject, is to be considered as a voluntary act on the part of the individual; but the actual exercise of it is influenced in a great measure by his previous intellectual habits. Of four individuals, for example, who are giving an account of a journey through the same district, one may describe chiefly its agricultural produce; another, its mineralogical characters; a third, its picturesque beauties; while the fourth may not be able to give an account of any thing except the state of the roads and the facilities for travelling. The same facts or objects must have passed before the senses of all the four; but their remembrance of them depends upon the points to which their attention was directed. Besides the manner here alluded to, in which the attention is influenced by previous habits or pursuits, some persons have an active inquiring state of mind, which keeps the attention fully engaged upon whatever is passing before them; while others give way to a listless, inactive condition, which requires to be strongly excited before the attention is roused to the degree required for remembrance. The former, accordingly, remember a great deal of all that passes before them, either in reading or observation. The latter are apt to say that they are deficient in memory; their deficiency, however, is not in memory, but in attention and this appears from the fact that they do not forget any thing which deeply engages their feelings, or concerns their interest.

Different objects of attention? Effects of inattention?

The habit of listless inactivity of mind should be carefully guarded against in the young; and the utmost care should be taken to cultivate the opposite, namely, the habit of directing the mind intensely to whatever comes before it, either in reading or observation. This may be considered as forming the foundation of sound intellectual character.

Next to the effect of attention, is the remarkable influence produced upon memory by ASSOCIATION. This principle holds so important a place in relation to the mental operations, that some philosophers have been disposed to refer to it nearly all the phenomena of mind; but without ascribing to it this universal influence, its effects are certainly very extensive, and the facts connected with it present a subject of peculiar interest.

The principle of association is founded upon a remarkable tendency, by which two or more facts or conceptions, which have been contemplated together, or in immediate succession, become so connected in the mind that one of them at a future time recalls the others, or introduces a train of thoughts which, without any mental effort, follow each other in the order in which they were originally associated. This is called the association of ideas, and various phenomena of a very interesting kind are connected with it.

But besides this tendency, by which thoughts formerly associated are brought into the mind in a particular order, there is another species of association into which the mind passes spontaneously, by a suggestion from any subject which happens to be present to it. The thought or fact which is thus present suggests another which has some kind of affinity to it; this suggests a third, and so on, to the formation of a train or series which may be continued to a great length. A remarkable circumstance likewise is, that such a train may go on with very little consciousness of, or attention to it; so that the particulars of the series are scarcely remembered, or are traced only by an effort. This singular fact every one must have experienced in that state of mind which is called a revery. It goes on for some time without effort and with little attention; at length the attention is roused, and directed to a particular thought which is

Caution to the young. Association. Its foundation? Trains of thought. Embracing them?

in the mind, without the person being at first able to recollect what led him to think of that subject. He then, by a voluntary effort, traces the chain of thoughts backwards, perhaps through a long series, till he arrives at a subject of which he has a distinct remembrance as having given rise to it.

It is impossible distinctly to trace the principles which lead to the particular chain of thoughts which arise in a case of this kind. It is probably much influenced by the previous intellectual habits of the individual; and perhaps in many instances is guided by associations previously formed. There are also among the facts or thoughts themselves certain principles of analogy, by which one suggests another without that kind of connection which is established by previous proximity. These have usually been called *principles of association*, or, according to the phraseology of Dr. Brown, principles of simple suggestion. They have been generally referred to four heads,—namely, resemblance, contiguity in time and place, cause and effect, and contrast: and others have reduced them to three, considering contiguity and cause and effect as referable to the same head. On these principles, then, one thought may suggest another which has some relation to it, either in the way of resemblance, contiguity, cause, effect, or contrast. But still the question recurs, What gives rise to the occurrence of one of these relations in preference to the others? This may depend, in some instances, on previous habits of thought and peculiarities of mental temperament; and in other cases associations may be more apt to occur, according as some analogous association may have been more recently formed, more lively, or more frequently repeated. When the common topic of the weather, for example, is introduced in conversation, or presented to the mind, the agriculturist will naturally refer to its influence on vegetation; the physician to its effect on the health of the community; the man of pleasure may think only of its reference to the sports of the field; the philosopher may endeavor to seek for its cause in some preceding atmospheric phenomena; and another person of certain habits of ob-

---

Explanation? Principles of association? Form used by Dr. Brown? Classification? Effects of habit? Illustration?

servation may compare or contrast it with the weather of the same period in a preceding year. Thus, in five individuals, the same topic may give rise to five trains of thought, perfectly distinct from each other, yet each depending upon a very natural and obvious principle of suggestion. In other instances it is impossible to trace the cause which leads the mind off into peculiar and unusual associations. The following example from Hobbes has been frequently referred to:—"In a company in which the conversation turned on the civil war, what could be conceived more impertinent than for a person to ask abruptly what was the value of a Roman denarius? On a little reflection, however, I was easily able to trace the train of thought which suggested the question; for the original subject of discourse naturally introduced the history of the king, and of the treachery of those who surrendered his person to his enemies; this again introduced the treachery of Judas Iscariot, and the sum of money which he received for his reward. And all this train of ideas passed through the mind of the speaker in a twinkling in consequence of the velocity of thought." Mr. Stewart adds, in relation to this anecdote, "It is by no means improbable, that if the speaker had been interrogated about the connection of ideas which led him aside from the original topic of discourse, he would have found himself, at first, at a loss for an answer."

In the mental process now referred to it is evident that the term *suggestion* is much more correct than *association*, which has often been applied to it. For in the cases which belong to this class, the facts or thoughts suggest each other, not according to any connection or association which the mind had previously formed between them, but according to some mental impression or emotion, which by a law of our constitution proves a principle of analogy or suggestion. We readily perceive how this takes place in regard to circumstances which are allied to each other by resemblance, contiguity, cause, or effect; and the suggestion of contrast must also occur to every one as by no means unnatural. Thus, the sight of a remarkably fat man may recall to us the thought of another man we had

Hobbes' example? Mr. Stewart's remark? Terms. Which preferable?

lately seen, who was equally remarkable for his leanness the playfulness and mirth of childhood may suggest the cares and anxieties of after life; and an instance of conduct which we greatly disapprove may lead us to recollect how very differently another individual conducted himself in similar circumstances.

In a practical view, the subject of association leads us chiefly to a consideration of the manner in which facts are so associated in the mind as to be recalled by means of the connection; in other words, the influence of association upon memory. In this view, associations are distinctly referable to three classes:

I. Natural or philosophical association.
II. Local or incidental association.
III. Arbitrary or fictitious association.

A variety of mental phenomena of the most interesting kind will be found connected with the subjects referred to under these classes. The principle on which they all depend is simply the circumstance of two or more facts, thoughts, or events being contemplated together by the mind, though many of them may have no relation to each other except this conjunction. The strength of the association is generally in proportion to the intensity of the mental emotion; and is likewise in a great measure regulated by the length of time, or the number of times, in which the facts have been contemplated in this connection. Astonishing examples may be often met with of facts or occurrences which have long ceased to be objects of simple memory, being brought up in this manner by association, though they had not passed through the mind for a very long time.

I. Natural or Philosophical Association takes place when a fact or statement on which the attention is fixed, is by a mental process associated with some fact previously known to which it has a relation, or with some subject which it is calculated to illustrate. The fact so acquired is thus, to use a figurative expression, put by in its proper

---

Why? Association, how classified? Foundation of all. The strength of it depends on what? Philosophical association

place in the mind, and can afterward be recalled by means of the association.

The formation of associations, in this manner, is of course influenced in a very great degree by previous mental habits, pursuits, or subjects of reflection; and, according to the nature and the variety of these pursuits or subjects of thought, facts which by some are passed by and instantly forgotten may be fixed upon by others with eager attention, and referred to some principle which they are calculated to illustrate. Examples of this kind must be familiar to every one; I may mention the following:—In a party of gentlemen, the conversation turned on the warlike character of the Mahrattas, as compared with the natives of Lower India, and the explanation given of it by an author who refers it to their use of animal food, from which the Hindoos are said to be prohibited by their religion. A doubt was started respecting the extent to which Hindoos are prohibited from the use of animal food: some were of one opinion and some of another, and the point was left undecided. Reading soon after the Journal of bishop Heber, I found it stated, that on one occasion during his journey, when a large supply of meat was brought to him, he ordered three lambs to be sent to his Hindoo attendants, and that the gift was received with every expression of gratitude. On another occasion such a fact might have been passed by without producing any impression; or it might have been slightly associated with the good bishop's attention to the comfort of all around him, but not remembered beyond the passing moment. In connection with the discussion now mentioned it became a fact of great interest, and never to be forgotten; and led to inquiry after more precise information on the subject to which it related.

This trifling example may serve to illustrate the principle, that the remembrance of insulated facts does not depend merely upon the degree of attention directed to them, but also on the existence in the mind of subjects of thought with which the new fact may be associated. Other facts, as they occur, will afterward be added from time to time, giving rise to a progressive increase of knowledge in a

---

Influence of previous habits. Example? Inference? Theory of progress in knowledge?

mind in which this mental process is regularly carried on. This habit of attention and association ought therefore to be carefully cultivated, as it must have a great influence on our progress in knowledge, and likewise on the formation of intellectual character, provided the associations be made upon sound principles, or according to the true and important relations of things. It is also closely connected with that activity of mind which is ever on the alert for knowledge, from every source that comes within its reach; and that habit of reflection which always connects with such facts the conclusions to which they lead, and the views which they tend to illustrate. On this principle, also, every new fact which is acquired, or every new subject of thought which is brought before the mind, is not only valuable in itself, but also becomes the basis or nucleus of further improvement. Minds which are thus furnished with the requisite foundation of knowledge, and act uniformly upon these principles of enlarging it, will find interesting matter to be associated and remembered, where others find only amusement for a vacant hour, which passes away and is forgotten. There is also another respect in which the habit of correct and philosophical association assists the memory, and contributes to progress in knowledge. For by means of it, when applied to a great mass of facts relating to the same subject, we arrive at certain general facts, which represent a numerous body of the individuals, and the remembrance of which is equivalent to the remembrance of the whole

The associations referred to under this first head arise out of the real relations of facts to each other, or to subjects of thought previously existing in the mind. The particular train of association, therefore, which is formed from the same facts by different individuals, may vary exceedingly. Thus, the same facts may often admit of various applications, or, in other words, of being associated in various ways, by different persons, according to their intellectual habits, or by the same person at different times, according to the subject of thought which happens to be more immediately present.

Influence of correct habits of association? Of previous attainments? Of classification?

When a variety of facts have been associated in the mind in the manner now referred to, they form a series which hang together and recall each other in a very remarkable manner. There are two ways in which this takes place, which may be called voluntary and spontaneous. (1.) We call up facts by a voluntary effort, by directing the mind into particular trains of thought calculated to lead to those which we are in search of. This is what we call recollecting ourselves on a particular subject. We have an impression, perhaps, that the mind is in possession of information which bears upon the subject, but do not at the moment remember it; or we remember some circumstances, and wish to recall a more full and complete remembrance. We therefore commence a mental process which consists in putting in motion, to speak figuratively, a train of thoughts, or a series of associated facts, which we think calculated to lead us to the facts we wish to recall. (2.) Associations recur spontaneously, either when particular topics naturally leading to them are brought before the mind, in reading or conversation, or in that state in which the mind is left to follow, without any effort, the current of thoughts as they succeed each other. In the healthy state of the mind, we can give way to this spontaneous succession of thoughts; or we can check it at our pleasure, and direct the mind into some new train connected with the same subject, or arising out of it; or we can dismiss it altogether. While we allow it to go on, it does so, not only without effort, but often without consciousness; so that when the attention is, after some time, arrested by a subject of thought which is in the mind, we do not at first remember what led us to think of it, and begin to recollect ourselves by tracing the series backwards. In this state of mind, it is most interesting to observe the manner in which old associations are revived, and old recollections renewed, which seemed to have been lost and forgotten; and how facts and occurrences come into the mind which had not been thought of for many years. They are recalled, we scarcely know how, by some train of association which we can hardly trace, and which had long ceased to

---

Recalling facts. First mode? Second mode? Our power to control our train of thought? Old associations revived.

be the subject of any voluntary effort of attention. We shall again allude to this most interesting subject, in relation to the manner in which associations, long forgotten, are sometimes brought into the mind in dreaming, and in certain states of delirium.

The voluntary power over the succession of thoughts and associations which has now been alluded to is a subject of extreme interest. We shall have occasion to refer to it again when we come to speak of a remarkable condition in which it is lost; and in which the mind is left entirely under the influence of the series of thoughts as they happen to succeed each other, according probably to old associations, without the power of arresting or varying it. This occurs in two very interesting mental conditions to be afterward more particularly mentioned; namely, dreaming and insanity.

II. LOCAL OR INCIDENTAL ASSOCIATION.—In the mental process referred to under the preceding head, facts or thoughts are associated according to certain real relations; though these, we have seen, may be various, and the particular relation which is fixed upon, in particular cases, depends upon the intellectual habits of the individual. In the class now to be mentioned, the associations are formed according to no other relations than such as are entirely local or casual. Thus, a fact, a thought, or a mental impression is associated with the person by whom it was communicated, or the place where the communication was made; and is recalled to the mind when the place or person is seen, mentioned, or thought of. Some persons seem to form almost no other associations than those of this description. When a place which they had visited, for example, is spoken of, they immediately relate, in connection with it, the persons whom they met there, incidents which occurred in their company, and opinions or statements which were mentioned in conversation with them; and from this, perhaps, they may branch off to other circumstances relating to these individuals, their families, or connections.

These mere local associations, however, often make a

Is the power over the succession of thoughts ever lost? In what cases? Local association. Definition? Examples.

very deep impression upon the mind; more vivid, certainly, than simple memory of the facts or transactions connected with them. Thus, we avoid a place which is associated with some painful recollection; yet the very fact of avoiding it shows that we have a full remembrance of the circumstances, and, at the same time, a conviction that the sight of the spot would make the impression more vivid and more painful. After the death of a beloved child or a much valued friend, we may retain a lively remembrance of them, and even anxiously cherish the impression of their endearing qualities; yet, after time has in some measure blunted the acuteness of feeling, the accidental discovery of some trifling memorial strongly associated with the lamented object of our affection produces a freshness and intensity of emotion, known only to those who have experienced it. This feeling is peculiarly strong if the memorial has been long lost sight of, and discovered by accident; because, as has been well remarked by Dr. Brown, it in this case presents the unmixed image of the friend with whom it is associated; whereas, a memorial which has become familiar to us is associated with other feelings not relating exclusively to him. Philosophers have endeavored to explain the mental phenomenon here referred to by supposing, that in such cases the mingling of mental emotion with actual perception gives a feeling of reality to the emotion, and for the time a kind of belief of the existence of the object of it. This is sufficiently plausible, but, after all, amounts to little more than expressing the fact in other words, without conveying any real explanation.

Similar impressions, whether of a pleasurable or painful character, according to the original feeling which is thus recalled, are excited by the sight of a spot which we have visited while under the influence of strong emotion; by a tune, a piece of poetry, an article of dress, or the most trifling object with which, from incidental circumstances, the association was made. The effect of a particular tune on the Swiss regiments in foreign service is familiar to every one; and a similar effect has been remarked, from a similar cause, among the Highland regiments of our own

---

Vividness of some local associations. When peculiarly strong? Proposed explanation? Amount of it? The Swiss soldiers.

country. The feelings thus produced may be so vivid as even to overpower present emotions; to excite pleasure amid circumstances of pain or depression; and to produce depressing and painful emotions, when all present circumstances are calculated to give satisfaction. Hence, it is probable that the principle might often be employed with much advantage, as a moral remedy, in various circumstances of depressing disease, as in the low state of fever, and certain conditions of insanity. A pleasing anecdote of this kind is mentioned by Dr. Rush. "During the time that I passed at a country school in Cecil county in Maryland, I often went on a holyday, with my schoolmates, to see an eagle's nest upon the summit of a dead tree, in the neighborhood of the school, during the time of the incubation of the bird. The daughter of the farmer in whose field the tree stood, and with whom I became acquainted, married, and settled in this city about forty years ago. In our occasional interviews, we now and then spoke of the innocent haunts and rural pleasures of our youth, and among others, of the eagle's nest in her father's field. A few years ago, I was called to visit this woman when she was in the lowest stage of typhus fever. Upon entering the room, I caught her eye, and with a cheerful tone of voice said only, *The eagle's nest.* She seized my hand, without being able to speak, and discovered strong emotions of pleasure in her countenance, probably from a sudden association of all her early domestic connections and enjoyments with the words which I uttered. From that time she began to recover. She is now living, and seldom fails when we meet, to salute me with the echo of—'The eagle's nest.'"

There is even something in these mere local associations which fixes an impression upon the mind, almost independent of memory, and upon a principle with which we are little acquainted. The following anecdote is, I believe authentic, though I cannot at present refer to the work in which it is related. It is certainly one of the most extraordinary of its kind, and yet we see enough of the principle, in various instances, to give it a high degree of probability.—A lady, in the last stage of a chronic disease, was

Story of the eagle's nest? Permanence of these impressions?

carried from London to a lodging in the country; there her infant daughter was taken to visit her, and, after a short interview, carried back to town. The lady died a few days after, and the daughter grew up without any recollection of her mother, till she was of mature age. At this time, she happened to be taken into the room in which her mother died, without knowing it to have been so; she started on entering it, and when a friend who was along with her asked the cause of her agitation, replied, "I have a distinct impression of having been in this room before, and that a lady, who lay in that corner, and seemed very ill, leaned over me and wept."

The singular influence of local association is often illustrated by the most trivial occurrences. Walking in the street lately, I met a lady whose face was familiar to me, but whom I could not name. I had, at the same time, an impression that I ought to have spoken to her, and to have inquired for some relative who had lately been my patient; but, notwithstanding repeated efforts, I could not recognise her, and passed on. Some time after, in passing along the road a few miles from town, my eye caught a cottage, to which I had been taken about six months before, to see a gentleman who had been carried into it in a state of insensibility, in consequence of being thrown from a gig. The sight of the cottage instantly recalled the accident, and the gentleman who was the subject of it; and, at the same instant, the impression that the lady whom I had passed in the manner now mentioned was his wife. In this case no recollection was excited by the sight of the lady, even after repeated and anxious attempts; and I believe I should not have recognised the patient himself, had he been long with her; whereas the whole was recalled in an instant by the sight of the cottage. Similar illustrations must have occurred to every one. We meet a person in the street, who stops and speaks to us; but we cannot recognise him. We are unwilling to tell him so, and walk along with him conversing on various topics; at length, he makes an allusion to some person or some circumstance, by means of which we instantly recollect who he is, and where we met with him. On the same principle, when we are endeavoring

Anecdote illustrating it? Anecdote of the author? Common examples?

to remind a person of a transaction which he has forgotten, and which we are anxious to call to his recollection, we mention various circumstances connected with it, until at length we mention one which, by association, instantly brings the whole distinctly before him. There are even facts which seem to show that the impression recalled by local association may affect the bodily organs. Van Swieten relates of himself, that he was passing a spot where the dead body of a dog burst and produced such a stench as made him vomit; and that, happening to pass the same spot some years after, he was affected by sickness and vomiting from the recollection.

Finally, to the influence of local association we are to refer the impressions produced by the monuments of the illustrious dead; the trophies of other times; the remains of Greece and Rome; or by the visitation of spots distinguished by illustrious deeds, as Thermopylæ, Bannockburn, or Waterloo. "Far from me," says Dr. Johnson, "and from my friends, be such frigid philosophy, as may conduct us, indifferent and unmoved, over any ground which has been dignified by wisdom, bravery, or virtue. That man is little to be envied whose patriotism would not gain force upon the plains of Marathon, or whose piety would not grow warmer among the ruins of Iona."

III. Arbitrary or Fictitious Association.—This association is generally produced by a voluntary effort of the mind; and the facts associated are not connected by any relation except what arises out of this effort. The process is exemplified in the connection we establish between something which we wish to remember, and something which we are in no danger of forgetting; as in the common expedients of tying a thread about the finger, or making a knot on the pocket-handkerchief. A Roman, for the same purpose, turned the stone of his ring inwards towards the palm of his hand. There is an analogous expedient which most people probably have employed for enabling them to remember the names of persons. It consists in forming an association between the name to be remembered and that

---

Monuments? On what principle does their interest depend? Arbitrary association Common examples.

of some intimate friend or public character of the same name, which is familiar to us. The remarkable circumstance in these cases is, that whatever difficulty a person may have in simply remembering a name, he never forgets who the individual was with whose name he formed the association.

On this principle have been founded various schemes of artificial memory. One of the most ancient consisted in associating the divisions of a discourse to be delivered with the various apartments of a building, and the leading sentiments with articles of furniture. This is said to have been much practised by the ancient orators, and to have given rise to the phraseology by which we speak of the divisions of a discourse, as the first *place*, the second *place*, &c. I have repeatedly made experiments on this method in remembering the discourses of public speakers, and the effect is certainly astonishing; for though it is many years since the experiments were made, I still find articles of furniture associated in the clearest manner with sentiments delivered by some of the speakers. Other systems of artificial memory are founded upon the same general principle, though the particular applications of it may vary; and some of them are extremely absurd. One of the last which attracted notice in this country was that of a German of the name of Feinagle, who delivered lectures on memory to crowded and fashionable audiences, about the year 1809 or 1810. A leading part of his system was the memory of dates, and it consisted in changing the figures in the date into the letters of the alphabet corresponding to them in number. These letters were then formed into a word to be in some way associated with the date to be remembered. One example, which I happen to recollect, will be sufficient to illustrate the peculiarity of the system, and at the same time its efficiency for its purpose. Henry IV., king of England, was born in the year 1366. This date, changed into letters, gives *mff*, which are very easily formed into the word *muff*. The method is not so obvious of establishing with this a relation to Henry IV. "Henry IV.," says M. Feinagle, "is four hens, and we put them into the muff.

Artificial memory. Supposed practice of the ancients? Feinagle's system? Example.

one in each corner." No one, certainly, after hearing this is in any danger of forgetting the date of the birth of Henry IV.; but whether the remembrance is worth such a process is a separate question.

There is a very obvious and decisive objection to all plans for remembering history by means of any such artificial systems. It is this; the object of studying history is to enlarge and elevate the mind, to fill it with useful thoughts and clear conceptions, extended views of human character and conduct, and interesting recollections of the past. If history is read as a story, and remembered as a story, this is the effect; but on M. Feinagle's plan, all this effect is destroyed, and the student of history stores his mind with many incongruous and ridiculous ideas. The name of Henry IV., for example, ought to bring to the recollection of the pupil the real events of his reign, the moral or political truths which it illustrates, and the important persons or events with which it was connected. Instead of this, however, this system connects with the name of the monarch only the absurd and ridiculous idea of four hens in the four corners of a muff. So with all the other applications of the system. It proceeds on altogether erroneous ideas, or rather on a total forgetfulness of the real design with which the history of the past is to be studied. The real objects ought to be the intellectual, moral and political lessons which it teaches. A knowledge of names and dates is only of service in assisting the pupil to obtain clearer and more connected views, and thus in enabling him to feel more fully the moral effect.

It is unnecessary to enlarge upon the subject of arbitrary association, as the observation of every one will furnish numerous examples of it. There is one application of the principle, however, which deserves to be referred to in a more particular manner. I allude to the practice of commemorative rites or periodical observances, for transmitting the remembrance of remarkable events. These are in their nature, in general, entirely arbitrary; or, if they have any analogy to the events, the relation is only figurative. But the influence of such celebrations is of the most extensive and most important kind. If the events, particularly, are of a very uncommon character, these rites remove any feeling of uncertainty which attaches to traditional testimony, when it has been transmitted through a long period of time, and consequently through a great number of indi-

Objection to system of artificial memory. Object of history? Effect of Feinagle's plan? Example; case of Henry IV. Error on which such systems are founded? Commemorative rites. Their influence.

viduals. They carry us back, in one unbroken series, to the period of the events themselves, and to the individuals who were witnesses of them.

The most important application of the principle in the manner now referred to is in the observances of religion which are intended to commemorate those events which are connected with the revelation of the Christian faith. The importance of this mode of transmission has not been sufficiently attended to by those who have urged the insufficiency of human testimony to establish the truth of events which are at variance with the common course of nature. We have formerly alluded to one part of this sophism, and have stated the grounds on which we contend that no objection to the credibility of these events can be founded upon our observation of what we call the course of nature. We have admitted that a much higher species of evidence is required for them than would be required for events which correspond with our previous observation; and this high and peculiar evidence is confirmed in a striking manner by the periodical rites now referred to. By means of these we are freed entirely from every impression of the fallibility of testimony, and the possibility of the statements having been fabricated; as we are conducted in one uninterrupted series to the period when the events took place, and to the individuals who witnessed them. This will appear if we state in a few words a hypothetical case. Let us conceive a person attempting to impose upon the world by an account of some wonderful or miraculous event, which he alleges occurred five hundred years ago. He, of course, exerts every possible ingenuity in fabricating documents, and framing the appearance of a chain of testimony in support of his statement. It is quite possible that he might thus deceive a considerable number of credulous persons; and that others, who did not believe his statement, might yet find difficulty in proving its fallacy. But if the report were further to bear, that ever since the occurrence of the alleged event it had been regularly and specially celebrated by a certain periodical observance, it is clear that this would bring the

Important case. Case supposed for illustration.

statement to the test of a fact open to examination, and tha the fallacy of the whole would be instantly detected.

On these principles it must appear that the statements of the sacred writings, respecting miraculous events which are said to have occurred upwards of 1800 years ago, could not have been fabricated at any intermediate era during that period. It is unnecessary to state how much more improbable it is that they could have been fabricated at the very time and place in which they are said to have occurred, and in the midst of thousands who are said to have witnessed them, many of whom were deeply interested in detecting their fallacy. This part of the question is not connected with our present inquiry, but it is impossible to dismiss the subject without one reflection:—that if we are to proceed upon the principle of probabilities, we must balance fairly the probabilities of fabrication. If we do so, we hesitate not to assert, that the probability of the world being imposed upon, under all the circumstances now alluded to, is more at variance with our firm and unalterable experience than all that we are called upon to believe.

It does not appear necessary to say much of that modification of memory which is called CONCEPTION. It is the recalling of a perception. If, for example, we have passed a person in the street whose face we think we have seen, but without being able to recognise him, we can recall the impression of his countenance, and endeavor to recollect who he is. By a higher exercise of this faculty a painter can draw from conception a landscape or a building long after he has visited them, and even the portrait of a friend who is dead or absent, and whom he has not seen for a considerable time. By another modification of this power we can imbody into a conception a scene, a figure, or a transaction which has been described to us by another. The vividness of our conception, in such cases, does not depend upon the accuracy or even the truth of the description, but upon the degree of liveliness with which it is given, or the intensity with which our attention is directed to it. Thus,

---

Argument. Conception, what? Examples. Important modification of this power Upon what the vividness depends.

it has been remarked that we have a more clear conception of Don Quixote or Sancho than of any characters in real history, unless they have been made familiar to us by paintings. The business of the novelist being to create his hero, he gives a more full and graphic delineation of him than the authentic historian finds it necessary to do, hence, the former begins his narrative by an impression made upon our conception; the latter disregards this, and proceeds at once to the facts which he has to address to our attention and memory.

There is no intellectual habit which can be more immediately improved by cultivation, than this power of painting distinctly to the mind scenes described by another. Both the enjoyment and the improvement which is derived from reading depend very much upon it. One person will read a narrative, such a one for instance as the story of Robinson Crusoe, and the *mental pictures,* which the descriptions bring up in his mind, are cold, and meagre, and barren Nothing comes to view which is not expressly described; and even that is very faintly and confusedly sketched by the mind. In the case of another individual, all is clear and distinct. The slight sketch which the description gives is filled up by the imagination, and clothed with beauty; so that while the printed words which meet the eye, in both cases, are the same, the real scenes to which they introduce the reader are entirely dissimilar. This is one great cause of the differences of opinion about the interest excited by a story. One reader praises and one condemns. They *speak* of the book. But the real object of the censure and of the praise, is, on the one hand, the meagre conceptions of a reader whose imagination has not been cultivated; and on the other, the glowing pictures which are formed by a mind of higher imaginative powers.

Now the habit of forming distinct and vivid conceptions of what an author describes, will not only very much increase the interest with which his description is read, but it will cause it to be very much more strongly impressed on the memory. What we see we remember much more distinctly than what we merely hear described; but by the power of strong and vivid conception, we can sometimes almost realize the effect of actual sight.

There are two modes of cultivating this power. 1. Occasionally pausing and making an effort to paint distinctly to the mind the scenes described by an author. Think of it as a reality, and dwell upon it until you have completed it, in its details, and made all the parts consistent with one another, and with the whole. Practice of this

---

Conceptions formed of imaginary persons? Why more distinct? Influence of cultivation upon it? Example of the difference in different individuals. Effect of this on opinions about books? Double advantage from the habit of forming vivid conceptions? Modes of cultivating this power? First mode?

kind will very soon lead to decided improvement. 2. Carefully observing scenery, as exhibited in prints and in nature, and impressing its features, both of beauty and grandeur, upon the mind, so as to provide the memory with a store of images, which are to be employed as elements or materials, to enter into the composition of imaginary scenes. Strictly speaking, there is nothing new or original in the conceptions we form of scenes described. They may be new combinations, but the elements from which they are composed are all furnished from memory. The memory then should be provided with a supply.

Conception, properly so called, or the recalling of a perception, does not appear to be necessarily connected with the impression of past time, but rather to be at first accompanied by a feeling of the present existence of the object. Connecting the impression with past time seems to be a distinct act of the mind; and the conception may be so strong, as, for the moment, almost to exclude all idea of the past. That degree of conception by which a painter can take the likeness of a friend who has been long dead, or delineate a scene visited at a remote period, must amount to something of this nature. In the active and healthy state of the other faculties of the mind this impression is but momentary, being almost instantly corrected by impressions received from the external world. We shall afterward have occasion to refer to a remarkable state of mind in which it is not thus corrected, but in which objects which exist only in conception are believed to have a real and present existence. On this condition depend many of the peculiarities of dreaming, insanity, and spectral illusions.

Different individuals possess the faculty of conception in different degrees; and, connected with the degree of it, there is generally a corresponding talent for lively description. The faculty itself, or the formation of the conception, probably follows nearly the same laws with memory, and depends in a great measure upon the degree of attention which was originally directed to the objects. This, again, is influenced, as in the case of memory, partly by the general activity of mind of the individual, and partly by his particular habits and pursuits. Thus, as formerly

Second mode? Reason for this rule? Connection of conception with the idea of time. Conception, when most vivid? Power of conception in different individuals. Depends upon what?

remarked, in describing the features of a country which they have passed over, one person will give a clear and lively description of its general characters, so as to place it, as it were, before you; a second will describe chiefly its pastures and produce; a third may include both; while a fourth may not be able to give an intelligible account of any one feature of the scene.

There are particular situations in which conception is apt to be most intensely brought into exercise, especially those of seclusion and the absence of all external impressions. A beautiful example of this occurs in the Life of Niebuhr, the celebrated Danish traveller. When old, blind, and so infirm that he was able only to be carried from his bed to his chair, he used to describe to his friends the scenes which he had visited in his early days with wonderful minuteness and vivacity. When they expressed their astonishment, he told them, "that as he lay in bed, all visible objects shut out, the pictures of what he had seen in the East continually floated before his mind's eye, so that it was no wonder he could speak of them as if he had seen them yesterday. With like vividness the deep intense sky of Asia, with its brilliant and twinkling host of stars, which he had so often gazed at by night, or its lofty vault of blue by day, was reflected, in the hours of stillness and darkness, on his inmost soul." This may perhaps be considered as an example of what we may call the highest degree of healthy conception. Something a little beyond this leads to that state on which depends the theory of apparitions or spectral illusions.

In concluding this brief allusion to the subject of conception, I shall only add the following example of another application of this mental process. In the church of St. Peter at Cologne the altar-piece is a large and valuable picture by Rubens, representing the martyrdom of the apostle. This picture having been carried away by the French in 1805, to the great regret of the inhabitants, a painter of that city undertook to make a copy of it from recollection; and succeeded in doing so in such a manner, that the most delicate tints of the original are preserved

---

Power of description various? Anecdote of Niebuhr? What illustrated by this? story of the picture?

with the most minute accuracy. The original painting has now been restored, but the copy is preserved along with it; and even when they are rigidly compared, it is scarcely possible to distinguish the one from the other. I am not aware that this remarkable anecdote has been recorded by any traveller; I am indebted for it to my friend Dr. Duncan, of the university of Edinburgh, who heard it on the spot in a late visit to the Continent, and saw both the pictures.

OF THE CULTURE AND IMPROVEMENT OF ATTENTION AND MEMORY.

The facts which have been briefly referred to, in regard to the phenomena of memory, lead to some remarks of a practical nature. These relate to the improvement of attention and memory in persons of adult years, and the cultivation of these powers in the education of the young.

The rules from which benefit is to be derived for the improvement of memory, in persons of adult years, may be chiefly referred to the following heads.

I. The cultivation of habits of attention, or of intense application of the mind to whatever is at the time its more immediate object of pursuit.

II. Habits of correct association. These consist in the constant practice of tracing the relation between new facts and others with which we are previously acquainted; and of referring facts to principles which they are calculated to illustrate, or to opinions which they tend to confirm, modify, or overturn. This is the operation of what we call a reflecting mind; and that information which is thus fully contemplated and associated is not likely to be forgotten.

III. Intimately connected with both the former rules is the cultivation of that active, inquiring state of mind which

---

Authority for it. First rule? Rule in regard to association, what? Correct association what?

is always on the watch for knowledge from every source that comes within its reach, either in reading, conversation, or observation. Such a mind is ever ready to refer newly-acquired knowledge to its proper place. It is thus easily retained, and made to yield those conclusions which are legitimately deduced from it.

IV. Method; that is, the pursuit of particular subjects, upon a regular and connected plan.

All these principles are opposed to that listless, inactive state of mind which is occupied with trifles, or with its own waking dreams; or which seeks only amusement in desultory pursuits which pass away and are forgotten. They are likewise opposed to habits of irregular and desultory application, which even intellectual persons are apt to fall into, by means of which the mind loses the train of investigation, or of argument, in which it had made some progress, and may not be able to recover it in a satisfactory manner. Nothing, indeed, appears to contribute more to progress in any intellectual pursuit than the practice of keeping the subject habitually before the mind, and of daily contributing something towards the prosecution of it.

V. Attention and memory are greatly promoted by writing on a subject, especially if it be done in a distinct and systematic manner; also, by conversing on the subject, and by instructing others in it. These exercises, indeed, may perhaps be considered rather as aids to attention, or a clear comprehension of the subject, than to memory. For in regard to memory, it is remarkable how much its power is increased in many instances by that kind of exercise by which it is alone trusted to, without any aid from writing. I have known medical men, for example, who had to recollect numerous appointments, do so with perfect accuracy by trusting to memory, to which they had habituated themselves, but blunder continually when they kept a written memorandum. The mental power which is in some cases acquired by constant and intense exercise, is indeed asto-

What state of mind best promotes the memory? Method. Habits of mind to which these rules are opposed? Influence of writing? What its mode of operation? Exceptions.

nishing. Bloomfield the poet relates of himself, that nearly one half of his poem, the Farmer's Boy, was composed, revised, and corrected, without writing a word of it, while he was at work with other shoemakers in a garret.

Similar rules apply to the cultivation of these powers in young persons. They may be chiefly referred to the following heads:

I. Exciting constant attention and constant interest. For this purpose it is of essential importance that whatever reading is presented to children shall be of a kind which they understand, and in which they can feel interest and pleasure. This will be greatly promoted by directing their attention to the meaning of words, and explaining them by familiar illustrations. The practice of setting tasks as punishments cannot be alluded to in terms adequate to its extreme absurdity. On this ground also it must be considered as a great error in education, to make children attempt too much; that is, more than they can do with close attention. When a sense of weariness or mental languor takes place, what follows is not merely a loss of time, but an important injury done to the mental constitution; and it appears to be of the utmost consequence that the time of children should be as much as possible divided between intense attention and active recreation. By a shorter time occupied in this manner, not only is more progress made than by a longer, with listless and imperfect application, but an important part of mental discipline is secured, which by the other method is entirely neglected. Similar observations, indeed, apply to persons at every period of life, and we are fully persuaded that progress in any intellectual pursuit does not depend so much upon protracted laborious study, as on the practice of keeping the subject habitually before the mind, and on the intensity of mental application.

II. Cultivating habits of association, by pointing out to children the relation of facts to each other, the manner in which they illustrate one another, or lead to some general

---

Anecdote of Bloomfield. Means of cultivating the memory in the young. Influence of attention and interest? Errors in education? Habits of association.

conclusion. By directing them in this manner from any particular fact to recollect similar or analogous facts which had formerly passed before them, they will be trained at once to attention, memory and reflection.

III. Cultivating that general activity of mind which seeks for information on every subject that comes in its way. The most common and trivial occurrences may thus be made the source of mental improvement: the habits of animals; the natural history of the articles that are constantly before us, in clothes, food, furniture; articles of manufacture from a watch to a pin; the action of the mechanic powers, as illustrated by various contrivances in constant use; the structure of a leaf, a flower, a tree. To those farther advanced, a constant source of interest may be found in history, geography, and memoirs of eminent individuals; and in the leading principles of natural history, natural philosophy, and chemistry. Every new subject of thought which is thus presented to the mind is both valuable in itself by the powers which it calls into action, and by proving a nucleus to which new facts may be afterward associated.

IV. Memory and attention are greatly promoted in young persons by writing; provided it be done, not merely in the form of extracts from books, but in their own words: in history, for example, in the form of chronological tables; and on other subjects in clear and distinct abstracts, neatly and methodically written.

V. These exercises of mind are greatly promoted in the young by verbal communication. Hence the importance of frequent examination. The teacher is thereby enabled, not only to ascertain their progress, but to explain what they do not understand; to impress upon them important points to which they may not have sufficiently attended; to excite attention, inquiry, and interest; and so to cultivate the habits of association and reflection. These, in fact, ought to be the objects to be kept in view in all such exercises, as of much greater moment than the mere putting of

---

Activity of mind. Means of awakening it? Written exercises: of what kind? Verbal communication—how secured? Advantages of it?

questions. On the same principle, a most useful exercise for young persons is instructing others still younger, on subjects which they have themselves recently acquired.

VI. In the cultivation of the mental powers in the young, a point of essential importance is the selection of proper and worthy objects of acquirement. In the general conduct of education in this respect, the chief error appears in general to have been, devoting too much time and attention in females to superficial accomplishments, and in males to mere acquirement in languages and mathematics; and the great object to be kept in view from the very earliest period is the paramount importance of the actual knowledge of things on subjects of real utility, the actual cultivation of habits of observation, inquiry, association and induction; and, as the foundation of the whole, the habit of steady and continued attention. The cultivation of these mental habits is of greater value by far than any one acquirement whatever; for they are the basis of all future improvement, and are calculated to give a tone to the whole character.

In this brief outline I have said nothing on the subject of religious instruction; for the same rules apply to it as to branches of inferior importance, in as far as it is to be considered as engaging the intellectual powers. The chief error here appears to be, the practice of trusting too much to the mere repetition of tasks or catechisms, without that kind of direct personal instruction which is calculated to interest the attention, to fix the truths upon the understanding, and to cultivate the habits of association and reflection. A leading branch of this subject, the culture of the moral feelings, does not belong to our present inquiry; but it is impossible to mention it without alluding to its intense interest even in a philosophical point of view. One of the most striking phenomena, certainly, in the science of the human mind, is the high degree of culture of which the moral powers are susceptible, even in the infant mind, long before the powers of intellect are developed for the investigation of truth.

Mutual instruction. Influence of a proper selection of objects? Prevalent errors What is really of paramount importance? Religious instruction. Common error here Culture of moral feelings?

In reference to the whole science of education, nothing is of greater importance than the principle of association, which, we have formerly seen, exerts a most extensive influence, not in the remembrance of facts alone, but in perpetuating and recalling mental emotions. We take a very limited view, indeed, of this great subject, if we confine education entirely or chiefly to the acquisition of knowledge, or even to the culture of the intellectual powers. That system is deficient in its most essential part which does not carry on along with these a careful and habitual culture and regulation of the passions and emotions of the young; their attachments and antipathies, their hopes and fears, their joys and sorrows; the cultivation of the social and benevolent affections; the habit of repressing selfishness, and bearing inconveniences and disappointments without murmuring; a disposition to candor and ingenuousness, and a sacred regard to truth. Their future character as social and moral beings will be greatly influenced by the manner in which they are taught from an early period to regulate their emotions, by directing them to adequate and worthy objects, and controlling them by the great principles of wisdom and virtue. In this important process the principle of association exerts a most extensive influence. The stern lessons of morality, and even the sublime truths of religion, may be rigidly impressed upon the minds of the young, and may, in after-life, recur from time to time, as a mere matter of remembrance; but many must have experienced how different is the impression when they recur in close association with a father's affection and a mother's tenderness,—with the lively recollection of a home, where the kindest sympathies of the human heart shed around the domestic circle all that is lovely in life, while a mild and consistent piety habitually pointed the way to a life which is to come.

Influence of association in regard to the moral feelings? Essential objects to be secured? What principle most effectual in securing them? Example.

OF THF INFLUENCE OF DISEASE UPON ATTENTION AND MEMORY.

THE preceding imperfect outline of the subject of memory naturally leads us briefly to investigate the manner in which this function is impaired in connection with bodily disease. This takes place chiefly from injuries of the head, affections of the brain, fever, and diseases of extreme debility. Similar effects arise from intemperance and other habits of dissipation. Our present purpose, however, is, not to investigate the peculiar effects of these various causes, but to endeavór to trace the manner in which attention and memory—and we may include perception—are affected by any or all of them.

The first mental function which is impaired by bodily disease, is usually the power of attention; this we see illustrated in all febrile affections. The patient, in the early or milder stages, is incapable of fixing his mind upon any thing that requires much attention, of following out an argument, or of transacting business which calls for much thought or consideration. He is acute and intelligent as to all common occurrences, and shows no want of recollection or of the power of reasoning when his attention is excited; but he feels it an exertion that is painful to him. In a higher degree of this condition, he is still intelligent as to what is said or done at the time, or in recognising persons; but in a short time forgets every thing in regard to the person or the occurrence. He is incapable of that degree of attention which is necessary for memory, though the powers of perception are entire. In the next stage he becomes incapable of receiving the full impression from external things; and, in consequence of this, he mistakes the objects of his own thoughts for realities. This is delirium, and there are various degrees of it. In some cases the atten tion of the patient can be roused for a time, and directed to

What bodily affections influence the memory? Object of this discussion? What function first impaired? First stage, effects what? Second stage? Third stage? Its name?

the true relations of external things, though he relapses into his delirious impressions when he is left undisturbed: in others, the false impression is constant, and cannot be corrected by any effort which is made to direct the attention; and in a third modification of this remarkable condition, he mixes up his hallucinations with external impressions in a most singular manner. He is still capable, however, of describing his impressions,—that is, of talking so as to be understood, though what he speaks of relates only to his erroneous conceptions, or mere bodily feelings. In the next stage he either does not attempt to express himself at all, or is entirely unintelligible. He is now cut off from communication with external things and with other sentient beings; and the highest degree of this is what we call coma, or stupor, which resembles profound sleep.

This description refers chiefly to the gradations in the state of the mental functions which we observe in continued fever. It is particularly interesting to trace them in this disease, because we see the various grades passing into one another, and thus showing in a connected series the leading peculiarities which, in other affections, we have to contemplate separately. These peculiarities may be chiefly referred to the following heads.

It will be observed that these heads are substantially a repetition and more full examination of those in the preceding paragraphs. The pupils will be very much assisted in understanding and remembering them, by calling to mind cases which have occurred within their own observation, and arranging them under their respective heads.

I. A state in which the attention cannot be steadily directed to a long and connected train of thought, or to any thing requiring a continued effort of mind. This takes place, as already stated, in the earlier stages of all febrile diseases. It likewise occurs in connection with the debility which succeeds acute diseases, in persons broken down by intemperance, and in the first approaches of old age. It is also often observed in a remarkable degree in connection with a disordered state of the stomach.

II. A state in which the impression made by external

Three modifications of this stage? Fourth stage? Its name? In what disease most commonly observed. First state? In what disease does it occur? Second state?

things is not sufficient to produce remembrance, though there appears to be, at the time, a perfect perception. A person so affected understands what is said to him, and answers correctly, but very soon forgets what has passed; he knows a friend, and is happy to see him, but in a short time forgets the occurrence. This is met with in a more advanced state of febrile diseases, in the higher degrees of the condition which results from habitual intemperance, and in the more advanced periods of age. It also occurs in diseases of the brain, and in cases of injuries of the head. A lady whom I attended some time ago, on account of an injury produced by a fall from a horse, lay, for the first week, in a state of perfect stupor; she then gradually revived, so as to be sensible to external impressions, and after some time to recognise her friends. But afterward, when she was entirely recovered, she had no recollection of this period of her convalescence, or of having seen various friends who then visited her, though, at the time, she recognised them, conversed with them sensibly, and was very happy to see them.

III. The third condition is that in which external impressions are either not perceived at all, or are perceived in a manner which cannot convey any distinct notion of their relations to the mind. On this account the conceptions or trains of ideas existing in the mind itself are believed to be realities. This remarkable condition belongs properly to another part of our subject. It occurs in various forms of delirium, and constitutes the peculiar characters of insanity and dreaming. The ideas or conceptions which occupy the mind in this condition are various. They may be trains of thought excited by some passing event or some bodily sensation; and frequently the patient repeats something which is said in his hearing, and then branches off into some other train to which that has given rise. In other cases the impression is one which has been brought up by some old associations, even relating to things which the person when in health had not recollected. Of this kind there are various remarkable examples on record, especially in

---

Describe the effects. Diseases in which it occurs? Case described. Third state what? Describe its effects.

regard to the memory of languages. A man, mentioned by Mr. Abernethy, had been born in France, but had spent the greater part of his life in England, and for many years had entirely lost the habit of speaking French. But when under the care of Mr. Abernethy, on account of the effects of an injury of the head, he always spoke French. A similar case occurred in St. Thomas' hospital, of a man who was in a state of stupor in consequence of an injury of the head. On his partial recovery, he spoke a language which nobody in the hospital understood, but which was soon ascertained to be Welsh. It was then discovered that he had been thirty years absent from Wales, and, before the accident, had entirely forgotten his native language. On his perfect recovery, he completely forgot his Welsh again, and recovered the English language. A lady, mentioned by Dr. Prichard, when in a state of delirium spoke a language which nobody about her understood; but which also was discovered to be Welsh. None of her friends could form any conception of the manner in which she had become acquainted with that language; but after much inquiry it was discovered, that in her childhood she had a nurse, a native of a district on the coast of Brittany, the dialect of which is closely analogous to the Welsh. The lady had at that time learned a good deal of this dialect, but had entirely forgotten it for many years before this attack of fever. The case has also been communicated to me of a lady who was a native of Germany, but married to an English gentleman, and for a considerable time accustomed to speak the English language. During an illness, of the nature of which I am not informed, she always spoke German, and could not make herself understood by her English attendants, except when her husband acted as interpreter. A woman who was a native of the Highlands, but accustomed to speak English, was under the care of Dr. Macintosh of Edinburgh, on account of an attack of apoplexy. She was so far recovered as to look around her with an appearance of intelligence, but the doctor could not make her comprehend any thing he said to her, or answer the most simple question.

Case described by Mr. Abernethy? The patient at St. Thomas' hospital. The lady mentioned by Dr. Prichard. Explanation of it? The German lady. Dr. Macintosh's patient

He then desired one of her friends to address her in Gaelic, when she immediately answered with readiness and fluency. An Italian gentleman, mentioned by Dr. Rush, who died of the yellow fever in New York, in the beginning of his illness spoke English, in the middle of it French, but on the day of his death he spoke only Italian. A Lutheran clergyman of Philadelphia informed Dr. Rush that Germans and Swedes, of whom he had a considerable number in his congregation, when near death always prayed in their native languages, though some of them he was confident had not spoken these languages for fifty or sixty years.

A case has been related to me of a boy, who at the age of four received a fracture of the skull, for which he underwent the operation of trepan. He was at the time in a state of perfect stupor, and after his recovery retained no recollection either of the accident or the operation. At the age of fifteen, during the delirium of a fever, he gave his mother a correct description of the operation, and the persons who were present at it, with their dress, and other minute particulars. He had never been observed to allude to it before, and no means were known by which he could have acquired the circumstances which he mentioned. An eminent medical friend informs me, that during fever, without any delirium, he on one occasion repeated long passages from Homer, which he could not do when in health; and another friend has mentioned to me, that in a similar situation there were represented to his mind, in a most vivid manner, the circumstances of a journey in the Highlands, which he had performed long before, including many minute particulars which he had entirely forgotten.

In regard to the memory of languages as influenced by these affections of the brain, a condition occurs, the reverse of that now mentioned, and presenting some singular phenomena: the cause of the difference is entirely beyond our researches. The late Dr. Gregory was accustomed to mention in his lectures the case of a clergyman, who, while laboring under a disease of the brain, spoke nothing but Hebrew, which was ascertained to be the last language that he had acquired. An English lady, mentioned by Dr. Pri-

---

Other examples. Case of the boy? Things which he remembered? Peculiar phenomena connected with the memory of languages?

chard, in recovering from an apoplectic attack, always spoke to her attendants in French, and had actually lost the knowledge of the English language: this continued about a month.

IV. The fourth condition is the state of stupor, or coma, in which the mind is entirely cut off from intercourse with the external world. This occurs in the worst states of fever, in various diseases of the brain and injuries of the head; and the same condition takes place, from a very different cause, in the state of fainting. In such cases there is seldom any recollection of mental impressions; yet there are facts which tend to show, that the patient is not in such a state of total insensibility to external things as his appearance would indicate. A gentleman whom I attended in a state of perfect apoplexy, from which he did not recover, was frequently observed to adjust his nightcap with the utmost care, when it got into an uncomfortable state; first pulling it down over his eyes, and then turning up the front of it in the most exact manner. Another, whom I saw lately in a state of profound apoplexy, but from which he recovered, had a perfect recollection of what took place during the attack, and mentioned many things which had been said in his hearing when he was supposed to be in a state of perfect unconsciousness. A lady, on recovering from a similar state, said she had been asleep and dreaming, and mentioned what she had dreamed about. Facts are wanting on this curious subject; but there can be little doubt, that many of the stories related of things seen by persons in a state of trance are referable to this head, and that their visions consisted of the conceptions of the mind itself, believed for the time to be real, in a manner analogous to dreaming. That such impressions should not be more frequently remembered in the ordinary cases of stupor, probably arises from the higher degree and greater permanency of the affection than that which occurs in sleep. For we have reason to believe that dreams which are remembered occur only in imperfect sleep, and that in very profound

Fourth state—what? It occurs when? The phenomena it exhibits? Is the patient totally insensible? Facts in proof. Trances; supposed explanation of them? These impressions not always remembered, and why?

sleep we do not remember any mental impressions, though we have satisfactory proof that they exist. Thus, a person will talk in his sleep so as to be distinctly understood by another, but without having the least recollection of the mental impression which led to what he said.

In the preceding observations we have referred chiefly to the temporary influence of disease, in impairing or suspending the powers of attention and memory. But there is a part of the subject quite distinct from this, namely, the effect of certain diseases in obliterating impressions formerly received and long retained. The higher degrees of this condition amount to that state which we call idiotism, and this we find supervening both upon affections of the brain and protracted febrile diseases. The condition so produced is sometimes permanent, but frequently is recovered from; and recovery takes place in some cases gradually, in others very suddenly. A man, mentioned by Willis, on recovering from a putrid fever, was found to have so entirely lost his mental faculties, that he knew nobody, remembered nothing, and understood nothing: "vix supra brutum sâperet." He continued in this state for two months, and then gradually recovered. Some years ago I attended a young man, who, on recovering from a tedious fever, was found to be in a state bordering upon idiotism; and this continued, even after his bodily health was entirely restored. In this state he was taken to the country, where he gradually recovered, after several months. A gentleman, mentioned by Wepfer, on coming out of an apoplectic attack, was found to know nobody, and remember nothing. After several weeks he began to know his friends, to remember words, to repeat the Lord's Prayer, and to read a few words of Latin, rather than German, which was his own language. When urged to read more than a few words at a time, he said that he formerly understood these things, but now did not. After some time he began to pay more attention to what was passing around him; but, while thus making slight and gradual progress, he was, after a few months, suddenly cut off by an attack of apoplexy.

These observations refer to what? Another effect of disease? Its name? Case mentioned. Point illustrated by all?

The sudden recoveries from this condition of the mental powers, are still more remarkable. Dr. Prichard, on the authority of the late Dr. Rush of Philadelphia, mentions an American student, a person of considerable attainments, who, on recovering from a fever, was found to have lost all his acquired knowledge. When his health was restored, he began to apply to the Latin grammar, had passed through the elementary parts and was beginning to construe, when, one day, in making a strong effort to recollect a part of his lesson, the whole of his lost impressions suddenly returned to his mind, and he found himself at once in possession of all his former acquirements.

In slighter injuries of the head, accompanied by loss of recollection, we observe the circumstances gradually recalled in a very singular manner. Some years ago I saw a boy who had fallen from a wall, and struck his head against a stone which lay at the foot of it. He was carried home in a state of insensibility, from which he soon recovered, but without any recollection of the accident. He felt that his head was hurt, but he had no idea how he had received the injury. After a short time he recollected that he had struck his head against a stone, but had no recollection how he had come to do so. After another interval, he recollected that he had been on the top of a wall, and had fallen from it and struck against the stone, but could not remember where the wall was. After some time longer, he recovered the recollection of all the circumstances. Dr. Prichard mentions a gentleman who suffered a severe injury by a fall from his horse, and who, on his recovery, had no recollection of any thing relating to the accident, or for some time before it. A considerable time elapsed before his recollection of it began to return, and it was only as he repeatedly rode over the country where the accident had happened, that the sight of the various objects gradually recalled the circumstances of the journey in which it occurred, and of the accident itself.

A still more remarkable phenomenon connected with cases of this kind, occurs in some instances in which there is perfect intelligence in regard to recent circumstances, but

---

Still more remarkable examples? The American student. Story of the boy. Narrate all the circumstances.

an obliteration of former impressions. Of this I have received the following striking example from an eminent medical friend. A respectable surgeon was thrown from his horse while riding in the country, and was carried into an adjoining house in a state of insensibility. From this he very soon recovered, described the accident distinctly, and gave minute directions in regard to his own treatment. In particular, he requested that he might be immediately bled; the bleeding was repeated, at his own desire, after two hours; and he conversed correctly regarding his feelings and the state of his pulse with the medical man who visited him. In the evening he was so much recovered as to be able to be removed to his own house, and a medical friend accompanied him in the carriage. As they drew near home, the latter made some observation respecting precautions calculated to prevent unnecessary alarm to the wife and family of the patient, when, to his astonishment, he discovered that his friend had lost all idea of having either a wife or children. This condition continued during the following day, and it was only on the third day, and after further bleeding, that the circumstances of his past life began to recur to his mind. On the other hand, remarkable instances occur of the permanency of impressions made upon the mind previously to such injuries, though the mental faculties are entirely obscured as to all subsequent impressions. An affecting example is mentioned by Dr. Conolly:—a young clergyman, when on the point of being married, suffered an injury of the head, by which his understanding was entirely and permanently deranged. He lived in this condition till the age of eighty; and to the last talked of nothing but his approaching wedding, and expressed impatience for the arrival of the happy day.

It is chiefly in connection with attacks of an apoplectic nature that we meet with singular examples of loss of memory on particular topics, or extending only to a particular period. One of the most common is loss of the memory of words, or of names, while the patient retains a correct idea of things and persons. The late Dr. Gregory used to mention a lady who, after an apoplectic attack, recovered cor-

---

Case of the surgeon. Narrate the circumstances. The clergyman. What disease occasions most numerous examples? Case of the lady who forgot names?

rectly her ideas of things, but could not name them. In giving directions respecting family matters, she was quite distinct as to what she wished to be done, but could make herself understood only by going through the house, and pointing to the various articles. A gentleman whom I attended some years ago, after recovering from an apoplectic attack, knew his friends perfectly, but could not name them. Walking one day in the street, he met a gentleman to whom he was very anxious to communicate something respecting a mutual friend. After various ineffectual attempts to make him understand whom he meant, he at last seized him by the arm and dragged him through several streets to the house of the gentleman of whom he was speaking, and pointed to the name-plate on the door.

A singular modification of this condition has been related to me. The gentleman to whom it referred could not be made to understand the name of an object if it was spoken to him, but understood it perfectly when it was written. His mental faculties were so entire, that he was engaged in most extensive agricultural concerns, and he managed them with perfect correctness, by means of a remarkable contrivance. He kept before him, in the room where he transacted business, a list of the words which were most apt to occur in his intercourse with his workmen. When one of these wished to communicate with him on any subject, he first heard what the workman had to say, but without understanding him further than simply to catch the words. He then turned to the words in his written list, and whenever they met his eye he understood them perfectly. These particulars I had from his son, a gentleman of high intelligence. Another frequent modification consists in putting one name for another, but always using the words in the same sense. An example of this also occurred in the gentleman last mentioned. He uniformly called his snuff-box a hogshead, and the association which led to this appeared to be obvious. In the early part of his life he had been in Virginia, and connected with the trade in tobacco; so that the transition from snuff to tobacco, and from tobacco to a hogshead, seemed to be natural. Another gentleman affect-

Case of recollecting writing, but not words. The patient's mode of understanding his workmen? Mistaking names.

ed in this manner, when he wanted coals put upon his fire, always called for paper, and when he wanted paper, called for coals; and these words he always used in the same manner. In other cases, the patient seems to invent names, using words which to a stranger are quite unintelligible; but he always uses them in the same sense, and his immediate attendants come to understand what he means by them.

Another remarkable modification of this condition of the mental powers is found in those cases in which there is loss of the recollection of a particular period. A clergyman, mentioned by Dr. Beattie, on recovering from an apoplectic attack, was found to have lost the recollection of exactly four years; every thing that occurred before that period he remembered perfectly. He gradually recovered, partly by a spontaneous revival of his memory, and partly by acquiring a knowledge of the leading events of the period. A young lady who was present at a late catastrophe in Scotland, in which many people lost their lives by the fall of the gallery of a church, escaped without any injury, but with the complete loss of the recollection of any of the circumstances; and this extended, not only to the accident, but to every thing that had occurred to her for a certain time before going to church. A lady whom I attended some years ago in a protracted illness, in which her memory became much impaired, lost the recollection of a period of about ten or twelve years, but spoke with perfect consistency of things as they stood before that time.

As far as I have been able to trace it, the principle in such cases seems to be, that when the memory is impaired to a certain degree, the loss of it extends backwards to some event or some period by which a particularly deep impression had been made upon the mind. In the lady last mentioned, for instance, the period of which she lost the recollection was that during which she had resided in Edinburgh, and it extended back to her removal from another city in which she had lived for many years. During her residence in the latter, she had become the mother of a large family, and other events had occurred likely to make

---

Loss of recollection of a particular period. What example? General principle in regard to such cases? Proposed explanation.

a deep impression on her mind. The period of her residence in Edinburgh had been uniform and tranquil, and without any occurrence calculated to excite much attention in a person of rather slender mental endowments. I do not know whether we can give a similar explanation of cases in which the loss of memory has extended only to particular subjects; namely, by supposing that these subjects had been more slightly impressed upon the mind than those which were retained. A gentleman is mentioned by Dr. Beattie, who, after a blow on the head, lost his knowledge of Greek, and did not appear to have lost any thing else.

While we thus review the manner in which the manifestations of mind are affected, in certain cases, by diseases and injuries of the brain, it is necessary that we should refer briefly to the remarkable instances in which the brain has been extensively diseased without the phenomena of mind being impaired in any sensible degree. This holds true both in regard to the destruction of each individual part of the brain, and likewise to the extent to which the cerebral mass may be diseased or destroyed. In another work I have mentioned various cases which illustrate this fact in a very striking manner; particularly the case of a lady in whom one-half of the brain was reduced to a mass of disease; but who retained all her faculties to the last, except that there was an imperfection of vision,—and had been enjoying herself at a convivial party in the house of a friend a few hours before her death. A man, mentioned by Dr. Ferriar, who died of an affection of the brain, retained all his faculties entire till the very moment of death, which was sudden: on examining his head, the whole right hemisphere,—that is, one-half of his brain,—was found destroyed by suppuration. In a similar case recorded by Diemerbroek, half a pound of matter was found in the brain; and in one by Dr. Heberden, there was half a pound of water. A man, mentioned by Mr. O'Halloran, suffered such an injury of the head that a large portion of

Applicability of it to other cases? Is disease of the brain always attended by disorder of the mind? Case of the lady. Did she enjoy all her faculties? Case mentioned by Dr. Ferriar. These cases similar, in what respect? Frequency of such cases?

the bone was removed on the right side; and extensive suppuration having taken place, there was discharged at each dressing, through the opening, an immense quantity of matter mixed with large masses of the substance of the brain. This went on for seventeen days, and it appears that nearly one-half of the brain was thrown out mixed with the matter; yet the man retained all his intellectual faculties to the very moment of dissolution; and through the whole course of the disease, his mind maintained uniform tranquillity. These remarkable histories might be greatly multiplied if it were required, but at present it seems only necessary to add the very interesting case related by Mr. Marshall. It is that of a man who died with a pound of water in his brain, after having been long in a state of idiocy, but who, a very short time before death, became perfectly rational.

The facts which have been thus briefly referred to, present a series of phenomena of the most remarkable kind, but on which we cannot speculate in the smallest degree without advancing beyond the sphere of our limited faculties; one thing, however, is certain, that they give no countenance to the doctrine of materialism, which some have presumptuously deduced from a very partial view of the influence of cerebral disease upon the manifestations of mind. They show us, indeed, in a very striking manner, the mind holding intercourse with the external world through the medium of the brain and nervous system; and, by certain diseases of these organs, they show this intercourse impaired or suspended; but they show nothing more. In particular, they warrant nothing in any degree analogous to those partial deductions which form the basis of materialism. On the contrary, they show us the brain injured and diseased to an extraordinary extent, without the mental functions being affected in any sensible degree. They show us, further, the manifestations of mind obscured for a time, and yet reviving in all their original vigor, almost at the very moment of dissolution. Finally, they exhibit to us the mind, cut off from all intercourse with the external world,

---

Danger of speculating on these facts. Certain inference from them—what? They show us what? Summary of the facts stated in this section.

recalling its old impressions, even of things long forgotten; and exercising its powers on those which had long ceased to exist, in a manner totally irreconcilable with any idea we can form of a material function.

SECTION II.

ABSTRACTION.

By Abstraction we separate various facts from each other, and examine them individually. We separate, for example, the qualities of a substance, and contemplate one of them apart from the rest. This act of the mind is employed in two processes of the utmost importance. By the one, we examine a variety of objects, select the properties in which certain numbers of them agree, and thus arrange them into classes, genera, and species. By the other, we take a more comprehensive view of an extensive collection of facts, and select one which is common to the whole. This we call generalizing, or deducing a general fact or general principle; and the process is of extensive application in all philosophical inquiries. The particular points to be attended to in conducting it, will come under view in another part of our subject. The most important is, that the fact assumed as general really belongs to all the individual instances, and has not been deduced from the examination of only a part of them.

The process of classification is of so great practical importance that it deserves to be carefully considered. To show how the definition given above applies, let us take a particular case.

A person has made, we will imagine, a large collection of sea-shells, which lie promiscuously on tables before him. He proposes to *classify* them. This, according to the definition, consists "*in examining them with reference to selecting the properties in which certain numbers of them agree, that they may be arranged in classes according to their properties.*"

Let us suppose the property he first examines is color. He looks

---

Its definition. Classification—what? Generalization—what? Example illustrating the process of classification. Definition—what? How applicable?

over the whole, and takes out all that are *spotted*, and places them by themselves. He next takes all which are white, and forms of them another class, and so on, arranging them in classes, according as they agree in the property of color. Or they might, in the same way, be classified with reference to any other property, or, as the more common phrase is, on any other principle. Take, for example, form. All those which are in two parts, as the oyster, the clam, &c., might be arranged by themselves, in one class, and those which consist of a single part, in another. These classes might be easily subdivided on the same principle, i. e., with reference to form alone. All the spiral shells might form one division, the conical ones another, and those of some different form still, a third. This would be classifying them on the principle of form.

Now it must be observed that this classification would entirely break up and destroy the other. For the spotted shells, which were before arranged together, in one class, would now be scattered among several, according to their various forms. In other words, they agreed in the property of color, so that when considering them with reference to color they were put together; but they disagree in respect to form.

The *principle of classification*, which is thus adopted in the case of any collection of individual objects, may be varied almost indefinitely. The shells, for example, might be classified with reference to the habits of the animals, i. e., all which lived in fresh water might form one division, and salt water shells another. Each of these might be subdivided with reference to the food or the habits of the animal.

Or the principle of classification might be *geographical*. Those from Africa might be placed on one shelf, those from Asia on another, and American specimens on a third. Thus the principle might be varied indefinitely.

In determining on the principle of classification to be adopted in any case, that is, the property or peculiarity in which those placed together are to be similar, we must have regard to the object in view Sometimes it is necessary to classify the same individual objects in several different ways, for different purposes. Words, for example are classified in a common dictionary with reference to similarity in the initial letters—in a rhyming dictionary, the sound of the last syllable determines their place—in a grammar and in a spelling book, two other principles are adopted, entirely distinct from the preceding, and each other. Thus the same things, that is, the words of the English language, are classified on four entirely different principles, according to the end in view.

In some cases it is very difficult to determine what principle of classification will best answer the purpose. A common case of this kind is the question of arranging the books of a library. Shall they

---

First mode of classification? Based upon what property? Second mode; on what property? Subdivision on the same principle, how effected? Relation of these modes to one another? Extent to which the principle of classification may be varied? Examples. Geographical arrangement? Various classifications of words, why made? Arranging a library; what difficulty?

be classified according to the subjects of the works, or in the alphabetical order of their titles, or in the alphabetical order of the authors' names, or according to the languages or countries in which they were written. It is plain that a library may be arranged in perfect order on each of these plans, though each is entirely different from the rest, and altering the arrangement from one to the other would perhaps change the place of every book in the whole collection. Each, too, would have its ground of preference over the others, depending on the object which the reader has in view in consulting the collection. The advantages of all are sometimes in a good degree secured by arranging the books, on the shelves, on one principle, and making out two or three catalogues, in which the other methods of classification are respectively adopted.

A classification cannot, however, in any case, be carried into full effect, except in the exact sciences; for, from the very nature of the case, the several classes will run into each other, whatever may be the principle adopted, and consequently there will be many individual objects, of which it will be impossible to say unhesitatingly where they belong. Some shells will be neither decidedly white nor decidedly spotted, but something between. A librarian may be perplexed in considering whether to class Marshall's Life of Washington as history or biography, and a writer on English grammar may, in the same manner, hesitate whether to call a certain word a pronoun or an adjective, when it partakes of the nature of both. This difficulty does not apply to the exact sciences. If a figure is either a triangle or a quadrangle, it will be very clear which of the two it is. It cannot be intermediate. It must have either three sides or four. In the exact sciences, therefore, the classification may be exact, but in others it cannot always be, and in doubtful cases we may arrange the object in *either* of the classes which seem to claim it. There are often, in such cases, very idle disputes, especially on the subject of grammar True philosophy, in such cases, requires us to consider either as right, when the nature of the case leaves it doubtful.

These remarks, then, naturally lead us to the following practical rules, which are worthy of very careful consideration, since there is perhaps no process, a thorough understanding of which is more essential to a well disciplined mind than classification.

1. In determining upon a principle of classification, there should be a careful regard to the object in view, in making the classification itself.

2. The classes should be bounded by as distinct and well defined lines as the nature of the case will allow.

3. The classes should be such as to include all the individuals, i. e., so that every individual object shall belong to some one or other of them.

Various modes. How may they be combined? Difficulty in carrying a classification into full effect. Examples. Exact sciences. Example? Inferences from these remarks? Rules. To the boundaries.

4. The classification, when completed, should be considered in its true light, viz. as an artificial arrangement, resorted to merely as a matter of convenience, and therefore not a proper subject for angry disputes. Questions arising from this source are substantially no more nor less than this,—whether a mineral in a cabinet shall be placed on one shelf or another, when it is admitted that it is doubtful to which it belongs.

"Generalizing is to be distinguished from classification, though the mental process concerned is in both essentially the same. We class together a certain number of substances by a property in which they agree; and, in doing so, we specify and enumerate the individual substances included in the class. Thus, we may take a number of substances differing widely in their external and mechanical properties, some being solid, some fluid, and some gaseous, and say they are all acids. The class being thus formed, and consisting of a defined number of substances which agree in the property of acidity, we may next investigate some other property which is common to all the individuals of the class, and belongs to no other, and say, for example, that all acids redden vegetable blues. The former of these operations is properly classification; the latter is generalizing in reference to the class. In the former, we take or exclude individual substances, according as they possess or not the property on which the classification rests; in performing the latter, the property which is assumed must belong to all the individuals without a single exception, or, if it does not, it must be abandoned as a general fact or general principle in reference to the class. In classifying, we may use every freedom regarding individuals in taking or excluding them. In generalizing, we must not exclude a single individual; for the principle which does not include every one of them,—that is, the proposed fact which is not true of all the individuals, is not a general fact, and consequently cannot be admitted as a general principle. For in physical science, to talk of exceptions to a general rule, is only to say, in other words, that the rule is not general, and, consequently, is unworthy of confidence. If one acid were discovered which does not redden vegetable blues, it would belong to a history of these substances to state that a certain number of them have this property; but the property of reddening vegetable blues would require to be abandoned as a general fact or general principle applicable to the class of acids.

"A general law, or general principle, then, is nothing more than a general fact, or a fact which is invariably true of all the individual cases to which it professes to apply. Deducing such facts is the great object of modern science; and it is by this peculiar character that it is distinguished from the ancient science of the schools, the constant aim of which was to discover causes. The general law of

---

Proper view of the nature and object of classification? Distinction between generalizing and classification. Process in forming a class? Process in deducing its properties? Differences resulting from this distinction? Exceptions to a general law? Objects of modern science? Of ancient science? Example

gravitation, for example, is nothing more than the general fact, or fact invariably true, that all bodies when left unsupported fall to the ground. There were at one time certain apparent exceptions to the universality of this law, namely, in some very light bodies, which were not observed to fall. But a little farther observation showed that these are prevented from falling by being lighter than the atmosphere, and that in vacuo they observe the same law as the heaviest bodies. The apparent exceptions being thus brought under the law, it became general, namely, the fact universally true, that all unsupported bodies fall to the ground. Now, of the cause of this phenomenon we know nothing; and what we call the general law, or general principle of gravitation, is nothing more than a universal fact, or a fact that is true without a single exception. But having ascertained the fact to be invariably and universally true, we assume it as a part of the established order of nature, and proceed upon it with as much confidence as if we knew the mysterious agency on which the phenomenon depends. The establishment of the fact as universal brings us to that point in the inquiry which is the limit of our powers and capacities, and it is sufficient to the purposes of science. On the same principle, it is familiar to every one that extensive discoveries have been made in regard to the properties and laws of heat; but we do not know what heat is, whether a distinct essence, or, as has been supposed by some philosophers, a peculiar motion of the minute atoms of bodies.

"In the same manner, the person who first observed iron attracted by the magnet, observed a fact which was to him new and unaccountable. But the same phenomenon having been observed a certain number of times, a belief would arise that there existed between it and the substances concerned a connection of cause and effect. The result of this belief would be, that when the substances were brought together, the attraction would be expected to take place. Observations would then probably be made with other substances; and farther observations with the same substances; and it being found that the attraction took place between iron and the magnet only, and that between these it took place in every instance, the general principle would be deduced, or the fact universally true in all instances, that the magnet attracts iron. The same observation applies to the other remarkable property derived from the magnet, namely, pointing to the north. The phenomenon received the name of magnetism, and the laws were then investigated by which it was regulated; but what we call magnetism is still nothing more than a mode of expressing the universal fact, that the magnet attracts iron, and points to the north.

"On what hidden influence these remarkable phenomena depend, we are still as ignorant as the man who first observed them; and, however interesting it would be to know it, the knowledge is not necessary to the investigation of the laws of magnetism.

"These may, perhaps, be considered as fair examples of the inductive philosophy, as distinguished from the hypothetical systems of the era

---

Law of gravitation. Apparent exceptions. Another example; nature and effects of heat. The magnet. Process for ascertaining its general laws. In what respect are we still ignorant in regard to it?

which preceded it. According to these, the constant aim of the inquirer was the explanation of phenomena; and in the case before us a theory would have been constructed calculated to account for the attraction by the fluxes and refluxes of some invisible fluid or ether, which would have been described with as much minuteness as if there had been real ground for believing it to exist. Strikingly opposed to all such speculations is the leading principle of the inductive philosophy, that the last object of science is to 'ascertain the universality of a fact.'"—*Abercrombie on Medical Science.*

There have been disputes among writers on the science of mind, whether abstraction is to be considered as a distinct mental operation, or is referable to judgment. But I have already stated that my object in this outline is to avoid all such discussions, and to allude simply to the actual processes of the mind in a practical view. One thing at least is clear, namely, that our abstractions must be corrected by reason, the province of which is to judge whether the process is performed correctly, and on sound principles. This, however, is distinct from the primary act of the mind to which I now apply the term abstraction, which is simply the power of contemplating one property of a substance apart from its other properties. It thus disjoins things which by nature are intimately united, and which cannot be separated in any other manner. Reason does not appear to be immediately concerned in this, though it is most closely connected with the purposes to which the process is afterward applied; namely, classifying substances according to a certain agreement of properties, and fixing upon those which are common to all the individuals of a numerous series, in the act of generalizing, or deducing a general fact or general principle.

I have formerly alluded to a period in the science of mind when our ideas of external things were supposed to be certain actual essences, separated from the substances and conveyed to the thinking principle. In connection with this theory there arose a controversy, whether, when we perform the mental act of generalizing, there exists in nature any essence corresponding to a general idea; or whether, in generalizing, we merely make use of an abstract

---

Method by which the subject of magnetism would probably have been treated in former times? Disputes on this subject. The author avoids them, how? Connection of abstraction with reason. Distinction between them? Former dispute on this subject?

term; whether, for example, in using the word *man*, we only employ a term, or whether we have the power of forming an idea of man in the abstract, without thinking of any individual man; and, in the same manner, whether we can reason respecting a class of substances, without thinking of any of the individuals composing it. Hence arose two sects, whose disputes make a most remarkable figure in the history of intellectual science, namely, the Nominalists and Realists.

The controversies of these sects we now consider as little more than a matter of historical curiosity; but, for several centuries, they divided the learned of Europe, and were often carried on with an asperity amounting to actual persecution. "The Nominalists," says Mosheim, "procured the death of John Huss, who was a Realist; and in their letter to Lewis, king of France, do not pretend to deny that he fell a victim to the resentment of their sect. The Realists, on the other hand, obtained, in the year 1479, the condemnation of John de Wesalia, who was attached to the party of the Nominalists. These contending sects carried their fury so far as to charge each other with the sin against the Holy Ghost." "The dispute," says Mr. Stewart, "was carried on with great warmth in the universities of France, Germany, and England, more particularly in the two former countries, where the sovereigns were led by some political views to interest themselves deeply in the contest, and even to employ the civil power in support of their favorite opinions. The emperor Lewis, of Bavaria, in return for the assistance which in his disputes with the pope Occam had given him by his writings, sided with the Nominalists; Lewis the Eleventh, of France, on the other hand, attached himself to the Realists, and made their antagonists the objects of a cruel persecution."

We find some difficulty in believing, in the present day, that the controversy which thus embroiled the continent of Europe in all the rancor of actual persecution, related to the question, whether, in employing general terms, we use words or names only, or whether there is in nature any

---

Example. Names of the sects—what? These controversies, how now considered? Their violence? Results of it? In what countries chiefly carried on? Connection with politics. Real question at issue?

thing corresponding to what we mean by a general idea. It is well designated by Mr. Stewart as "one of the most curious events whieh occur in the history of the human mind."

The question is one of no practical importance, and when it is cleared from its connection with the ancient doctrine of ideas, appears to be one of no difficulty. Without supposing that there is in nature any actual essence corresponding to a general idea, the truth seems to be, that we do form a certain notion or conception of a quality in which several substances agree, distinct from any one substance to which the quality belongs. Hence some have proposed the term Notionalist, or Conceptualist, as designating opinions distinct from those both of the Nominalist and Realists. But, according to the principles of modern science, we cannot consider the discussion as any thing more than an ingenious arguing on points of no real importance. The process which the mind really carries on in that mental operation to which these remarks have referred, consists simply in tracing relations or points of resemblance in which certain individual things agree, though they may in others be remarkably different. We then give a name to this common quality, and thus form the individuals into a class of which this quality is the distinguishing character. Thus we may take a number of animals differing remarkably from each other, and say they are all quadrupeds. We may take a number of substances very dissimilar in their external and mechanical properties, and say they are all acids. Some of these substances are solid, some fluid, and some gaseous; but the property of acidity is common to them all, and this accordingly becomes the name and the distinguishing character of the class into which we now arrange them.

Character of the controversy? What is the real process in such a case? Examples

SECTION III.

IMAGINATION.

In the exercise of Imagination, we take the component elements of real scenes, events, or characters, and combine them anew by a process of the mind itself, so as to form compounds which have no existence in nature. A painter by this process, depicts a landscape combining the beauties of various real landscapes, and excluding their defects. A poet or a novelist, in the same manner, calls into being a fictitious character, endowed with those qualities with which it suits his purpose to invest him, places him in contact with other beings equally imaginary, and arranges, according to his will, the scenes in which he shall bear a part, and the line of conduct which he shall follow. The compound in these cases is entirely fictitious and arbitrary; but it is expected that the individual elements shall be such as actually occur in nature, and that the combination shall not differ remarkably from what might really happen. When this is not attended to, as in a picture or a novel, we speak of the work being extravagant or out of nature. But, avoiding combinations which are grossly at variance with reality, the framer of such a compound may make it superior to any thing that actually occurs. A painter may draw a combination of beauties in a landscape superior to any thing that is actually known to exist; and a novelist may delineate a more perfect character than is met with in real life. It is remarked by Mr. Stewart, that Milton, in his garden of Eden, "has created a landscape more perfect, probably, in all its parts, than has ever been realized in nature, and certainly very different from any thing that this country exhibited at the time when he wrote." "It is a curious remark of Mr. Walpole," he adds, "that Milton's Eden is free from the defects of the old English garden, and is imagined on the same principles which

Nature of imagination? Examples. How much fictitious, and how much true? Superiority of such creations. Examples. Stewart's remark?

it was reserved for the present age tc carry into execut.on."

The mode of artificial combination which results from the exercise of imagination is applicable chiefly to four kinds of composition.

1. Fictitious narrative, in which the author delineates imaginary scenes or transactions; and paints imaginary characters, endowing them with such qualities as may suit the purpose which he has in view.

2. Composition or verbal address, directed to the passions, and intended to excite particular mental emotions. To this head are referable many of the combinations of the poet, and addresses calculated to operate upon the feelings of a popular assembly; also, those which derive their character from the language of trope and metaphor. The genius of the orator, and the inventive powers of the poet, are exhibited in the variety and the novelty of the analogies, resemblances, illustrations, and figures, which he thus brings to bear upon his subject.

3. Those unexpected and peculiar associations which form the basis of wit and humor.

4. Combinations of objects of sense, calculated to produce mental emotions of a pleasurable or painful kind, as our impressions of the sublime, the beautiful, the terrible, or the ludicrous. The combinations of this class are chiefly referable to the head of objects of taste, or the fine arts; and are exemplified in the inventions of the painter and the statuary, in decorative architecture and artificial gardening, —we may add, theatrical exhibitions and music.

The facility of rapidly forming in these several departments combinations calculated to produce the effect which is intended, constitutes what we call *inventive genius*. Similar powers of invention, founded on an exercise of imagination, may also be applied to the investigations of science. It may be employed, for example, in the contrivance of experiments calculated to aid an investigation or to illustrate a doctrine; and in the construction of those legitimate hypotheses which have often led to the most important discoveries.

Kinds of composition, how many and what? First kind, what? Second kind? How different from the first? Third kind? Fourth kind? Examples. Inventive genius, what? How applicable to science?

The union of elements, in all such productions of the imagination, is regulated by the knowledge, the taste, and the intellectual habits of the author; and, we must add, by his moral principles. According to the views, the habits, and the principles of him who frames them, therefore, they may either contribute to moral and intellectual improvement, or they may tend to mislead the judgment, vitiate the taste, and corrupt the moral feelings.

Similar observations apply to the conduct of the imagination in individuals, and its influence in the cultivation of moral and intellectual character. There is certainly no power of the mind that requires more cautious management and stern control; and the proper regulation of it cannot be too strongly impressed upon the young. The sound and proper exercise of it may be made to contribute to the cultivation of all that is virtuous and estimable in human character. It leads us, in particular, to place ourselves in the situation of others, to enter into their feelings and wants, and to participate in their distresses. It thus tends to the cultivation of sympathy and the benevolent affections; and promotes all those feelings which exert so extensive an influence in the duties of friendship and the harmonies of civil and social intercourse. We may even say that we exercise imagination when we endeavor to act upon that high standard of morals which requires us "to do to others as we would that they should do unto us:" for in this mental act we must imagine ourselves in the situation of other men, and, in their character, judge of our own conduct towards them. Thus a man deficient in imagination, though he may be free from any thing unjust or dishonorable, is apt to be cold, contracted, and selfish,—regardless of the feelings and indifferent of the distresses of others. Further, we may be said to exercise imagination when we carry our views beyond present and sensible objects, and endeavor to feel the power of "things which are not seen," and the reality of scenes and times which are yet to come. On the other hand, imagination may be employed for calling into being evils which have no existence, or for exaggerating those which

---

The exercise of imagination, how regulated? Effects? Importance of a proper regulation of it? Its useful effects? Moral effects of a deficiency of imagination? Perverted imagination. Its effects?

are real; for fostering malevolent feelings, and for imputing to those with whom we are connected motives and intentions which have no foundation in truth. Finally, an ill-regulated imagination may be employed in occupying the mind with waking dreams and vain delusions, to the exclusion of all those high pursuits which ought to employ the faculties of a rational being.

There has been considerable difference of opinion in regard to the effects produced upon the mind by fictitious narrative. Without entering minutely upon the merits of this controversy, I think it may be contended, that two evils are likely to arise from much indulgence in works of fiction. The one is a tendency to give way to the wild play of the imagination; a practice most deleterious, both to the intellectual and moral habits. The other is a disruption of the harmony which ought to exist between the moral emotions and the conduct,—a principle of extensive and important influence. In the healthy state of the moral feelings, for example, the emotion of sympathy excited by a tale of sorrow ought to be followed by some efforts for the relief of the sufferer. When such relations in real life are listened to from time to time without any such efforts, the emotion gradually becomes weakened, and that moral condition is produced which we call selfishness, or hardness of heart. Fictitious tales of sorrow appear to have a similar tendency;—the emotion is produced without the corresponding conduct; and when this habit has been much indulged the result seems to be, that a cold and barren sentimentalism is produced, instead of the habit of active benevolence. If fictitious narratives be employed for depicting scenes of vice, another evil of the greatest magnitude is likely to result from them, even though the conduct exhibited should be shown to end in remorse and misery: for by the mere familiarity with vice an injury is done to the youthful mind, which is in no degree compensated by the moral at the close.

Imagination, therefore, is a mental power of extensive influence, and capable of being turned to important purposes

---

Fictitious narrative. Two evils resulting from it? Example. What evils from fictitious tales of sorrow? From fictitious tales of vice? Inference from these views?

in the cultivation of individual character. But to be so, it must be kept under the strict control both of reason and of virtue. If it be allowed to wander at discretion, through scenes of imagined wealth, ambition, frivolity, or pleasure it tends to withdraw the mind from the important pursuits of life, to weaken the habit of attention, and to impair the judgment. It tends, in a most material manner, to prevent the due exercise of those nobler powers which are directed to the cultivation both of science and virtue. The state of a mind which has yielded itself to the influence of this delusive habit cannot be more forcibly represented than in the words of an eloquent writer:—"The influence of this habit of dwelling on the beautiful fallacious forms of imagination will accompany the mind into the most serious speculations, or rather musings, on the real world, and what is to be done in it, and expected; as the image which the eye acquires from looking at any dazzling object still appears before it wherever it turns. The vulgar materials that constitute the actual economy of the world will rise up to its sight in fictitious forms, which it cannot disenchant into plain reality, nor will even suspect to be deceptive. It cannot go about with sober, rational inspection, and ascertain the nature and value of all things around it. Indeed, such a mind is not disposed to examine with any careful minuteness the real condition of things. It is content with ignorance, because environed with something more delicious than such knowledge in the paradise which imagination creates. In that paradise it walks delighted, till some imperious circumstance of real life call it thence, and gladly escapes thither again when the avocation is past. There every thing is beautiful and noble as could be desired to form the residence of an angel. If a tenth part of the felicities that have been enjoyed, the great actions that have been performed, the beneficent institutions that have been established, and the beautiful objects that have been seen in that happy region, could have been imported into this terrestrial place,—what a delightful thing it would have been to awake each morning to see such a world once more."*

* Foster's Essays.

State of mind induced by a perverted imagination? Foster's description of its effects?

To the same purpose are the words of another writer of the highest authority:—"To indulge the power of fiction, and send imagination out upon the wing, is often the sport of those who delight too much in silent speculation. He who has nothing external that can divert him must find pleasure in his own thoughts, and must conceive himself what he is not,—for who is pleased with what he is? He then expatiates in boundless futurity, and culls from all imaginable conditions that which for the present moment he should most desire; amuses his desires with impossible enjoyments, and confers upon his pride unattainable dominion. The mind dances from scene to scene, unites all pleasures in all combinations, and riots in delights which nature and fortune, with all their bounty, cannot bestow. In time, some particular train of ideas fixes the attention; all other intellectual gratifications are rejected; the mind, in weariness or leisure, recurs constantly to the favorite conception, and feasts on the luscious falsehood whenever she is offended with the bitterness of truth. By degress the reign of fancy is confirmed; she grows first imperious, and in time despotic. Then fictions begin to operate as realities, false opinions fasten upon the mind, and life passes in dreams of rapture or of anguish."*

SECTION IV.

OF REASON OR JUDGMENT.

The most simple view which we can take of reason probably is, that it is the exercise of mind by which we compare facts with each other, and mental impressions with external things. The applications of this mental process may be referred to the following heads:—

I. We compare facts with each other, so as to trace their relations, connections, and tendencies; and to distinguish

* Johnson's Rasselas.

Johnson's description. Definition of reason? How many general applications?

the connections which are incidental from those which are fixed and uniform.

What we call the relations of things, whether referring to external events or mental processes, comprehend all those facts which form the great objects of human knowledge, with respect either to the individuals, or their tendencies towards each other. They may be briefly enumerated in the following manner:—

1. Relations of character,—or those marks, characters, or properties by which a substance may be recognised, and may be distinguished from all others; for example, the botanical characters of a plant—the chemical properties of a mineral—the symptoms of a disease—sensible properties of color, taste, smell, &c.—the mental endowments and moral qualities of individual men.

2. Relations of resemblance and analogy, arising out of a comparison of the qualities of various individual substances or events. These admit of various degrees. When there is a close agreement between two events or classes of events, it constitutes resemblance: when there are points of difference, it is analogy. In the latter case, we then trace the degrees of analogy, depending upon the number of points in which the resemblance holds and the number of points in which there is a difference. On the relations of resemblance also depend the arts of arrangement and classification; and the use of those general terms by which we learn to express a great number of individual objects by a single term, derived from certain characters in which they agree, such as solids, fluids, quadrupeds, &c. We find a certain number of substances which agree so much in their properties, that we class them together as one species. We then find other substances, which agree with these in a certain number of their properties, but differ in others. We dismiss the latter, and retain those only in which they all agree, and so form the whole into a genus. The individuals forming the genus are still found to agree in some of their properties with various other substances, and by leaving out of view those in which they differ, we again form this still larger number into a class or order.

First? What comprehended under the phrase *relations of things?* First class? Examples? Second class? Distinction between resemblance and analogy? Arts depending upon these relations? Process of classification.

3. Nearly connected with the former, but still more extensive, is that important process by which, among a great series of facts, we trace an accordance, and thus deduce from the whole a general fact or general principle.

4. Relations of composition; comprehending the resolution of a substance into its elements or constituent parts,—the connection of the parts as constituting a whole—of the whole to the parts, and of the parts to each other.

5. Relations of causation, or the tendencies of bodies to produce or be followed by certain actions upon each other in certain circumstances. These refer chiefly to that uniform sequence of events from which we derive our idea of the one being the cause of the other. But the class likewise includes other relations arising out of the same subject; such as the relation of two events as the joint causes of a common effect, or the joint effects of a common cause; or as forming links in a chain of sequences in which we have still to look for other events as the true antecedents or final results. It includes also that most important mental process by which, from the properties of a known effect, we infer the powers and properties of an unknown cause.

6. Relations of degree and proportion, as in those truths and relations which are the subjects of mathematics.

7. The important question of moral relations, which does not properly belong to the present part of our inquiry—including the relation of certain actions to the great standard of moral rectitude, and to those principles which bind men together in the harmonies of social and domestic intercourse.

These appear to include the principal relations of things which the mind requires to investigate in an intellectual point of view. The facts respecting them are acquired by attention and memory; but it is the province of reason to separate from the mass so acquired those which are incidental and temporary from those which are uniform,—to ascertain, for example, those characters by which a substance may be certainly recognised,—the symptoms by

---

Third class? Relations of composition? Relations of causation? What included? Relations of degree and proportion? Moral relations? Province of reason, as distinguished from that of attention and memory?

which a disease may be distinguished from other diseases which resemble it,—and the actions which a substance may be confidently expected to produce upon other substances in particular circumstances. When the mental process required for doing so is performed in a legitimate manner, the deduction constitutes *truth*, in regard to the particular point which is the immediate subject of it; when the contrary, it leads to fallacy or *falsehood*. Hence reason has sometimes been defined that exercise of mind by which we distinguish truth from falsehood.

II. Having by the preceding processes ascertained the uniform tendencies of bodies to be followed by certain actions upon each other, we bring these tendencies into operation for the production of certain results. Hence reason has been considered also to be that power by which we combine means for accomplishing an end; but this, perhaps, may be regarded rather as the practical application of the knowledge to which reason leads us, than as a primary part of the province of reason itself.

III. We compare mental impressions with external things, so as to correct the impressions of the mind in regard to the external world. Mental processes of the most important kind are connected with this application of reason.

Reason or judgment, when duly exercised, conducts us through these various mental operations, and guides us towards the discovery of truth. It does so by enabling us to compare facts with facts, and events with events; to weigh their relations, bearings, and tendencies; and to assign to each circumstance its proper weight and influence in the conclusions which we are to deduce from them. The person who does so we call a man of sound judgment, whose opinions and conclusions we receive with confidence. On the contrary, we receive with distrust and suspicion the conclusions of a man of an opposite character, who forms his opinions and deductions hastily,—that is, from a limited number of facts, or a hasty and imperfect examination of their relations.

Truth and falsehood? Second general application of reason? Third general application? General view of reason?

A distinction has sometimes been made between the term reason, as used in the language of science, and as employed in the common affairs of life; but there seems to be no real ground for the distinction.

Reason, in the language of intellectual science, appears to be that process by which we judge correctly of the true and uniform relations of facts, or events, and give to each circumstance its due influence in the deductions. It is chiefly opposed to imagination, in which the mind is allowed to ramble through chains of events which are connected by loose and casual associations, leading to no true results. It is also distinguished from simple memory, in which facts or events are connected in the mind by certain principles of association, without a full view of their relations. Thus, when we find a person remembering an extensive collection of facts, and forming certain combinations among them, or deductions from them, without attending to points of difference which tend to other deductions, we say, his memory is better than his judgment.

Reasoning, again, appears to be the continued exercise of reason, when applied to the investigation of a particular subject, or a certain series of facts or events, so as to trace their relations or to establish a particular conclusion as deduced from such a series. This process, however, which is commonly called the discursive faculty, is to be distinguished from the simple exercise of reason. It ought to be guided by reason; that is, by a full view of the real relations of the facts about which it is exercised; but it is often allowed to fix on a slight and partial view of them; or is applied ingeniously to discover relations of a particular kind only. Thus, we speak of a man who reasons closely, or with a correct attention to the real relations of things, and the true weight of every fact in the investigation; of another who reasons loosely, or who is led away by casual relations and partial views, affording no true deductions; and of a third, who reasons ingeniously and plausibly, but not soundly,—that is, who argues on one side of a question, and contemplates facts in particular relations only, or as

---

Distinction commonly made? Ground for it? Reason as opposed to imagination? To memory? Reasoning in contradistinction from reason? Kinds of reasoning?

supporting particular opinions, neglecting those views of them which tend to a different conclusion. This art of ingenious reasoning or disputation, accordingly, we shall afterward have occasion to show, is not only to be distinguished from the sound exercise of reason or judgment, but is often found directly opposed to it.

In the language of theology, reason is distinguished from revelation; and means that exercise of the mind by which we deduce a certain knowledge of the Deity from the power and wisdom displayed in the works of creation, apart from any direct revelation of his character and will.

In the language of common life, the mental process which we term reason or judgment appears to be the same, though the facts on which it is exercised may be different. A reasonable man is one who, both in the formation of his opinions and the regulation of his conduct, gives the due weight and influence to all the facts and considerations which ought to influence his decision. A man of the opposite character is one who takes up his opinions upon slight, partial, and inadequate grounds; and then cannot, or will not, admit the impression of facts or arguments which are calculated to correct these unsound deductions; or who, in the regulation of his conduct, is led away by hasty impressions, or feeble and inadequate motives, without giving due consideration to those which are calculated to lead him into a different course. The former we call a reasonable, considerate, thinking man; the latter we say is an unreasonable, inconsiderate man, who cannot or will not think. It also very often happens that the latter, having formed his conclusions, is obstinately tenacious of them; while the former is still open to the true and full impression of any new fact or argument that is proposed to him. Solomon has expressed in a very striking manner the leading features of two such characters, namely, of the man who takes up opinions with little examination, and then adheres to them with inaccessible pertinacity; and him who forms them only after full and candid examination, and with a clear conception of the grounds on which they are formed:—

Disputation. Reason as distinguished from revelation? Reason compared with Judgment. Character of a reasonable man? The opposite character? Tenacity with which the two characters hold their opinions? Solomon's remark?

"The sluggard is wiser in his own conceit than seven men that can render a reason."

The process of mind which we call reason or judgment, therefore, seems to be essentially the same, whether it be applied to the investigation of truth, or the affairs of common life. In both cases, it consists in comparing and weighing facts, considerations, and motives, and deducing from them conclusions, both as principles of belief and rules of conduct. In doing so, a man of sound judgment proceeds with caution, and with a due consideration of all the facts which he ought to take into the inquiry. Having formed his conclusions, he is still open to the influence of new facts, by which they may be corrected or modified; but he is not to be shaken in his confidence by trivial statements or frivolous objections. Opposed to this there are two modifications of character which present an interesting subject for observation. Both form their conclusions hastily, and without due examination of the facts and considerations which ought to influence them; but their subsequent conduct is widely different. The one is shaken in his conclusions by every new fact that is presented to him, and every slight objection that is brought against his inductions; and the consequence is, that his opinions and his principles of conduct are constantly changing. The other, having framed his opinions, though on grounds the most inadequate, adheres to them with inaccessible firmness; and seems totally proof against the force of any facts or arguments that can be brought against them. The former is the more hopeful character of the two, his error consisting in a want of attention, rather than of judgment; or in a habit of framing his conclusions too hastily. By education or attention on his own part, his habit may be corrected in a greater or less degree; but the latter appears to labor under a radical defect of judgment, which makes him insensible to the due force of the considerations and arguments which influence other men. In the affairs of life, the former, after perhaps committing various indiscretions, acquires wisdom from experience; that is, by having the fallacy of his conclusions in many instances forced upon him.

Operation of sound judgment? Characters opposed to this? Fickleness and obstinacy compared? Which character most hopeful? Why?

The latter remains unchanged; retaining the same confidence in his own conclusions, and the same contempt for every thing that can be opposed to them. This unfortunate condition of mind, though it may have had its origin in peculiarity of mental constitution or deficient education. is fostered and increased by indulgence, and by a neglect of cultivating the important habit of calm and candid investigation. The man seems at last to become totally insensible to the motives and evidences which influence other men; and the more striking and convincing these are to others, the more remarkable appears the condition of that mind which does not feel or estimate their importance. This state of mind is emphatically ascribed, in the sacred writings, to the man who denies the existence of a great First Cause:—"The fool hath said in his heart, there is no God." By some process of mind, known to himself, he has arrived at this conclusion; and he is totally insensible to the manifold evidence, which meets him wherever he turns his eye, of its futility and folly. And surely, if there be in human things an affecting representation of a mind lost to every function of a healthy understanding, incapable of rising from effects to causes, or of tracing the relations of things,—a mind deserted by its rightful guardian, and left the unprotected victim of every wild delusion that flutters by,—it is to be found in him who, possessed of the senses of a living man, can stand before the fair face of creation, and say in his heart, "There is no God."

In every exercise of judgment, it is of essential importance that the mind shall be entirely unbiassed by any personal feeling or emotion which might restrain or influence its decisions. Hence the difficulty we feel in deciding on a subject in which we are deeply interested, especially if our inclinations and the facts and motives presented by the case be in any degree opposed to each other. Thus, we speak of a man who allows his feelings to influence his judgment; and of another, of a cool head, who allows no feeling to interfere with his decisions. Any particular emotion, which has been deeply indulged and fostered, comes

---

Results of the latter character. Instance mentioned in the Bible? Circumstance essential to the exercise of the judgment? Sources of bias?

in this manner to influence the judgment in a most extraordinary degree. It is thus that a vitiated and depraved state of the moral feelings at last misleads the judgment, in regard to the great principles of moral rectitude; and terminates in a state of mind emphatically described in the sacred writings, in which a man puts evil for good and good for evil, and is left to the influence of strong delusion, so that he "believes a lie." This remarkable condition of the power of reasoning and judging we cannot refer to any principle with which we are acquainted; but we must receive it as a fact in the history of our moral constitution which is not to be questioned. A poet has sung, that vice, which at first is hated as an odious monster, is, when seen too oft, endured, then pitied, then embraced: and he has only added his evidence to a fact which has been received upon the testimony of the philosopher and the moralist in every age, and is acted upon as a fixed and uniform principle of our nature by all classes of men.

Upon the grounds which have been briefly referred to in the above observations, it will appear that the principles on which a man should form his opinions are essentially the same with those by which he ought to regulate his conduct. If this conclusion be admitted, it will enable us to perceive the fallacy of a dogma which has often been brought forward with much confidence,—that a man is not responsible for his belief. When taken abstractly, this is true; but in the practical application of it there is a great and dangerous fallacy. In the opinions which a man forms on any particular subject, he is indeed influenced, not by his own will, but by the facts or evidence by which the doctrines are supported; and, in this sense, a man may justly be said not to be responsible for his belief. But when we apply the principle to practical purposes, and especially to those truths of religious belief to which the dogma has been pointed, it may easily be seen to be as fallacious as it is dangerous. A man is undoubtedly responsible for the care with which he has informed himself of the facts and evidences by which his belief on these subjects ought to be influenced; and for the care and anxiety with which he gives to

---

Responsibility of a man for his belief? Common dogma in regard to it? In what sense true? In what sense not true? For what is a man really responsible?

each of these facts and evidences its due weight in the momentous inquiry. He is further responsible for any degree of that vitiated and corrupted state of the moral feelings by which his judgment may have been biassed, so as to prevent him from approaching the subject with the sincere desire for truth of a pure and uncontaminated mind. If, in this sense, we say that a man is not responsible for his belief, we may quite as reasonably allege that he is not responsible for his conduct, because he chooses on some slight and partial grounds to frame for himself principles of action, without taking into consideration those fundamenta rules of moral rectitude by which mankind in general are expected to be influenced. We may as well contend that the man is not responsible for his conduct who, by long familiarity with vice, has lost sight of its malignity, and has come to approve and love that which he once contemplated with abhorrence.

It appears, then, that the exercise of reason is precisely the same, and is guided by the same laws, whether it be applied to the investigation of truth or to the regulation of conduct. The former is more particularly connected with the further prosecution of our inquiry: but the leading principles apply equally to the great questions of morals, and the important subject of religious belief. In prosecuting the subject as a branch of intellectual science, it seems to resolve itself into two parts:—

I. The use of reason in the investigation of truth.

II. The use of reason in correcting the impressions of the mind in regard to external things.

Before proceeding to these branches of the subject, however, this may perhaps be the proper place for again stating, in a few words, that in the preceding observations my object has been to confine myself to facts, respecting the processes which the mind actually performs, without entering on the question how it performs them. On this subject we find great differences among philosophers, which I have alluded to only in an incidental manner. Some ap-

---

Consequences resulting from any other view. Reason as applied to opinions and to conduct? Grand divisions of this subject; how many and what?

pear to have spoken in too unqualified terms respecting various and distinct FACULTIES of the mind, and have enumerated a variety of these, corresponding to the various mental operations. Dr. Brown, on the other hand, has followed a very different course, by referring all our mental processes to the two principles of simple and relative suggestion. According to this eloquent and ingenious writer, we have no direct voluntary power over the succession of our thoughts; but these follow each other in consequence of certain principles of suggestion, by which conceptions, in certain circumstances, call up or suggest other conceptions, which are in some manner related to them. We have the power only of fixing the mind more intensely upon some images of this series, when they arise, in consequence of approving of them, as referring to some subject of thought which is before us, while we disapprove of others of the series as less allied to it. The former become more fixed and vivid in consequence of this approbation, while the latter are allowed to sink back into oblivion. What systematic writers have called the faculty of conception is, according to this system, the simple presence in the mind of one of these suggested or recalled images. Memory is this simple suggestion combined with the impression of past time. In imagination, again, which has been considered as a voluntary power of forming conceptions or images into new combinations by a peculiar mental process, Dr. Brown belives that we have only the power of perceiving images as they are brought up by established principles of suggestion, approving of some which thus become fixed, and disapproving of others which thus pass away. In thus approving or disapproving of the suggested images, we are guided by a perception of their relation to any particular subject which is before us, and which we may desire to cultivate or illustrate. According to this writer, therefore, what is usually called conception is simple suggestion; memory is simple suggestion with a feeling of past time; imagination is simple suggestion combined with desire and with a perception of relation. The relative suggestion of Dr. Brown, again, is that perception of relations arising out

---

Differences among philosophers? Dr. Brown's view? His view of conception? Of memory? Of imagination?

of the comparison of different facts or objects which we have treated of under the more familiar name of judgment; and the mental process usually called abstraction he resolves simply into a perception of resemblances. Various objections might be urged against this system; and we may, perhaps, be allowed to doubt whether by means of it any thing has been gained to the science of mind. But the plan which I proposed to myself in this outline does not lead me into any consideration of it, or of those systems to which it is opposed. My object has been simply to inquire *what* the mind does, without entering on the question *how* it does so. On this ground, the division which has been adopted of distinct mental operations, not distinct faculties, appears to be that best calculated for practical utility.

---

§ I.

OF THE USE OF REASON IN THE INVESTIGATION OF TRUTH.

In applying our reason to the investigation of truth in any department of knowledge, we are, in the first place, to keep in mind that there are certain intuitive articles of belief which lie at the foundation of all reasoning. For, in every process of reasoning, we proceed by founding one step upon another which has gone before it; and when we trace such a process backwards, we must arrive at certain truths which are recognised as fundamental, requiring no proof and admitting of none. These are usually called First Truths. They are not the result of any process of reasoning, but force themselves with a conviction of infallible certainty upon every sound understanding, without regard to its logical habits or powers of induction. The force of them is accordingly felt in an equal degree by all classes of men; and they are acted upon with absolute confidence in the daily transactions of life. This is a subject of great and extensive importance. The truths or articles of

---

Remarks upon this system? The foundation of all reasoning? Name given to these truths? Their universal authority.

belief which are referable to it were briefly mentioned in a former part of our inquiry; they are chiefly the following:—

I. A conviction of our own existence, as sentient and thinking beings; and of mind, as something distinct from the functions of the body. From the first exercise of perception we acquire a knowledge of two things; namely, the thing perceived, and the sentient being who perceives it. In the same manner, from the exercise of any mental operation, such as memory, we acquire an impression of the thing remembered, of an essence or principle which remembers it, and of this essence as something entirely distinct from any function of the body. This last conviction must be considered as a first truth, or intuitive article of belief, standing on the same ground with the other truths which are referable to this class. It does not, as was formerly stated, rest upon any metaphysical or physiological argument, but upon an appeal made to the conviction of every man who attends to what is passing within. It resolves itself into a consciousness of the various mental processes, impressions, and emotions, as referable to one permanent and unchanging essence, while the body is known to be in a constant state of change; and of these processes as being exercised without any necessary dependence upon present impressions from external things. Like other truths of this class, it is, consequently, unaffected by sophisms which are brought against it; and the answer to these does not properly consist in any process of reasoning, but in this appeal to every man's absolute conviction. If brought into comparison, indeed, the evidence which we have for the existence of mind is perhaps less liable to deception than that which we have for the existence of matter.

II. A confidence in the evidence of our senses in regard to the existence and the properties of external things; or a conviction that they have a rea existence independently of our sensations. We have formerly referred to a celebrated doctrine, by which it was maintained that the mind perceives

---

How many classes? First? intuitive conviction? Nature and foundation of our belief of our own existence? Proper answer to sophisms against it? Second conviction?

only its own ideas or impressions; and that, consequently, we derive from our senses no evidence of the existence of external things. The only answer to such a sophism is, that a confidence in the evidence of our senses is a first truth, or intuitive principle of belief, admitting of no other proof than that which is derived from the universal conviction of mankind.

III. A confidence in our own mental processes; that facts, for example, which are suggested to us by our memory really occurred.

IV. A belief in our personal identity. This is derived from the combined operation of consciousness and memory; and it consists in a remembrance of past mental feelings, and a comparison of them with present feelings as belonging to the same sentient being. There were formerly many disputes on this subject; some maintaining that the notion of personal identity is inconsistent with the different states in which the mind exists at different times, as love and hatred, joy and sorrow; and also with the remarkable changes of character which often take place at different periods of life. This was one of the sophisms of the schools, founded upon an obscure analogy with changes which take place in material things, and is not at all applicable to mind. The only answer to the paradox is, that every man, under every variety of mental emotion, and every possible change of character, retains an absolute conviction that the sentient being whom he calls himself remains invariably the same; and that in all the affairs of life, whether referring to the past or the future, every man acts upon this conviction.

V. A conviction that every event must have a cause, and a cause adequate to the effect; and that appearances, showing a correct adaptation of means to an end, indicate design and intelligence in the cause. These, as fundamental truths, are quite distinct from the question relating to the connection of any two specified events as cause and effect. The latter belongs to another part of our inquiry.

Answer to sophisms against it? Third conviction? Fourth conviction, relating to personal identity? Former disputes? Answer? Fifth conviction, relating to cause and effect

VI. A confidence in the uniformity of nature; or, that the same substance will always exhibit the same characters; and that the same cause, under the same circumstances, will always be followed by the same effect. This, as a first truth, is a fundamental and instinctive conviction. The province of experience, we have already seen, is to ascertain the particular events which are so connected as to be included under the law.

Our confidence in the uniformity of nature is the foundation of all the calculations which we make for the future in regard to our protection or comfort, or even for the continuance of our existence; and without it the whole system of human things would be thrown into inextricable confusion.

It is referable to the two heads now stated; namely, uniformity of characters, and uniformity of sequences or operations.

By uniformity of characters, in any substance, we mean that the substance will always continue to exhibit the same combination of characters; so that, when we have ascertained its presence by some of them, we conclude that it also possesses the others. These characters may be numerous, and referable to various classes; such as the botanical characters of a plant, the chemical properties of a mineral, sensible qualities of smell, taste, and color, and capabilities of action upon other bodies. Such is our confidence in the undeviating uniformity of nature, that whatever number of these qualities we have ascertained to belong to a substance, we expect to find in every specimen of it in all time coming. For example, I find a substance which, by its smell and color, I know to be opium. Without any further information, I decide with confidence on its taste, its composition, its chemical affinity, its action on the human body, and the characters of the plant from which it was derived; and I never calculate upon the possibility of being deceived in any of these particulars.

Our confidence in the uniformity of the sequences or operations of nature resolves itself into a conviction of the continuance of that order which experience has shown us to

Sixth conviction, relating to the uniformity of nature? What calculations founded upon it? How many branches, and what? Uniformity of characters? Examples? Uniformity of operations?

exist in a uniform manner in the succession of phenomena. The conviction itself is an original or instinctive principle, felt and acted upon by all classes of men in the daily transactions of life. It is from experience that we learn the particular cases to which we are warranted in applying it; or, in other words, the successions of phenomena which, there is sufficient ground for believing, have occurred in a certain order in time past. These we expect with perfect confidence to continue to be equally uniform, or to occur in the same order in time to come. The error to be guarded against in such investigations is, assuming the past uniformity of phenomena on insufficient grounds; or, in other words, concluding that events have always occurred in a certain order because we have seen them occur in that order in a few instances. A principle assumed in this manner may of course disappoint us if applied to future phenomena; but in this case there is no deviation from the uniformity of nature; the error consisted in assuming such a uniformity where none existed.

The uniformity of the sequences of phenomena is the foundation of our idea of causation in regard to these phenomena; that is to say, when we have observed one event uniformly follow another event, we consider the first as cause, and the second as effect; and, when this relation has been ascertained to be uniform, we conclude that it will continue to be uniform; or that the same cause in the same circumstances will always be followed by the same effect. This expectation will of course disappoint us if we have assumed the relation on inadequate grounds; or have considered two events as cause and effect which have been only accidentally combined in a few instances. To entitle us to assume that the relation will be uniform in time to come, we must have full and adequate grounds for believing that it has been uniform in time past.

In the great operations of nature a very extensive observation often enables us to trace a remarkable uniformity even in regard to events which at first sight appear to be most irregular and uncertain. Thus, the most uncertain of

---

Error to be guarded against? Foundation of our idea of cause and effect. Caution necessary? Remarkable uniformity among events apparently irregular? Example. Duration of human life?

all things is human life, as far as respects individuals; but the doctrine of the continuance of life in regard to a large body of men is, by extensive observation, reduced almost to a certainty. Nothing is more uncertain than the proportion of males and females that shall be born in one family; but in great communities this also is uniform. There is much uncertainty in the character of different seasons, but there are facts which give probability to the conjecture that in a long series of years there may also be discovered a remarkable uniformity. An impression of this kind was carried so far by the ancients as to lead to the doctrine of the Annes Magnus, or Platonic year, in which it was believed that the whole series of human events would be acted over again.

The uniform successions of phenomena are, with reason able care, easily ascertained in regard to material things; and when they are ascertained, we rely upon their uniform continuance; or, if we find a deviation in any instance, we easily ascertain the incidental cause by which the sequence is interrupted, and can provide against the interference of the same or any similar cause in future instances. There is greater uncertainty when our researches refer to the phenomena of mind, or the actions of living bodies. The causes of this uncertainty were formerly mentioned. It arises partly from the greater difficulty of ascertaining the true relations; that is, of tracing causes to their true effects, and effects to their true causes; and partly from the tendency to these being interrupted in future instances by some new cause, in regard to which we cannot calculate either the existence or the precise effects. Hence, for example, the uncertainty of human laws; one of the contingencies by which they are interrupted being the chances of evading hem. If we could conceive a case in which every crime was with certainty detected, and every criminal brought to punishment, it is probable that the effect of human laws would be nearly as certain as the operation of material causes. But the criminal, in the first instance, calculates on the chance of evading detection, and, even in the event of detection, of escaping punishment; and thus the tendency of the wisest laws is constantly interrupted in a manner which no human

---

Proportion of males and females? Notion of the ancients? Facility of ascertaining the laws of material things? The laws of mind? Why more difficult? Operation of human laws? Calculation of the criminal in violating them?

wisdom can calculate upon or prevent. There is often a similar uncertainty in human character in other situations: for example, in judging how an individual will act in particular circumstances, or be influenced by particular motives; for a motive which we have found to induce a particular line of conduct in one individual may fail in producing the same result in another, being prevented by circumstances in his moral condition which entirely elude our observation.

Yet there is a uniformity in moral phenomena which, though it may be ascertained with greater difficulty than the order of natural phenomena, we calculate upon with similar confidence when it has been ascertained. Thus, a man may have acquired such a character for integrity, that we rely upon his integrity in any situation in which he may be placed, with the same confidence with which we rely on the uniformity of nature; and there is a man distinguished by veracity and fidelity to his promise, of whom we say, in common language, that his word is as good as his bond. In such examples as these, indeed, our confidence is founded, not upon any laws which have been observed in regard to the whole species, but on a uniformity which has been observed in regard to the individuals, or rather a class to which the individuals belong. There are also, however, laws which apply to mankind in general, and on which we rely as far as they go,—namely, principles of conduct in which we confide, as regulating every man of a sane mind, whatever may be our knowledge of his previous habits of judging or acting. It is in this manner, for example, as formerly stated, that we regulate our confidence in testimony. If a man who is either a stranger to us or bears a character of doubtful veracity, relates circumstances which tend greatly to promote his own purposes, we calculate on the probability of fabrication, and reject his testimony; and if we even suspect that he has a purpose to serve, a similar impression is produced. If, on the contrary, we are satisfied that the circumstances are indifferent to him, and that he has no purpose to answer, we give greater credit to his testimony. If, further than this, we

---

Similar uncertainty in other cases? Can the uniformity of moral phenomena be relied upon in any cases? Example. General principles of human conduct.

perceive that the statement operates against himself, conveying an imputation against his own conduct, or exposing him to contempt, ridicule, or personal injury, we are satisfied that nothing could make him adhere to such a testimony but an honest conviction of its truth. Under the former circumstances, we believe only a man whom we consider as a person of known and established veracity; under the latter, we believe any man whom we consider to be of a sane mind. Thus, in both instances, we proceed upon a certain uniformity of moral phenomena; only that we refer them to two classes,—namely, one which is ascertained to be uniform in regard to the whole species, and another which is uniform only in regard to a certain order, that is, all men of integrity and veracity. In the one case, we rely upon the uniformity in every instance; in the other, we do not rely upon it until we are satisfied that the individual example belongs to that order in which the other kind of moral uniformity has been ascertained.

There are other inquiries closely connected with the uniformity of moral relations; but at present we must allude to them very briefly. We have every reason to believe that there are moral causes, that is, truths and motives, which have a tendency to influence human volition and human conduct with a uniformity similar to that with which physical agents produce their actions upon each other. These moral causes, indeed, do not operate in every instance, or in all circumstances; but neither do physical causes. Substances in chemistry, for example have certain tendencies to act upon each other, which are uniform and necessary; but no action takes place unless the substances are brought into certain circumstances which are required for bringing these tendencies into operation. They must, in the first place, be brought into contact; and, besides this, many of them require other collateral circumstances, as a particular temperature, or a particular state of concentration or dilution. It is the same with moral causes: their tendencies are uniform, and there are principles in the mind of man which these are adapted for

---

Example; laws of testimony? Influence of the circumstances of the case on the credibility of witnesses? Other cases of the uniformity of moral relations? Moral and physical causes compared. Influence of circumstances in both cases?

acting upon. But they require certain circumstances in the man on whom they are expected to act, without which they produce no influence upon him. It is necessary, for example, that he be fully informed in regard to them as truths; and that his attention be directed to them with such a degree of intensity as shall bring him fully under their influence as statements addressed to his understanding; also, that there be a certain healthy state of his moral feelings,—for this has a most extensive influence on the due operation of moral causes. Without these the most powerful moral causes may produce no effect upon a man; as the most active chemical agents may fail entirely of their actions, if the substances are not placed in the requisite circumstances of temperature, dilution, or concentration.

These considerations seem to bear an important reference to a question which has been much argued, namely that respecting liberty, necessity, and the freedom of the will. On a subject on which some of the wisest and the best of men have been found on opposite sides, I would express myself with becoming caution and diffidence; but perhaps some of the obscurity in which the question has been involved arises from the want of a clear definition of the terms in which it has been argued; and by not fully distinguishing between *will* or *simple volition*, and *desire* or *inclination*. Will, or simple volition, is the state of mind which immediately precedes action; and the action following upon this is not only free, but it is absolutely impossible to suppose it should be otherwise. A man is not only free to do what he wills, but we cannot conceive a case in which he could exert a power of not doing what he wills, or of doing what he wills not. Impulse or restraint from without, acting upon his bodily organs, could alone interfere with his following, in this sense, the tendency of his [illegible] or simple volition. The only idea, indeed, that [illegible] form of free agency, or freedom of the will, is, that [illegible]sists in a man being able to do what he wills, or to abstain from doing what he wills not. Necessary agency, on

---

Circumstances essential to the full operation of moral causes? Important question connected with this subject? Terms used? Distinction between them? The *will*—what? Proper idea of free agency? Necessary agency?

the other hand, would consist in the man being compelled, by a force from without, to do what he wills not, or prevented from doing what he wills.

The real bearing of the inquiry does not lie in this connection between the volition and the act, but in the origin or cause of the volition, or in the connection between the volition and the desire; and this will be seen to be entirely distinct. A man, for example, may desire, or have an inclination to, that which he has not the power to will; because he may be under the influence of motives and principles which prevent the inclination from being followed by volition, with as absolute a necessity as we observe in the sequences of natural phenomena. Thus, also, we may say to a man of strict integrity and virtue that he has not the power to commit murder or robbery, or any act of gross injustice or oppression. He may reply that he has the power to do it if he willed; and this is granted, for this is free agency; but it is not the question in dispute. We do not say that he has not the power to do any or all of these acts if he willed, but that he has not the power to will such deeds. He is under the influence of motives and principles which make it as much a matter of necessity for him not to will such acts, as it is for a stone not to rise from the earth's surface contrary to its gravity. Such a necessity as this, if we must retain the term, so far from being unfavorable to the interests of virtue and morals, or opposed to the practice of exhorting men to virtue, seems, on the contrary, to hold out the strongest encouragement in doing so; and to be, in fact, the only scheme on which we can expect an argument or motive to have any influence upon human conduct. For it represents man as possessed of certain uniform principles in his nature which are capable of being acted upon by certain moral causes, truths, laws, or motives, with a uniformity similar to that which we observe in physical phenomena, provided he can be brought under their influence, and into those circumstances which are required for their due operation. These circumstances are,—that the moral causes, laws, motives, or

Real point of inquiry? Distinction between desire and will? Examples. Controlling influence of motives in such cases. Is this *necessity*? Influence of it on virtue and morals? How does this view represent man? Circumstances essential?

truths, shall be brought before his understanding; that he shall direct his attention to them with suitable intensity; and that he is free from that degree of corruption of his moral feelings, or any of those distorted moral habits which we know to produce a most extensive influence on the operation of moral causes. To suppose a kind of moral liberty opposed to such a necessity as this, would be to represent man as a being possessed of no fixed or uniform principles, —not to be calculated upon as to his conduct in any instance,—and not capable of being acted upon by any motive or principle except the blind caprice of the moment. To endeavor to act upon such a being, by persuading him to virtue or dissuading him from vice, would be like expecting fixed results in chemistry, by bringing substances to act upon each other, the actions of which we had previously found to be without any kind of uniformity. This is, in fact, precisely the situation of the maniac, whom, accordingly, we never expect to guide or influence by motives or arguments, but by external restraint. He may act harmlessly, or he may act mischievously; but we never can calculate upon his actions in any one instance; we therefore shut him up, so as to prevent him from being dangerous to the community.

Necessity, then, as applied to the operation of moral causes, appears simply to correspond with the uniformity which we observe in the operation of physical causes. We calculate that a man of a certain character will act in a particular manner in particular circumstances, or that he will be acted upon in a certain manner by particular truths and motives, when they are presented to him, by a principle of uniformity similar to that with which we expect an acid to act in a particular manner upon an alkali. The action of the acid we know to be uniform, but we know also, that no action will take place till the substances are brought fully in contact, and in certain circumstances which are required for their action;—and the action of moral causes is uniform, but they exert no influence on a man till he is fully acquainted with them,—directs his attention to them

Is man possessed of any moral liberty, inconsistent with this view? Why not Uniformity of the operations of moral causes? Compared with physical? Example.

with suitable care,—and is besides in a certain healthy state of moral feeling. It is thus that we calculate on the full and uniform operation of moral causes on some individuals, and not on others;-namely, by having previously ascertained that the former are in those intellectual and moral circumstances which are required for their action. When, in another individual, we find these causes fail in their natural actions, we endeavor, as far as may be in our power, to supply those collateral circumstances,—by instructing him in the facts, truths, or motives;—by rousing his attention to their importance;—by impressing them upon him in their strongest characters, and by all such arguments and representations as we think calculated to fix the impression. All this we do under a conviction, that these causes have a certain, fixed, uniform, or necessary action, in regard to human volition and human conduct; and it is this conviction which encourages us to persevere in our attempts to bring the individual under their influence. If we had not this conviction, we should abandon the attempt as altogether hopeless; because we could have no ground on which to form any calculation, and no rules to guide us in our measures. Precisely in the same manner, when we find a chemical agent fail of the effect which we expect from it, we add it in larger quantity, or in an increased state of concentration, or at a higher temperature, or with some other change of circumstances calculated to favor its action; and we persevere in these measures, under a conviction that its action is perfectly uniform or necessary, and will take place whenever these circumstances have been provided for. On the same principle, we see how blame may attach to the intelligent agent in both cases, though the actions of the causes are uniform and necessary. Such is the action of chemical agents,—but blame may attach to the chemist who has not provided them in the necessary circumstances as to quantity, concentration, and temperature. Such is the action of moral causes,—but deep guilt may attach to the moral agent, who has been proof against their influence. There is guilt in ignorance, when knowledge was within his reach;—there

Practical use of these principles. Conviction upon which such practice is based The same with physical processes. What constitutes guilt?

is guilt in heedless inattention, when truths and motives of the highest interest claimed his serious consideration;—there is guilt in that corruption of his moral feelings which impedes the action of moral causes, because this has originated, in a great measure, in a course of vicious desires, and vicious conduct, by which the mind, familiarized with vice, has gradually lost sight of its malignity. During the whole of this course, also, the man felt that he was a free agent; that he had power to pursue the course which he followed, and that he had power to refrain from it. When a particular desire was first present to his mind, he had the power immediately to act with a view to its accomplishment; or he had the power to abstain from acting, and to direct his attention more fully to the various considerations and motives which were calculated to guide his determination. In acting as he did, he not only withheld his attention from those truths which were thus calculated to operate upon him as a moral being; but he did still more direct violence to an impulse within, which warned him that he was wandering from the path of rectitude. The state of moral feeling which gradually results from this habitual violation of the indications of conscience, and this habitual neglect of the serious consideration of moral causes, every individual must feel to be attended with moral guilt. The effect of it is not only to prevent the due operation of moral causes on his future volitions, but even to vitiate and distort the judgment itself, respecting the great principles of moral rectitude. Without attempting any explanation of this remarkable condition of the mental functions, its actual existence must be received as a fact in the constitution of human nature, which cannot be called in question; and it offers one of the most remarkable phenomena that can be presented to him who turns his attention to the moral economy of man.

Before concluding this incidental allusion to a much controverted subject, I may be allowed to remark, that the term necessity, as applied to moral phenomena, is not fortunate, and perhaps not philosophical; and something would perhaps be gained in conducting the inquiry, if, for

In what sense the individual is free? Guilt of habitually violating conscience. Remarks upon the term *necessity*.

necessity, we were to substitute *uniformity*. In strict propriety, indeed, the terms necessity and necessary ought to be applied only to mathematical truth. Of physical relations, all that we know is the fact of their uniformity; and it would appear equally philosophical to apply the same term to mental phenomena. On this principle, therefore, we should say, that the tendency of moral causes or motives is not necessary, but uniform; and that on this depends all our confidence in the uniformity of human character, and in the power of truths, motives, or arguments, to produce particular results on human conduct. To suppose the mind possessed of a power of determining, apart from all the influence of moral causes or motives, would be to overthrow this confidence, and to reduce our whole calculations on human character to conjecture and uncertainty. When, indeed, we talk of a self-determining power of the will, we seem to use a combination of words without any definite meaning. For the will is not distinct from the being who wills; and to speak of an individual determining his will, is only saying, in other words, that he wills. He wills some act for some reason, which is known to himself; if communicated to another, the reason might not appear a satisfactory one; but still it is to him the reason which induced him to will the act, and this appears to be all that we can make of the subject. A power of determining, without any reason, appears to be not only unphilosophical, but, in point of fact, inapplicable to any conceivable case. Ignorance, inattention, or gross perversion of the moral feelings may make the worse reason appear the better; but we cannot conceive a case, in which an individual could exert a power of determining without any reason, or according to what appears to him at the time to be a weaker reason, in opposition to one which appears a stronger. It will also, I think, be found that the warmest advocates for philosophical liberty, and a self-determining power, in actual practice recognise as much as others the principle of the uniformity of moral causes. Thus, if we find a person acting in a manner widely different from that which we expected from him, all men concur in saying, "what motive could induce

---

Proposed substitute? Self-determining power of the will? Objections to that language? Uniformity of moral causes admitted in practice?

him to act in that manner?" and if we cannot reconcile his conduct to any conceivable motive, we say, "it really looks like insanity." Another may remark, "his conduct indicates a singular want of consideration;" thus clearly recognising the existence of certain motives or moral causes, which would have led the man into a different line of conduct, had he allowed his attention to fix upon them. The doctrine of a self-determining power should remove every difficulty in such a case to those who believe in it; but I am not aware that it ever was made use of for such a purpose. It will also be found to agree with the universal conviction of mankind, that the circumstance which gives to an action the character of merit or demerit is entirely the motive from which it was done; and that if we could conceive such a thing as an action performed by the impulse of a free self-determining power apart from any influence of motives or moral causes, no man of sane mind would for a moment allow to such an act the character of virtue. On the contrary, it is familiar to every one, that we often find in a man's motive an excuse for conduct in which we think he has acted wrong. We say, he erred in judgment, but his motive was good; and this mode of reasoning meets with the cordial concurrence of the whole mass of mankind.

The First Truths, or intuitive principles of belief, which have been the subject of the preceding observations, are of the utmost practical importance, as they furnish the true and only answer to many of the sophisms of the scholastic philosophy, and to many sceptical arguments of more modern times. They admit of no other evidence than an appeal to the consciousness of every man, that he does and must believe them. "We believe them," says Dr. Brown, "because it is impossible not to believe them." "In all these cases," says Mr. Stewart, "the only account that can be given of our belief is, that it forms a necessary part

---

Evidence of it? Moral character of an action without motive? Only evidence of these First Truths? Dr. Brown's remark?

of our constitution, against which metaphysicians may argue, so as to perplex the judgment, but of which it is impossible to divest ourselves for a moment, when we are called to employ our reason, either in the business of life or in the pursuits of science."

It is likewise to be kept in mind, as was formerly stated, that our idea of reasoning necessarily supposes the existence of a certain number of truths, which require and admit of no evidence. The maxim, indeed, is as old as the days of Aristotle, and has never been called in question, "that, except some first principles be taken for granted, there can be neither reason nor reasoning; that it is impossible that every truth should admit of proof, otherwise proof would extend *in infinitum*, which is incompatible with its nature; and that, if ever men attempt to prove a first principle, it is because they are ignorant of the nature of proof."* As these truths, therefore, do not admit of being called in question by any sound understanding, neither do they admit of being supported by any process of reasoning; and, when paradoxes or sophisms in opposition to them are proposed, any attempt to argue with such, upon logical principles, only leads to discussions as absurd as themselves. Of attempts of both kinds many examples are to be met with among the writers of the sixteenth and seventeenth centuries, as Des Cartes and Hobbes; and even some eminent persons, of more modern times, are not entirely free from them. Thus, Des Cartes, Malebranche, and others, thought it necessary to prove that external objects, and the sentient beings with whom we are connected, have a real existence whether we think of them or not, and are not merely ideas in our own minds. Berkeley showed the weakness of this argument, and on this founded the well-known doctrine by which he denied the real existence of material things.

Many of the dogmas of modern sophistical writers, such as Mr. Hume, have consisted of attempts to overturn, by processes of argument, these fundamental or first truths.

* Aristotle's Metaphysics, book IV.

Mr. Stewart's remark? Impossibility of reasoning without the admission of such truths. They can neither be proved nor called in question. Former attempts to prove them? Example. Attempts to disprove them?

On the other hand, the unsatisfactory nature of some of the replies to these sophisms, depends upon the attempts to combat them having been made by reasonings, of which the subject is not susceptible. For these principles admit of no proof by processes of reasoning, and, consequently, are in no degree affected by demonstrations of the fallacy of attempts to establish them by such processes. An interesting illustration of this has been reserved by Mr. Stewart, in a correspondence between Mr. Hume and Sir Gilbert Elliot.* "From the reply to this letter," says Mr. Stewart, "by Mr. Hume's very ingenious and accomplished correspondent, we learn that he had drawn from Mr. Hume's metaphysical discussions the only sound and philosophical inference: that the lameness of the proofs offered by Des Cartes and his successors, of some fundamental truths, universally acknowledged by mankind, proceeded, not from any defect in the evidence, but, on the contrary, from their being self-evident, and consequently unsusceptible of demonstration." The same view of Mr. Hume's sceptical reasonings was taken by other eminent persons, by whom his system was attacked, particularly Reid, Beattie, and Oswald; and on the continent, the nature and importance of these first truths had been at an earlier period illustrated in a full and able manner by father Buffier.

Various characters have been proposed, by which these primary and fundamental truths may be distinguished. One of those given by father Buffier appears to be the best, and to be alone sufficient to identify them. It is, that their practical influence extends even to persons who affect to dispute their authority; in other words, that in all the affairs of life, the most sceptical philosopher acts, as much as the mass of mankind, upon the absolute belief of these truths. Let a person of this description, for example, be contending very keenly, in regard to something which deeply concerns his interest or his comfort, he would scarcely be satisfied by being told, that the thing about which

* Introductory Essay to the Appendix of the Encyclopædia Britannica.

Illustration of this? Effect of Hume's reasoning upon Elliot's mind? Upon other minds? Distinctive characters of these primary truths? Buffier's? Example?

he contends has no real existence, and that he who contends about it so eagerly is himself a nonenity, or, at best, nothing more than an idea. Let him be taking cognizance of an offence committed against him ten years ago, he never doubts that he is still the person against whom the offence was committed. Let him lay plans for future advantage or comfort, it is done under a full conviction that he is still to continue the individual who may enjoy them. Has a building started up on his premises, which he did not expect to see, he immediately asks who ordered the masons, and would be very ill-satisfied by being told, that the thing had appeared without any known cause, by a fortuitous combination of atoms. However much he may reason to the contrary, he shows no doubt, in his own practice, that every event must have an adequate cause. The same mode of reasoning will be seen to apply to the other truths which belong to the class under consideration, namely, that those who argue against them act in all cases on a belief of their truth.

The distinction between a process of reasoning and the act of the mind in arriving at these fundamental and instinctive truths, is a principle of the utmost practical importance. For a chain of correct reasoning requires logical habits, and a certain cultivation of the mental powers; and, consequently, it is confined to a comparatively small number of mankind. But the process here referred to is the spontaneous and immediate induction of the untutored mind, and a correct exercise of it requires only that the mind shall not be debased by depravity, nor bewildered by the refinements of a false philosophy. The truths which we derive from it accordingly do not concern the philosopher alone, but are of daily and essential importance to the whole class of mankind. Let us take, for example, the principle referred to under the fifth head, namely, our intuitive conviction that every change or event must have an adequate cause. This is a principle of daily application, and one which is acted upon with absolute confidence in the ordinary affairs of life by all classes of men. By the

---

Practical admissions of them in various cases? Important distinction? What essential to correct reasoning?—to intuitive belief? Universal influence of these truths? Example, inferring a cause from an effect.

immediate and unconscious exercise of it, we infer the skill of one workman from works indicating skill, and the vigor of another from works indicating strength. We infer from every work, not only a cause, but a cause which, both in degree and kind, is exactly proportioned to the effect produced. From a chronometer, which varies only a second in a year, we infer exquisite skill in the artist; and from the construction of the pyramids of Egypt, the united strength of a multitude of men. We never supposed for a moment that the minute skill of the artist raised the pyramid, or that the united force of the multitude constructed the chronometer; still less, that these monuments of art started into their present condition without a cause. We infer with absolute certainty in both cases an adequate cause; that is, a cause distinguished in the one case by design and mechanical power, in the other, by design, adaptation, and exquisite skill.

The principle which is thus acted upon, in the ordinary affairs of life, with a conviction of infallible certainty, is precisely the same by which, from the stupendous works of creation, we infer by the most simple step of reasoning the existence of a great First Cause. This cause also we conclude to be a designing and intelligent mind, infinite in wisdom and boundless in power; and by a very slight and natural extension of the same principle, we arrive with equal certainty at the conviction of this cause being the first,—not arising out of any thing preceding it, consequently self-existent and eternal. All this is not such a process of reasoning as requires logical habits, and admits of debate, deliberation, or doubt;—the metaphysician may bewilder himself in its very simplicity; but the uncontaminated mind finds its way to the conclusion with unerring certainty, and with a conviction which is felt to be not only satisfactory, but irresistible.

When we proceed from these first or intuitive articles of belief to the further investigation of truth in any department of knowledge, various mental processes are brought into

Instances in common life? Instance in regard to the works of creation.

operation; but in regard to all of them reason is our ultimate guide in judging whether they are performed in a legitimate manner, and upon principles calculated to lead to the discovery of truth. These processes may be chiefly referred to the following heads:—

I. To make a careful collection of facts relating to the subject, and to abstain from deducing any conclusions till we have before us such a series as seems calculated to warrant them. The first operation of reason therefore is, to judge when we have a sufficient number of facts for this purpose.

II. To separate from the mass those facts which are connected with it incidentally, and to retain those only which we have reason to consider as uniform and essential. In some sciences this is accomplished by repeated and varied experiments; and in those departments which do not admit of this, it is done by cautious and extensive observation. Our object in both cases is to ascertain how many of the circumstances observed, and what particular combinations of them uniformly accompany each other, or are really connected with the effects which are produced. In this careful clearing of our statement from all incidental combinations consists that faithful observation of nature which forms the first step in every scientific investigation. It is opposed to two errors, both equally to be avoided, namely, leaving out of view, or not assigning an adequate value to, important and essential facts; and giving a place and an importance to those which are incidental and trivial. In every scientific investigation this is a process of the utmost importance; and there is another nearly connected with it, namely, to judge of the authenticity of the facts. This also is a mental process of the utmost delicacy. In conducting it, there are two extremes from which the exercise of sound judgment ought equally to guard us, namely, receiving facts upon imperfect evidence, and rejecting those which have a sufficient title to credit; in other words, credulity and scepticism. Both these extremes are equally unworthy of a mind which is guided by sound reason.

Classification of mental processes necessary for the investigation of truth? First head; collecting facts. Second head; selecting those which are essential. Two errors to be avoided? Two extremes in regard to the admission of facts?

III. To compare facts with each other, so as to trace their resemblances, or to ascertain those characters or properties in which a certain number of facts or substances agree. We thus arrange them into classes, genera, and species.

IV. To compare facts or events with each other, so as to trace their relations and sequences; especially that relation of uniform sequence on which is founded our notion of cause and effect. This delicate and most important process consists entirely in a patient observation of facts, and of their relation to each other. When, in a certain number of instances, we find two events following one another without any exception, we come to consider the sequence as uniform, and call the one cause, and the other effect; and when, in other instances, we are disappointed in finding such a succession, this confidence is shaken, unless we can discover a cause by which the sequence was interrupted. Reason, acting upon extensive observation, must here guide us; on the one hand to judge of the uniformity of the sequences, and, on the other, to account for apparent deviations.

V. To review an extensive collection of facts, so as to discover some general fact common to the whole. This is the process which we call generalizing, or the induction of a general principle. The result of it is the last and greatest object of human science, and that to which all the other steps are preliminary and subservient. An ordinary mind is satisfied with the observation of facts as they pass before it, and those obvious relations which obtrude themselves upon its notice; but the philosopher analyzes the phenomena, and thus discovers their more minute relations. His genius is distinguished above the industry of the mere observer of facts, when he thus traces principles of accordance among facts which, to the vulgar eye, appear remote and dissimilar. A remarkable example of this is familiar to every one. Between the fall of an apple from a tree and

---

Third head; comparison of facts with reference to their nature. Fourth head; comparison of facts with reference to their causes and relations. Fifth head · generalizing The operation of an ordinary and of a philosophical mind compared.

the motions of the heavenly bodies a common mind would have been long ere it discovered any kind of relation; but on such a relation Newton founded those grand principles by which he brought to light the order and harmony of the universe. For it was this simple fact that first suggested to him the great principle of physical science, that matter attracts matter in the reciprocal ratio of their masses.

In a practical view, these processes may be referred to three heads,—namely, collecting authentic facts,—tracing causation,—and deducing general principles. Here various mental operations are brought into action, especially attention, memory, conception, and abstraction; but it is the province of reason to judge whether these are conducted in a legitimate manner, or, in other words, to distinguish truth from falsehood. It may, therefore, be important to keep in mind what those circumstances are in which consist truth and falsehood, in reference to any department of knowledge.

I. In collecting facts, it is required in the first place that they shall be authentic; secondly, that the statement shall include a full and fair view of all the circumstances which ought to be taken into our investigation of the case; and thirdly, that it shall not include any facts which are not connected with the subject, or whose connection is only incidental. When we have thus formed a collection of facts, authentic, full, and essential, the statement, in as far as relates to the facts, constitutes truth. When any of the facts are not authentic; when important facts are left out of the statement, or misrepresented; or when facts are taken into it which, though true, have no real relation to the subject; this constitutes fallacy or falsehood.

II. In considering two events as connected in the manner of cause and effect; when this relation is deduced from a full and extensive observation of the sequence being uniform,—this is truth. When it is assumed upon inadequate grounds, that is, from the observation of a connection which is only incidental or limited,—this is either falsehood or hy-

Example? More general classification of these processes? Three principles to be observed in collecting facts. Principles to be observed in determining the relation of cause and effect?

pothesis; for the relation may be assumed upon grounds which, though not actually false, are yet not sufficient to establish it as true—namely, on observation which is too limited in extent. This is conjecture or hypothesis; and it is in some cases a legitimate process, provided it be used only as a guide for further observation, and be not received as true until such observation shall have been sufficient to confirm it.

III. In deducing from a large collection of facts a general fact or general principle; when this induction is made from a full examination of all the individual cases to which the general fact is meant to apply, and actually does apply to them all,—this is truth. When it is deduced from a small number of observations, and extended to others to which it does not apply,—this is falsehood. As in the former case, however, a general principle may be produced hypothetically or by conjecture; that is, it may be assumed as general so far as we at present know. This process is often legitimate and useful as a guide in further inquiry, if it be employed for this purpose only, and the result be not received as truth until it be established by sufficient observation. A great and not unfrequent error is, that when such hypothetical principles are proposed in a confident manner, they are very often received as true; and the consequence is, that a degree of observation is required for exposing their fallacy, perhaps as extensive as, if properly employed, might have been sufficient to discover the truth. Those who are acquainted with the history of medical doctrines will be best able to judge of the accuracy of this observation, and to estimate the extensive influence which this error has had in retarding the progress of medical science.

The proper rules to be observed, in deducing a general principle, are therefore opposed, in the first place, to the error of hasty generalizing, or deducing such a principle from a limited number of facts. They are further opposed to another error, prevalent in the hypothetical systems of the old philosophy, by which phenomena were referred to principles altogether fictitious and imaginary, or, in other words,

---

Principles to be observed in deducing general laws. False deductions. Hypothesis; its legitimate use? Abuse of it? Common errors?

which could not be shown to be facts. In opposition to both these errors the great rule of induction in modern science is, that the principle which is assumed as general shall be itself a fact, and that the fact shall be universal. Thus, what we call the law of gravitation is primarily nothing more than the fact that bodies fall to the earth; and that this is true of all bodies, without a single exception. Of the cause of this fact, or the hidden principle on which it depends, we know nothing, and all the investigations of Newton were carried on independently even of the attempt to discover it. "When Newton," says Mr. Stewart, "showed that the same law of gravity extends to the celestial spaces, and that the power by which the moon and planets are retained in their orbits is precisely similar in its effects to that which is manifested in the fall of a stone; he left the efficient cause of gravity as much in the dark as ever, and only generalized still further the conclusions of his predecessors."

False investigation may be briefly referred to three heads --fallacies in facts,—false inductions,—and false reasoning.

I. Fallacies in Facts. A statement of facts is fallacious when any of the alleged facts are not true,—when it includes facts not relating to the subject,—and when important facts are omitted. This last error is most frequently exemplified in those cases in which facts are collected on one side of a question, or in support of a particular doctrine. To the same class we may likewise add those instances in which statements are received as facts which are not facts, but opinions.

II. False Induction includes false causation and false generalization. False causation is, when two events are considered as cause and effect without sufficient reason and which are, in fact, only incidentally combined; when events are considered as cause and effect which are only joint effects of a common cause; and when, of two events really connected as cause and effect, we mistake the order

Great rule of induction? Examples. False investigation; referred to how many and what heads? First head? Second head?

of the sequence, considering that as the cause which is really the effect, and that as the effect which is really the cause. The error of false causation is most apt to occur in those sciences in which there is peculiar difficulty in tracing effects to their true causes, and causes to their true effects. These, as formerly mentioned, are exemplified by medicine and political economy. A physician, for example, ascribes the cure of a patient to a remedy which he has taken, though it perhaps had no influence on his recovery; and a political declaimer refers some circumstance of national distress or commercial embarrassment to certain public measures which happened to correspond in time, but were in fact entirely unconnected. False generalization, again, as was lately stated, includes general principles which are deduced from a limited number of facts; and hypotheses which cannot be shown to be facts, but are entirely fictitious and imaginary.

III. False Reasoning. This consists either,—in applying to the explanation of facts principles which are unsound,—in applying sound principles to facts which have no relation to them,—or in deducing conclusions which do not follow from these facts and principles.

Reasoning is usually divided into two parts, which have been called the intuitive and the discursive. Intuitive reasoning, or intuitive judgment, is when the truth of a proposition is perceived whenever it is announced. This applies to axioms or self-evident truths, and to first truths or fundamental articles of belief, formerly referred to, which rest upon the absolute conviction of the whole mass of mankind. In discursive reasoning, again, some of these axioms or first truths are applied to particular facts, so as to deduce from the connection new conclusions. Thus, when we say that "every event must have an adequate cause," we state a principle of intuitive judgment. When we then collect from the phenomena of nature various examples of adaptation and design, and, applying that intuitive principle to these facts, arrive at the conclusion that the universe is the work of an intelligent and designing First Cause,—this is

Examples? Third head? Reasoning, how divided? Intuitive reasoning? Discursive reasoning? Example of each?

discursive reasoning. The new principle or conclusion thus deduced may be applied in a similar manner to the deduction of farther conclusions, and so on through what we call a chain of reasoning. Any particular piece of reasoning, then, may generally be resolved into the following elements :—

1. Certain principles or propositions which are stated either as axioms, as first truths, or as deductions from some former process of reasoning.

2. Certain facts or relations of facts, derived either from observation or testimony, which are stated as true, and to which the principles are to be in some manner applied.

3. Certain new conclusions deduced from the application of the principles to the facts.

In examining the validity of such a process, we have not only to attend to the correctness of the principles, and the authenticity of the alleged facts, but likewise to inquire whether the facts are of that class to which the principles are legitimately applicable; for the principles may be true and the facts authentic, and yet the reasoning may be unsound, from the principles being applied to the facts to which they have no relation.

This method of examining, separately, the elements of an argument, appears to correspond with the ancient syllogism; and this, accordingly, when divested of its systematic shape, is the mental process which we perform, whenever we either state or examine any piece of reasoning. If I say, for example, " the greatest kings are mortal, for they are but men;" I appear to state a very simple proposition; but it is in fact a process of reasoning which involves all the elements of the syllogism; namely,—

1. The general fact or proposition that all men are mortal.

2. The fact referable to the class of facts which are included under this proposition,—that kings are men.

3. The deduction from this connection, that kings are mortal.

Elements of reasoning? Axioms. Facts. Conclusions. Points to be attended to? Nature of the ancient syllogism. Example of simple reasoning and analysis of it How many and what parts?

For the validity and efficacy of such a process, two things are necessary, namely,—

1. That the general proposition which forms the first part of the statement, or, in logical language, the major proposition, be absolutely and universally true, or true without exception in regard to facts of a certain class, and be admitted as such by those to whom the reasoning is addressed.

2. That the fact referred to it, or the minor proposition, be admitted or proved to be one of that class of facts which are included under the general proposition.

The conclusion then follows by a very simple process. If either of the two former propositions be deficient or untrue, the argument is false. Thus, if I had varied the state ment as follows,—" Angels, like other human beings, are mortal;" there is a fallacy which, when put into the syllogistic form, is immediately apparent; thus,—

All human beings are mortal,
Angels are human beings;
Therefore, angels are mortal.

The general or major proposition here is true but the minor is not one of the class of facts which are included under it; therefore the conclusion is false. If I had said, again, " Angels, like other created beings, are mortal;' the fallacy is equally apparent, though from a different source; thus,—

All created beings are mortal,
Angels are created beings;
Therefore, angels are mortal.

Here the minor proposition is true, or is a fact included under the first; but the first, or major, is not true, for we have no ground to believe that all created beings are mortal. On the other hand, when a general fact is assumed as true of a certain class of cases, we must not assume the converse as true of those which are not included in the class; thus, from the proposition, that all human beings are mor-

---

What necessary for the validity of the process? The syllogistic form rendering false reasoning apparent. Example. Names of the propositions?

tal, we are not entitled to infer that angels, who are not human beings, are immortal. Whether this conclusion be true or not, the argument is false; because the conclusion does not arise out of the premises;—for, from the admitted general fact, that human beings are mortal, it does not follow, that all who are not human beings are not mortal. Yet this will be found a mode of fallacious reasoning of very frequent occurrence. The rule to be kept in mind for avoiding such fallacies is,—that a general truth, which applies invariably to a certain class, may be applied to any individual which can be shown to be included in that class; but that we are not entitled to extend it to any which cannot be shown to belong to the class; and that we are not to assume the reverse to be true of those which do not belong to it. On the other hand, we are not to assume a property as belonging to a class, because we have ascertained it to belong to a certain number of individuals. This error comes under another part of our subject, and has been already alluded to under the head of false generalization. The syllogism, therefore, cannot properly be considered an engine for the discovery of truth, but rather for enabling us to judge of the application of, and deductions from truths previously ascertained. For, before we can construct such a process as constitutes the syllogism, we require to have premised that most important process of investigation by which a fact is ascertained to be general in regard to all the individuals of a class; and, likewise, that certain individuals specified in the argument belong to this class. Thus, the syllogism was nothing more than that process of mind which we exercise every time when we examine the validity of an argument, though we may not always put it into this systematic form. And yet there may often be advantage in doing so, as it enables us to examine the elements of the arguments more distinctly apart. It is related of an eminent English barrister, afterward a distinguished judge, that, on one occasion, he was completely puzzled by an argument adduced by his opponent in an important case, and that he did not detect the fallacy till he went home and put it into the form of a syllogism. Though

---

General rules in all such reasoning? Real nature of the syllogism? Advantage of it? Anecdote of the English lawyer.

a syllogism, therefore, may not lead to any discovery of truth, it may be an important instrument in the detection of sophistry, by directing the attention distinctly and separately to the various elements which compose a statement or an argument, and enabling us to detect the part in which the sophistry is involved.

In every process of reasoning there are two distinct objects of attention, or circumstances to be examined, before we admit the validity of the argument. These are,—the premises or data which the reasoner assumes, and which he expects us to admit as true,—and the conclusions which he proposes to found upon these premises. The premises again consist of three parts, which we require to examine separately and rigidly. These are,—

1. Certain statements which he brings forward as facts, and which he expects to be admitted as such.

2. Certain principles or propositions which he assumes as first truths, or articles of belief universally admitted.

3. Certain other propositions which he refers to, as deductions from former processes of investigation, or processes of reasoning.

If the statements referable to these three heads are admitted as true, the argument proceeds, and we have only to judge of the validity or correctness of his farther deductions. If they are not at once admitted, the argument cannot proceed till we are satisfied on these preliminary points. If we do not admit his facts, we require him to go back to the evidence on which they rest. If we no not admit the general propositions which he assumes, we require the processes of reasoning or investigation on which these are founded. When we are at last agreed upon these premises, we proceed to judge of the conclusions which he proposes to deduce from them.

The circumstances now referred to may be considered as the essential parts of a process of reasoning, in a logical view; but there is another point which we require to keep carefully in mind in examining such a process, and that is,

---

Utility of the syllogism? Objects of attention in reasoning? How many and what? Premises; how many parts? Examination of these premises? Us of terms.

the use of terms. Much of the confusion and perplexity in reasoning consists in the ambiguity of the terms; this is referable to three heads, namely: 1. Terms of a vague and indefinite character, the precise import of which has not been defined. 2. Terms employed in a sense in some respect different from their common and recognised acceptation. 3. Varying the import of a term, so as to use it in different meanings in different parts of the same argument; or employing it at different times in degrees of comprehension and extension.

In examining the validity of a process of reasoning, then, the mental operation which we ought to perform may be guided by the following considerations:—

1. What statements does the author propose as matters of fact;—are these authentic; are they all really bearing upon, or connected with the subject; do they comprise a full and fair view of all the facts which ought to be brought forward in reference to the inquiry: or have we reason to suspect that any of them have been disguised or modified,—that important facts have been omitted or kept out of view,—that the author has not had sufficient opportunities of acquiring the facts which he ought to have been possessed of,—or that he has been collecting facts on one side of a question, or in support of a particular opinion?

2. What propositions are assumed, either as first or intuitive truths, or as deductions arising out of former processes of investigation; and are we satisfied that these are all legitimate and correct? In particular, does he make any statement in regard to two or more events being connected as cause and effect; and is this connection assumed on sufficient grounds:—does he assume any general principle as applicable to a certain class of facts; is this principle in itself a fact, and does it really apply to all the cases which he means to include under it; have we any reason to believe that it has been deduced from an insufficient number of facts; or is it a mere fictitious hypothesis, founded upon a principle which cannot be proved to have a real existence?

3. Do these assumed principles and facts really belong

Sources of ambiguity? Considerations which should guide in examining reasoning? As to matters of fact? Cautions? Proposition assumed? Cautions in regard to them. Connection between the principles and facts?

to the same subject,—or, in other words, do the facts belong to that class to which the principles apply?

4. Are the leading terms which he employs fully and distinctly defined as to their meaning; does he employ them in their common and recognised acceptation; and does he uniformly use them in the same sense; or does he seem to attach different meanings to the same term in different parts of his argument?

5. What are the new conclusions which he deduces from the whole view of the subject; are these correct and valid; and do they really follow from the premises laid down in the previous part of his argument? For on this head it is always to be kept in mind that a conclusion may be true, while it does not follow from the argument which has been brought to prove it; in such a case the argument is false.

Much of the confusion, fallacy, and sophistry of reasoning arises from these points not being sufficiently attended to, and distinctly and rigidly investigated. An argument may appear fair and consecutive, but when we rigidly examine it we may find that the reasoner has, in his premises, contrived to introduce some statement which is not true in point of fact, or some bold general position which is not correct, or not proved; or that he has left out some fact, or some principle, which ought to have been brought forward in a prominent manner, as closely connected with the inquiry. Hence the necessity for keeping constantly in view the various sources of fallacy to which every process of reasoning is liable, and for examining the elements rigidly and separately before we admit the conclusion.

A process of reasoning is to be distinguished from a process of investigation; and both may be illustrated in the following manner: All reasoning must be founded upon facts, and the ascertained relations of these facts to each other. The nature of these relations has already been mentioned, as referable to the various heads of resemblance, cause, effect, &c. The statement of an ascertained relation of two facts to each other is called a proposition, such as,—that A

Use of terms? Conclusions? Importance of attending to these points? Distinction between reasoning and investigation? Foundation of reasoning? Proposition.—what?

is equal to B; that C has a close resemblance to D; that E is the cause of F, &c. These statements, propositions, or ascertained relations are discovered by processes of investigation. In a process of reasoning, again, we take a certain number of such propositions or ascertained relations, and deduce from them certain other truths or relations, arising out of the mutual connection of some of these propositions to each other. Thus, if I state as propositions, ascertained by processes of investigation, that A is equal to B, and that B is equal to C, I immediately decide by a single step of reasoning that A is equal to C, in consequence of the mutual relation which both A and C have to B. Such a process may be rendered more complicated in two ways.

1. By the number of such ascertained relations, which we require to bear in mind and compare with each other before we arrive at the conclusion. Thus the relation that A is equal to E might rest on such a series of relations as the following:—A is equal to B; B is the double of C; C is the half of D; D is equal to E; therefore A is equal to E.

2. By propositions which are the conclusions of one or more steps in a process becoming the premises in a subsequent step. Thus,—I may take as one process A is equal to B, and B is equal to C; therefore A is equal to C;—and, as a distinct process, C is equal to D, and D is equal to E; therefore C is equal to E. The conclusions from these two processes I then take as the premises in a third process—thus: it has been proved that A is equal to C, and that C is equal to E; therefore A is equal to E.

In examining the validity of such processes, there are two circumstances or objects of inquiry which we ought to keep constantly in view. (1.) Have we confidence in the accuracy of the alleged facts, and ascertained relations, which form the premises? Can we rely on the process of investigation by which it is said to have been ascertained that A is equal to B, and that B is equal to C, &c.? (2.) Are the various propositions in the series so related as to

---

Example? Province of investigation? Province of reasoning? Ways in which the process becomes complicated. First way,—what? Example. Second way? Example. Objects of inquiry in examining the validity of such processes?

bring out a new truth or new relation? For it is to be kept in mind that a series of propositions may all be true, and yet lead to nothing; such propositions, for example, as that A is equal to B, C is equal to D, E is equal to F. There is here no mutual relation, and no new truth arises out of the series. But when I say A is equal to B, and B is equal to C, a new truth is immediately disclosed in consequence of the relation which both A and C have to B; namely, that A is equal to C.

Inventive genius, in regard to processes of reasoning consists in finding out relations or propositions which are thus capable of disclosing new truths or new relations; and in placing them in that order which is calculated to show how these new relations arise out of them. This is the exercise of a reflecting mind; and there may be much acquired knowledge, that is, many facts accumulated by memory alone, without any degree of this exercise or habit of reflection. But both are required for forming a well-cultivated mind; the memory must be stored with information, that is, ascertained facts and ascertained relations; and the power of reflection must be habituated to discover new truths or new relations by a comparison of these facts and ascertained relations with each other. For the discovery of new truths may consist either of new facts or of new relations among facts previously known. Thus, it might happen that we had long been familiar with two facts, without being aware that they had any particular connection. If we were then to ascertain that the one of these was the cause of the other, it would be a real and important discovery of a new truth, though it would consist only of a new relation between facts which had long been known to us.

A process of reasoning, as we have seen, consists of two parts, namely, the premises, and the conclusion deduced from them. If the premises be admitted as true, the remaining part of the process becomes comparatively simple. But it often happens that a reasoner must begin by establishing his premises. This is most remarkably exemplified

---

Inventive genius in reasoning? Knowledge of facts. Necessity of both? A process of reasoning consists of how many, and what parts?

in what we call a chain of reasoning, consisting of numerous distinct arguments or steps, so arranged that the conclusion from one step becomes an essential part of the premises in the next; and this may be continued through a long series. The process then becomes much more complicated, and in judging of the accuracy of the reasoning we require to examine carefully every part of it as we proceed, to guard against the introduction of fallacy. Without this attention it may often happen that the more advanced parts of an argument may appear fair and consecutive, while a fallacy has been allowed to creep into some part of it, which, in fact, vitiates the whole. In the preceding observations we have endeavored to point out some of the leading cautions to be observed in this respect, especially in regard to the admission of facts, the assumption of causation, and the deduction of general principles: and also the sources of fallacy to be kept in view in conducting these processes. But there is another class of fallacies which, though less immediately connected with our inquiries, it may be right briefly to point out in relation to this subject. These are what may be called logical fallacies, or perversions of reasoning. In regard to them, as well as to those formerly mentioned, it is to be kept in mind, that however obvious they may appear when simply stated, this is by no means the case when they are skilfully involved in a long process of reasoning. The fallacies of this class may be chiefly referred to the following heads :—

I. When a principle is assumed which, in fact, amounts to the thing to be proved; slightly disguised, perhaps, by some variation in the terms. This is commonly called *petitio principii*, or begging the question. When simply stated, it appears a fallacy not likely to be admitted; but will be found one of very frequent occurrence. It is indeed remarkable to observe the facility with which a dogma, when it has been boldly and confidently stated, is often admitted by numerous readers, without a single inquiry into the evidence on which it is founded.

Chain of reasoning? Cautions necessary. Two classes of fallacies. Logical fallacies—how divided? Begging the question.

A very common example of this is when a man's promises or statements are received with some suspicion, and he attempts to fortify them by asserting that he never told a falsehood or broke a promise in his life, or by solemn assurances that he would on no account violate his word. This, or something like this, is very common among men of doubtful veracity. The reasoning, however, when analyzed, is "begging the question." The very doubt is about the authority of his statements, and he offers you that very authority in proof of them.

II. When a principle is assumed without proof; when this is employed to prove something else; and this is again applied in some way in support of the first assumed principle. This is called reasoning in a circle; and the difficulty of detecting it is often in proportion to the extent of the circle, or the number of principles which are thus made to hang upon one another.

Such an argument as the following would be a fair example of this sort.

1. The Bible must be true, because miracles were wrought in attestation of it.

2. The miracles must have been wrought, because twelve honest men agree in bearing testimony to them.

3. We know that twelve honest men did unite in this testimony, for the Bible says that they did.

Here the reader will perceive that we come round exactly to our first position. The first proposition is proved by the second, the second by the third, and the third rests on the truth of the Bible, which is the very point to be proved. The propositions thus depend upon one another, and are without any common foundation.

To make the reasoning sound, the last proposition must be established on independent evidence; which is the course always pursued by writers on the subject, the fact that twelve honest men did thus testify being established by peculiar evidence, entirely distinct from the mere assertion of the book itself.

III. A frequent source of fallacy is when a reasoner assumes a principle, and then launches out into various illustrations and analogies, which are artfully made to bear the appearance of proofs. The cautions to be kept in mind in such a case are, that the illustrations may be useful and the analogies may be of importance, provided the principle has been proved; but that if it has not been proved, the illustrations must go for nothing, and even analogies seldom

Example of it? Reasoning in a circle. Example of it? What necessary in order to correct this reasoning? Declaration instead of reasoning.

have any weight which can be considered as of the nature of evidence. Fallacies of this class are most apt to occur in the declamations of public speakers; and when they are set off with all the powers of eloquence, it is often difficult to detect them. The questions which the hearer should propose to himself in such cases are, Does this really contain any proof bearing upon the subject, or is it mere illustration and analogy, in itself proving nothing?—if so, has the reasoner previously established his principle or has he assumed it, and trusted to these analogies as his proofs?

IV. A fallacy somewhat analogous to the preceding consists in arguing for or against a doctrine on the ground of its supposed tendency, leaving out of view the primary question of its truth. Thus, a speculator in theology will contend in regard to a doctrine which he opposes, that it is derogatory to the character of the Deity; and, respecting another which he brings forward, that it represents the Deity in an aspect more accordant with the benignity of his character. The previous question in all such cases is, not what is most accordant with our notions respecting the Divine character, but what is truth.

V. When a principle which is true of one case, or one class of cases, is extended by analogy to others which differ in some important particulars. The caution to be observed here is, to inquire strictly whether the cases are analogous, or whether there exists any difference which makes the principle not applicable. We have formerly alluded to a remarkable example of this fallacy in notions relating to the properties of matter being applied to mind, without attention to the fact that the cases are so distinct as to have nothing in common. An example somewhat analogous is found in Mr. Hume's objection to miracles, that they are violations of the established order of nature. The cases, we have seen, are not analogous; for miracles do not refer to the common course of nature, but to the operation of an agency altogether new and peculiar. Arguments founded

---

Tests to be applied. Arguing from tendencies? False reasoning from analogy? Examples? Mr. Hume's argument.

upon analogy, therefore, require to be used with the utmost caution, when they are employed directly for the discovery or the establishment of truth. But there is another purpose to which they may be applied with much greater freedom, namely, for repelling objections. Thus, if we find a person bringing objections against a particular doctrine, it is a sound and valid mode of reasoning to contend that he receives doctrines which rest upon the same kind of evidence; or that similar objections might be urged with equal force against truths which it is impossible to call in question. It is in this manner that the argument from analogy is employed in the valuable work of bishop Butler. He does not derive from the analogy of nature any direct argument in support of natural or revealed religion; but shows that many of the objections which are urged against the truths of religion might be brought against circumstances in the economy and course of nature which are known and undoubted facts.

VI. A fallacy the reverse of the former is used by sophistical writers; namely, when two cases are strictly analogous they endeavor to prove that they are not so by pointing out trivial differences not calculated in any degree to weaken the force of the analogy.

VII. When a true general principle is made to apply exclusively to one fact, or one class of facts, while it is equally true of various others. This is called, in logical language, the non-distribution of the middle term. In an example given by logical writers, one is supposed to maintain that corn is necessary for life, because food is necessary for life, and corn is food. It is true that food is necessary for life, but this does not apply to any one particular kind of food; it means only, that food of some kind or other is so. When simply stated, the fallacy of such a position is at once obvious, but it may be introduced into an argument in such a manner as not to be so immediately detected.

VIII. When an acknowledged proposition is inverted,

Proper use of analogy? Butler's use of it? The reverse of the former? Non-distribution of the middle term? Example.

and the converse assumed to be equally true. We may say, for example, that a badly governed country must be distressed; but we are not entitled to assume that every distressed country is badly governed; for there may be many other sources of national distress. I may say, "all wise men live temperately," but it does not follow that every man who lives temperately is a wise man. This fallacy was formerly referred to under the syllogism. It is, at the same time, to be kept in mind that some propositions do admit of being inverted, and still remain equally true. This holds most remarkably of propositions which are universally negative, as in an example given by writers on logic. "No ruminating animal is a beast of prey." It follows, as equally true, that no beast of prey ruminates. But if I were to vary the proposition by saying, "all animals which do not ruminate are beasts of prey," this would be obviously false; for it does not arise out of the former statement.

IX. A frequent source of fallacy among sophistical writers consists in boldly applying a character to a class of facts, in regard to which it carries a general aspect of truth, without attention to important distinctions by which the statement requires to be modified. Thus, it has been objected to our belief in the miracles of the sacred writings, that they rest upon the evidence of testimony, and that testimony is fallacious. Now, when we speak of testimony in general, we may say with an appearance of truth that it is fallacious; but, in point of fact, testimony is to be referred to various species; and, though a large proportion of these may be fallacious, there is a species of testimony on which we rely with absolute confidence;—that is, we feel it to be as improbable that this kind of testimony should deceive us, as that we should be disappointed in our expectation of the uniformity of nature. The kind of sophism now referred to seems to correspond with that which logical writers have named the fallacy of division. It consists in applying to facts in their separate state what only belongs

---

Inversion of a proposition? Examples? Can any propositions be inverted safely? Inattention to important distinctions? Example Reply to this? Fallacies of division and composition?

to them collectively. The converse of it is the fallacy of composition. It consists in applying to the facts collectively what belongs only to them, or to some of them, in their separate state;—as if one were to show that a certain kind of testimony is absolutely to be relied on, and thence were to contend that testimony in general is worthy of absolute confidence.

X. A frequent fallacy consists in first overturning an unsound argument, and thence reasoning against the doctrine which this argument was meant to support. This is the part of a mere casuist, not of a sincere inquirer after truth; for it by no means follows that a doctrine is false because unsound arguments have been adduced in support of it. We have formerly alluded to some remarkable examples of this fallacy, especially in regard to those important principles commonly called first truths; which, we have seen, admit of no processes of reasoning, and consequently are in no degree affected by arguments exposing the fallacy of such processes. We learn from this, on the other hand, the importance of avoiding all weak and inconclusive arguments, or doubtful statements; for, independently of the opening which they give for sophistical objections, it is obvious that on other grounds the reasoning is only encumbered by them. It is the part of the casuist to rest the weight of his objections on such weak points, leaving out of view those which he cannot contend with. It may even happen that a conclusion is true, though the whole reasoning may have been weak, unsound, and irrelevant. The casuist, of course, in such a case attacks the reasoning, and not the conclusion. On the other hand, there may be much in an argument which is true, or which may be conceded; while the most important part of it is untrue, and the conclusion false. An inexperienced reasoner, in such a case, thinks it necessary to combat every point, and thus exposes himself to sound replies from his adversary on subjects which are of no importance. A skilful reasoner concedes or passes over all such positions, and rests his attack on those in which

---

Confounding an argument with the doctrine it was intended to support. Practical direction arising from this. Course to be taken in regard to weak points. Skilful reasoning.

the fallacy is really involved. An example illustrative of this subject is familiar to those who are acquainted with the controversy respecting our idea of cause and effect. Mr. Hume stated in a clear manner the doctrine that this idea is derived entirely from our experience of a uniform sequence of two events; and founded upon this an argument against our belief in a great First Cause. This led to a controversy respecting the original doctrine itself; and it is not many years since it was contended by respectable individuals that it is nothing less than the essence of atheism to maintain that our notion of cause and effect originates in the observation of a uniform sequence. It is now, perhaps, universally admitted that this doctrine is correct, and that the sophism of Mr. Hume consisted in deducing from it conclusions which it in no degree warranted. This important distinction we formerly alluded to; namely, that our idea of cause and effect in regard to any two individual events is totally distinct from our intuitive impression of causation, or our absolute conviction that every event must have an adequate cause.

XI. A sophism somewhat connected with the former con sists in disproving a doctrine, and on that account assuming the opposite doctrine to be true. It may be true, but its truth does not depend upon the falsehood of that which is opposed to it; yet this will be found a principle of not unfrequent occurrence in unsound reasonings.

XII. Fallacies are often introduced in what may be termed an oblique manner; or, as if upon a generally admitted authority. The effect of this is to take off the appearance of the statement being made directly by the author, and resting upon his own authority, by which we might be led to examine its truth. For this purpose it is put, perhaps, in the form of a question; or is introduced by such expressions as the following:—"it is a remarkable fact,"—"it is somewhat singular,"—"it has

---

Example. Mr. Hume's doctrine, and his inference from it? Former opinion of his doctrine? Present opinion of the doctrine and the inference? Disproving a doctrine and inferring the opposite to be true? Fallacies introduced in an oblique manner? Examples.

been argued with much justice,"—"it will be generally admitted," &c.

XIII. Fallacy may arise from leaving the main subject of discussion, and arguing upon points which have but a secondary relation to it. This is one of the resources of the casuist when he finds himself in the worst of the argument. Nearly allied to this is the art of skilfully dropping part of a statement, when the reasoner finds he cannot support it, and going on boldly with the remainder as if he still maintained the whole.

XIV. Much of the fallacy and ambiguity of processes of reasoning depends entirely, as formerly stated, on the use of terms. This may consist in two contending parties using the same word in different meanings without defining what their meanings are; in one or both using terms in a sense different from their commonly recognised acceptation, or in using them in one sense in one part of the argument, and in another in a different part of it. Such disputes, accordingly, are often interminable; and this mode of disputation is one of the great resources of the casuist, or of him who argues for victory, not for truth. The remedy is, that every reasoner shall be required clearly to define the terms which he employs; and that in every controversy certain premises or preliminaries shall be fixed in which the parties are agreed. The ambiguity of terms is in fact so extensive a source of fallacy, that scarcely any sophistical argument will be found free from it; as in almost every language the same term is used with great diversity of meanings. Let us take, for example, the term faith. It means a mere system of opinions, confidence in testimony, reliance on the integrity, fidelity, and stability of character of other beings, an act of the understanding in regard to abstract truth presented to it, and a mental condition by which truths of another description exert a uniform influence over the moral feelings, the will, and the whole character. In the controversies which have arisen out of this word, it will probably be found that these various meanings have not been suffi-

Wandering from the question? Wrong use of terms? Consequences of it? Remedy? Example; term faith?

ciently distinguished from each other. A celebrated passage in the "Spirit of Laws" has been justly referred to as a remarkable example of the same kind of sophism. "The Deity," says Montesquieu, "has his laws; the material world, its laws; intelligences superior to man, their laws; the brutes, their laws; man, his laws." In this short passage the term laws is employed, probably, in four senses, remarkably different.

XV. There are various other sources of fallacy, consisting chiefly in the use of arguments which cannot be admitted as relevant in regard to the process of reasoning, though they may carry a certain weight in reference to the individuals concerned. Among these may be reckoned appeals to high authorities, to popular prejudices, or to the passions of the multitude; and what is called the *argumentum ad hominem.* If a person, for example, be arguing in support of a particular rule of conduct, we may retort upon him that his own conduct in certain instances was in direct opposition to it. This may be very true in regard to the individual, but can have no influence in the discussion of the question.

XVI. One of the most common sources of fallacy consists of distorted views and partial statements;—such as facts disguised, modified, or collected on one side of a question, or arguments and authorities adduced in support of particular opinions, leaving out of view those which tend to different conclusions. Misstatement, in one form or another, may indeed be considered as a most fruitful source of controversy; and, amid the contests of rival disputants, the chief difficulty which meets the candid inquirer after truth, is to have the subject presented to his mind without distortion. Hence the importance, in every inquiry, of suspending our judgment, and of patiently devoting ourselves to clear the subject from all imperfect views and partial statements. Without the most anxious attention to this rule, a statement may appear satisfactory, and a de-

---

Example from the "Spirit of Laws." The *argumentum ad hominem.* Example of this? Incorrect views and statements? Frequency of it?

duction legitimate, which are in fact leading us widely astray from the truth.

After every possible care in any process of reasoning we may still find, in many cases, a degree of doubt, and even certain varieties of opinion in regard to the import and bearing of the argument. This arises partly from actual differences in the power of judging, or what we call in common language, vigor of mind; and partly from differences in attention, or in the habit of applying the judgment closely to the elements of an inquiry. Hence the varieties of opinion that may be held by different individuals on the same subject, and with the same facts before them; and the degree of uncertainty which attends various processes of reasoning. There is one species of reasoning which is free from all this kind of uncertainty, namely, the mathematical; and the superiority of it depends upon the following circumstances:—

1. Nothing is taken for granted, or depends upon mere authority; and, consequently, there is no room for fallacy or doubt in regard to the premises on which the reasoning is founded. No examination of facts is required in any degree analogous to that which is necessary in physical science. The mathematician, indeed, proceeds upon assumptions of such a kind that it is in his own power to clear them from all ambiguity, and from every thing not connected with the subject.

2. In the farther progress of a mathematical argument, if we have any doubt of a proposition which is assumed as the result of a former process, we have only to turn to the demonstration of it, and be immediately satisfied. Thus, if any step of a process be founded upon the principle that all the angles of a triangle are equal to two right-angles, or that the square of the hypotenuse is equal to the sum of the squares of the two sides, should we have any doubt of the truth of these conclusions, the demonstration of them is before us. But if an argument be founded on the principle that the heavenly bodies attract one another with a force which is directly as their quantity of matter, and inversely

---

Some uncertainty unavoidable. Reason for it? Exception. Grounds of the superiority of mathematical science? Nature of the premises? Evidence easily accessible? Illustrations of this?

as the square of their distance; this great principle must be received on the authority of the eminent men by whom it was ascertained, the mass of mankind having neither the power nor the means of verifying it.

3. All the terms are fully and distinctly defined, and there is no room for obscurity or ambiguity in regard to them.

4. The various steps in a process of mathematical reasoning follow each other so closely and consecutively, as to carry a constant conviction of absolute certainty; and, provided we are in possession of the necessary premises, each single step is short, and the result obvious.

5. The proper objects of mathematical reasoning are quantity and its relations; and these are capable of being defined and measured with a precision of which the objects of other kinds of reasoning are entirely unsusceptible. It is, indeed, always to be kept in mind, that mathematical reasoning is only applicable to subjects which can be defined and measured in this manner, and that all attempts to extend it to subjects of other kinds have led to the greatest absurdities.

Notwithstanding the high degree of precision which thus distinguishes mathematical reasoning, the study of mathematics does not, as is commonly supposed, necessarily lead to precision in other species of reasoning, and still less to correct investigation in physical science. The explanation that is given of the fact seems to be satisfactory. The mathematician argues certain conclusions from certain assumptions, rather than from actual ascertained facts; and the facts to which he may have occasion to refer are so simple, and so free from all extraneous matter, that their truth is obvious, or is ascertained without difficulty. By being conversant with truths of this nature, he does not learn that kind of caution and severe examination which is required in physical science, for enabling us to judge whether the statements on which we proceed are true, and whether they include the whole truth which ought to enter into the investigation. He thus acquires a habit of too great facility in the admission of data or premises, which is

---

Use of terms. Regular succession of steps. Objects of mathematical reasoning? Effects of mathematical studies on the mind? Common error? Explanation of the facts?

the part of every investigation which the physical inquirer scrutinizes with the most anxious care, and too great confidence in the mere force of reasoning, without adequate attention to the previous processes of investigation on which all reasoning must be founded. It has been, accordingly, remarked by Mr. Stewart, and other accurate observers of intellectual character, that mathematicians are apt to be exceedingly credulous, in regard both to opinions and to matters of testimony; while, on the other hand, persons who are chiefly conversant with the uncertain sciences, acquire a kind of scepticism in regard to statements, which is apt to lead them into the opposite error. These observations, of course, apply only to what we may call a mere mathematician, a character which is now probably rare, since the close connection was established between the mathematical and physical sciences in the philosophy of Newton.

In the various steps constituting a process of reasoning or a process of investigation, in any department of knowledge, our guide is reason or judgment. Its peculiar province is to give to each fact or each principle a proper place and due influence in the inquiry, and to trace the real and true tendency of it in the conclusion. It is, of course assisted by other mental operations, as memory, conception, and abstraction, but especially by attention, or a deliberate and careful application of the mind to each fact and each consideration which ought to have a place in the inquiry. This is entirely a voluntary exercise of the mind, strengthened and made easy by habit, or frequent exercise, and weakened or impaired by disuse or misapplication; and there is, perhaps, nothing which has a greater influence in the formation of character, or in determining the place which a man is to assume among his fellow-men.

This sound exercise of judgment is widely distinct from the art of ingenious disputation. The object of the former is to weigh fully and candidly all the relations of things, and to give to each fact its proper weight in the inquiry;

Mr. Stewart's remark? To what class does this remark apply? The guide in reasoning. Other powers which assist. Distinction between sound judgment and ingenious disputation?

the aim of the latter is to seize with rapidity particular relations, and to find facts bearing upon a particular view of a subject. This habit when much exercised tends rather to withdraw the attention from the cultivation of the former. Thus, it has not unfrequently happened, that an ingenious pleader has made a bad judge; and that acute and powerful disputants have perplexed themselves by their own subtleties, till they have ended by doubting of every thing. The same observation applies to controversial writing; and hence the hesitation with which we receive the arguments and statements of a keen controvertist, and the necessity of hearing both sides. In making use of this caution, we may not accuse the reasoner of any unsound arguments or false statements. We only charge him with acting the part of an ingenious pleader, who brings forward the statements and arguments calculated to favor one side of a question, and leaves those of the opposite side out of view. The candid inquirer, like the just judge, considers both sides, and endeavors, according to the best of his judgment, to decide between them. To the same principle we trace the suspicion with which we receive the statements of an author, who first brings forward his doctrine, and then proceeds to collect facts in support of it. To a similar process we may ascribe the paradoxical opinions in which sophistical writers have landed themselves, often on subjects of the highest importance, and which they have continued to advocate, with much appearance of an honest conviction of their truth. It would be unjust to suppose that these writers have always intended to impose upon others; they have very often imposed upon themselves; but they have done so by their own voluntary act, in a misapplication of their reasoning powers. They have directed their attention, exclusively or chiefly, to one view of a subject, and have neglected to direct it, with the same care, to the facts and considerations which tend to support the opposite conclusions.

In regard to the sound exercise of judgment, it is farther to be remarked, that it may exist without the habit of observing the various steps in the mental process which is con-

Comparison of the two. Influence of the habit of disputation. Difference between a keen disputer and a candid inquirer. Self-deception common. Steps of a mental process sometimes unobserved.

nected with it. Thus we find men of that character to which we give the name of strong sound sense, who form just and comprehensive conclusions on a subject, without being able to explain to others the chain of thought by which they arrived at them; and who, when they attempt to do so, are apt to bewilder themselves, and fall into absurdities. Such persons, accordingly, are adapted for situations requiring both soundness of judgment and promptitude in action; but they make a bad figure in public speaking or reasoning. They are, indeed, possessed of a faculty more valuable than any thing that metaphysics or logic can furnish; but a due attention to these sciences might increase their usefulness, by enabling them to communicate to others the mental process which led to their decisions. A person of this description, according to a well-known anecdote, when appointed to a judicial situation in one of the colonies, received from an eminent judge the advice to trust to his own good sense in forming his opinions, but never to attempt to state the grounds of them. "The judgment," said he, "will probably be right, the argument will infallibly be wrong." When this strong sound judgment and correct logical habits are united in the same individual, they form the character of one who arrives at true conclusions on any subject to which his attention is directed, and, at the same time, carries others along with him to a full conviction of their truth.

We have, then, every reason to believe that, though there may be original differences in the power of judgment, the chief source of the actual varieties in this important function is rather to be found in its culture and regulation. On this subject there are various considerations of the highest interest, claiming the attention of those who wish to have the understanding trained to the investigation of truth. These are chiefly referable to two heads, namely, the manner in which the judgment suffers from deficient culture; and the manner in which it is distorted by want of due regulation.

I. The judgment is impaired by deficient culture. This

Example. Such individuals qualified for what duties? Means of increasing their usefulness? Anecdote. Importance of cultivation? Division of the subject? Deficient culture?

is exemplified in that listless and indifferent habit of the mind in which there is no exercise of correct thinking, or of a close and continued application of the attention to subjects of real importance. The mind is engrossed by frivolities and trifles, or bewildered by the wild play of the imagination; and, in regard to opinions on the most important subjects, it either feels a total indifference, or receives them from others without the exertion of thinking or examining for itself. The individuals who are thus affected either become the dupes of sophistical opinions imposed upon them by other men, or spend their lives in frivolous and unworthy pursuits, with a total incapacity for all important inquiries. A slight degree removed from this condition of mind is another, in which opinions are formed on slight and partial examination, perhaps from viewing one side of a question, or, at least, without a full and candid direction of the attention to all the facts which ought to be taken into the inquiry. Both these conditions of mind may perhaps originate partly in constitutional peculiarities or erroneous education; but they are fixed and increased by habit and indulgence, until, after a certain time, they probably become irremediable. They can be corrected only by a diligent cultivation of the important habit which, in common language, we call sound and correct thinking; and which is of equal value, whether it be applied to the formation of opinions, or to the regulation of conduct.

II. The judgment is vitiated by want of due regulation; and this may be ascribed chiefly to two sources, prejudice and passion. Prejudice consists in the formation of opinions before the subject has been really examined. By means of this, the attention is misdirected, and the judgment biassed, in a manner of which the individual is often in a great measure unconscious. The highest degree of it is exemplified in that condition of the mind in which a man first forms an opinion which interest or inclination may have suggested; then proceeds to collect arguments in support of it; and concludes by reasoning himself into the belief of what he wishes to be true. It is thus that the judg-

---

Its particular effects? Conditions of mind formed by it? Remedy. Want of regulation. Sources? Prejudice—what?

ment is apt to be misled, in a greater or less degree, by party spirit and personal attachments or antipathies; and it is clear that all such influence is directly opposed to its sound and healthy exercise. The same observations apply to passion, or the influence exerted by the moral feelings. The most striking example of this is presented by that depraved condition of the mind, which distorts the judgment in regard to the great principles of moral rectitude. "A man's understanding," says Mr. Locke, "seldom fails him in this part, unless his will would have it so; if he takes a wrong course, it is most commonly because he goes wilfully out of the way, or at least chooses to be bewildered; and there are few, if any, who dreadfully mistake, that are willing to be right."

These facts are worthy of much consideration, and they appear to be equally interesting to all classes of men, whatever may be the degree of their mental cultivation, and whatever the subjects are to which their attention is more particularly directed. There is one class of truths to which they apply with peculiar force,—namely, those which relate to the moral government of God, and the condition of man as a responsible being. These great truths and the evidence on which they are founded, are addressed to our judgment as rational beings; they are pressed upon our attention as creatures destined for another state of existence; and the sacred duty from which no individual can be absolved, is a voluntary exercise of his thinking and reasoning powers,—it is solemnly, seriously, and deliberately to consider. On these subjects a man may frame any system for himself, and may rest in that system as truth; but the solemn inquiry is, not what opinions he has formed, but in what manner he has formed them. Has he approached the great inquiry with a sincere desire to discover the truth; and has he brought to it a mind neither misled by prejudice, nor distorted by the condition of its moral feelings;—has he directed his attention to all the facts and evidences with an intensity suited to their momentous importance; and has he conducted the whole investigation with a deep and serious feeling that it carries with it an interest which reaches into

Passion? Locke's remark. Important application of these principles. The real question in regard to our opinions?

eternity? Truth is immutable and eternal, but it may elude the frivolous or prejudiced inquirer: and, even when he thinks his conclusions are the result of much examination, he may be resting his highest concerns in delusion and falsehood.

The human mind, indeed, even in its highest state of culture, has been found inadequate to the attainment of the true knowledge of the Deity; but light from heaven has shone upon the scene of doubt and of darkness, which will conduct the humble inquirer through every difficulty, until he arrive at the full perception and commanding influence of the truth;—of truth such as human intellect never could have reached, and which, to every one who receives it, brings its own evidence that it comes from God.

Finally, the sound exercise of judgment has a remarkable influence in producing and maintaining that tranquillity of mind which results from a due application of its powers, and a correct estimate of the relations of things. The want of this exercise leads a man to be unduly engrossed with the frivolities of life, unreasonably elated by its joys, and unreasonably depressed by its sorrows. A sound and well regulated judgment tends to preserve from all such disproportioned pursuits and emotions. It does so, by leading us to view all present things in their true relations, to estimate aright their relative value, and to fix the degree of attention of which they are worthy;—it does so, in a more especial manner, by leading us to compare the present life, which is so rapidly passing over us, with the paramount importance and overwhelming interest of the life which is to come.

The truth within the reach of every mind. Effect of sound judgment in producing mental tranquillity. How does it produce this effect?

OF THE USE OF REASON IN CORRECTING THE IMPRESSIONS OF THE MIND IN REGARD TO EXTERNAL THINGS.

THIS subject leads to an investigation of great and extensive interest, of which I cannot hope to give more than a slight and imperfect outline. My anxiety is, that what is attempted may be confined to authentic facts, and the most cautious conclusions; and that it may be of some use in leading to farther inquiry.

We have seen the power which the mind possesses of recalling the vivid impressions of scenes or events long gone by, in that mental process which we call conception. We have seen also its power of taking the elements of actual scenes, and forming them into new combinations, so as to represent to itself scenes and events which have no real existence. We have likewise observed the remarkable manner in which persons, events, or scenes, long past, perhaps forgotten, are recalled into the mind by means of association;—trains of thought taking possession of the mind in a manner which we often cannot account for, and bringing back facts or occurrences which had long ceased to be objects of attention. These remarkable processes are most apt to take place when the mind is in that passive state which we call a revery; and they are more rarely observed when the attention is actively exerted upon any distinct and continued subject of thought.

During the presence in the mind of such a representation, whether recalled by conception or association, or fabricated by imagination, there is probably, for the time, a kind of belief of its real and present existence. But, on the least return of the attention to the affairs of life, the vision is instantly dissipated; and this is done by reason comparing the vision with the actual state of things in the external world. The poet or the novelist, it is probable, feels him-

---

Caution in regard to the ensuing discussion? Conception? Imagination? Association? In what state of mind are these processes most frequently performed? Belief of the reality of these representations. How dispelled?

self, for the time, actually imbodied in the person of his hero, and in that character judges, talks, and acts in the scene which he is depicting. This we call imagination; but were the vision not to be dissipated on his return to the ordinary relations of life,—were he then to act in a single instance in the character of the being of his imagination,—this would constitute insanity.

The condition of mind here referred to does actually take place; namely, a state in which the visions or impressions of the mind itself are believed to have a real and present existence in the external world, and in which reason fails to correct this belief by the actual relations of external things. There are two conditions in which this occurs in a striking manner; namely, insanity and dreaming. Considered as mental phenomena, they have a remarkable affinity to each other. The great difference between them is, that in insanity the erroneous impression being permanent, affects the conduct; whereas, in dreaming, no influence on the conduct is produced, because the vision is dissipated upon awaking. The difference, again, between the mind under the influence of imagination, and in the state now under consideration, is, that in the former the vision is built up by a voluntary effort, and is varied or dismissed at pleasure; while in dreaming and insanity this power is suspended and the mind is left entirely under the influence of the chain of thoughts which happens to be present, without being able either to vary or dismiss it. The particular chain or series seems, in general, perhaps always, to depend upon associations previously formed; the various elements of which bring up one another in a variety of singular combinations, and in a manner which we often cannot trace, or in any degree account for. The facts connected with this branch of the subject form one of the most interesting parts of this investigation.

There are some other affections which come under the same class; but insanity and dreaming are the two extreme examples. In dreaming, the bodily senses are in a great measure shut up from external impressions; and the influence of the will upon bodily motions is also suspended, so

Example. The vision sometimes not dissipated. Two cases? State of the mind in these cases? State of the bodily senses in dreaming?

that no actions in general follow. We shall afterward see that there are exceptions to this; but it is the common state in dreaming. In insanity, on the other hand, the bodily senses are awake to impressions from without, and bodily motion is under the influence of the will; hence the maniac acts, under his erroneous impressions, in a manner which often makes him dangerous to the community. There is an affection which holds an intermediate place between these two extremes, and presents a variety of interesting phenomena. This is somnambulism. It differs from dreaming, in the senses being, to a certain degree, awake to external things; though that power is suspended by which the mental impressions are corrected by the influence of the external world. Thus, the somnambulist often understands what is said to him, and can converse with another person in a tolerably connected manner, though always with some reference to his erroneous mental impressions. He acts, also, under the influence of these; but the remarkable difference between him and the maniac is, that the somnambulist can be roused from his vision, and then the whole is dissipated. There are cases, indeed, in which the hallucination is more permanent, and cannot be at once interrupted in this manner:—these of course come to border on insanity.

There is still a fourth condition connected with this curious subject; namely, that in which a person awake, and in other respects in possession of his rational powers, perceives spectral illusions. This, we shall see, is allied in a singular manner to the affections now referred to.

The subject, therefore, divides itself into four parts, which will form the separate topics of the following observations:—

1. Dreaming.
2. Somnambulism.
3. Insanity.
4. Spectral Illusions.

The causes of these remarkable conditions of the mental functions are entirely beyond the reach of our inquiries;

In insanity? Somnambulism. Its nature? Illustration of this. More or less permanent. Fourth condition? Recapitulation.

but the phenomena connected with them present a subject of most interesting investigation.

I. DREAMING.

The peculiar condition of the mind in dreaming appears to be referable to two heads:—

1. The impressions which arise in the mind are believed to have a real and present existence; and this belief is not corrected, as in the waking state, by comparing the conception with the things of the external world.

2. The ideas or images in the mind follow one another according to associations over which we have no control; we cannot, as in the waking state, vary the series, or stop it at our will.

One of the most curious objects of investigation is to trace the manner in which the particular visions or series of images arise. When considered in this view, a great variety may be observed in dreams. Some of those which we are able to trace most distinctly, appear to be the following:—

I. Recent events, and recent mental emotions, mingled up into one continuous series with each other, or with old events, by means of some feeling which had been in a greater or less degree allied to each of them, though in other respects they were entirely unconnected. We hear, perhaps, of a distressing accident; we have received some unpleasant news of an absent friend; and we have been concerned in some business which gave rise to anxiety: a dream takes place, in which all these are combined together; we are ourselves connected with the accident; the absent friend is in our company; and the person with whom the business was transacted also appears in the scene. The only bond of union among these occurrences was, that each of them gave rise to a similar kind of emotion; and the train was probably excited by some bodily feeling of uneasiness, perhaps an oppression at the stomach, at the

Condition of the mind in dreaming, how referred? Sources of the images which arise in dreaming? Recent events or emotions. Examples?

time when the dream occurred. Without this, the particular series might not have take place at all; or some of the elements of it might have occurred in a totally different association. The absent friend might have appeared in connection with old and pleasing recollections, combined perhaps with persons and events associated with these, and without any reference to the painful intelligence by which the attention had been directed to him. We meet a person whom we have not seen for many years, and are led to inquire after old friends, and to allude to events long past. Dreams follow, in which these persons appear, and other persons and occurrences connected with them; but the individual, whose conversation gave rise to the series, does not appear in it, because he was not connected with the particular chain of events which was thus recalled into the mind.

A woman who was a patient in the clinical ward of the infirmary of Edinburgh, under the care of Dr. Duncan, talked a great deal in her sleep, and made numerous and very distinct allusions to the cases of other sick persons. These allusions did not apply to any patients who were in the ward at that time; but, after some observation, they were found to refer correctly to the cases of individuals who were there when this woman was a patient in the ward two years before.

II. Trains of images brought up by association with bodily sensations. Examples of this kind are of frequent occurrence. By the kind attention of my friend Dr. James Gregory, I have received a most interesting manuscript by his late eminent father, which contains a variety of curious matter on this subject. In this paper, Dr. Gregory mentions of himself that, having on one occasion gone to bed with a vessel of hot water at his feet, he dreamed of walking up the crater of mount Etna, and of feeling the ground warm under him. He had at an early period of his life visited mount Vesuvius, and actually felt a strong sensation of warmth in his feet when walking up the side of the crater; but it was remarkable that the dream was not of Ve-

---

Story of Dr. Duncan's patient. Images brought up by bodily sensations? Story of the effect of hot water at the feet.

suvius, but of Etna, of which he had only read Brydone's description. This was probably from the latter impression having been the more recent. On another occasion, he dreamed of spending a winter at Hudson's Bay, and of suffering much distress from the intense frost. He found that he had thrown off the bed-clothes in his sleep; and, a few days before, he had been reading a very particular account of the state of the colonies in that country during winter. Again, when suffering from toothache, he dreamed of undergoing the operation of tooth-drawing, with the additional circumstance that the operator drew a sound tooth, leaving the aching one in its place. But the most striking anecdote in this interesting document is one in which similar dreams were produced in a gentleman and his wife, at the same time, and by the same cause. It happened at the period when there was an alarm of French invasion, and almost every man in Edinburgh was a soldier. All things had been arranged in expectation of the landing of an enemy; the first notice of which was to be given by a gun from the castle, and this was to be followed by a chain of signals calculated to alarm the country in all directions. Further, there had been recently in Edinburgh a splendid military spectacle, in which five thousand men had been drawn up in Prince's street, fronting the castle. The gentleman to whom the dream occurred, and who had been a most zealous volunteer, was in bed between two and three o'clock in the morning, when he dreamed of hearing the signal gun. He was immediately at the castle, witnessed the proceedings for displaying the signals, and saw and heard a great bustle over the town from troops and artillery assembling, especially in Prince's street. At this time he was roused by his wife, who awoke in a fright in consequence of a similar dream, connected with much noise and the landing of an enemy, and concluding with the death of a particular friend of her husband's, who had served with him as a volunteer during the late war. The origin of this remarkable concurrence was ascertained, in the morning, to be the noise produced in the room above by the fall of a pair of tongs which had been left in some very awkward position in support of a clothes-screen. Dr. Reid relates

---

Other examples. Story of the Edinburgh gentleman and his wife?

of himself, that the dressing applied after a blister on his head having become ruffled so as to produce considerable uneasiness, he dreamed of falling into the hands of savages and being scalped by them.

To this part of the subject are to be referred some remarkable cases in which, in particular individuals, dreams can be produced by whispering into their ears when they are asleep. One of the most curious as well as authentic examples of this kind has been referred to by several writers: I find the particulars in the paper of Dr. Gregory, and they were related to him by a gentleman who witnessed them. The subject of it was an officer in the expedition to Louisburg in 1758, who had this peculiarity in so remarkable a degree, that his companions in the transport were in the constant habit of amusing themselves at his expense. They could produce in him any kind of dream by whispering into his ear, especially if this was done by a friend with whose voice he was familiar. At one time they conducted him through the whole progress of a quarrel, which ended in a duel; and, when the parties were supposed to be met, a pistol was put into his hand, which he fired, and was awakened by the report. On another occasion they found him asleep on the top of a locker or bunker in the cabin, when they made him believe he had fallen overboard, and exhorted him to save himself by swimming. He immediately imitated all the motions of swimming. They then told him that a shark was pursuing him, and entreated him to dive for his life. He instantly did so with such force as to throw himself entirely from the locker upon the cabin floor, by which he was much bruised, and awakened of course. After the landing of the army at Louisburg, his friends found him one day asleep in his tent, and evidently much annoyed by the cannonading. They then made him believe that he was engaged, when he expressed great fear, and showed an evident disposition to run away. Against this they remonstrated, but at the same time increased his fears by imitating the groans of the wounded and the dying; and when he asked, as he often did, who was down, they named his particular friends. At last they

Effect of a blister? Producing dreams, in particular individuals? Case of the officer? Various experiments tried upon him.

told him that the man next himself in the line had fallen when he instantly sprang from his bed, rushed out of the tent, and was roused from his danger and his dream together by falling over the tent-ropes. A remarkable circumstance in this case was, that after these experiments he had no distinct recollection of his dreams, but only a confused feeling of oppression or fatigue; and used to tell his friends that he was sure they had been playing some trick upon him. A case entirely similar is related in Smellie's Natural History, the subject of which was a medical student at the university of Edinburgh.

A singular fact has often been observed in dreams which are excited by a noise: namely, that the same sound awakes the person, and produces a dream which appears to him to occupy a considerable time. The following example of this has been related to me:—A gentleman dreamed that he had enlisted as a soldier, joined his regiment, deserted, was apprehended, carried back, tried, condemned to be shot, and at last led out for execution. After all the usual preparations a gun was fired; he awoke with the report, and found that a noise in an adjoining room had both produced the dream and awakened him. The same want of the notion of time is observed in dreams from other causes. Dr. Gregory mentions a gentleman, who, after sleeping in a damp place, was for a long time liable to a feeling of suffocation whenever he slept in a lying posture; and this was always accompanied by a dream of a skeleton which grasped him violently by the throat. He could sleep in a sitting posture without any uneasy feeling; and after trying various expedients he at last had a sentinel placed beside him, with orders to awake him whenever he sunk down On one occasion he was attacked by the skeleton, and a severe and long struggle ensued before he awoke. On finding fault with his attendant for allowing him to lie so long in such a state of suffering, he was assured that he had not lain an instant, but had been awakened the moment he began to sink. The gentleman after a considerable time recovered from the affection. A friend of mine

---

His recollections afterwards? Remarkable fact respecting persons awakened by a noise. Example? Dr. Gregory's instance? Instances illustrating mistakes as to time in sleep?

dreamed that he crossed the Atlantic, and spent a fortnight in America. In embarking on his return, he fell into the sea; and, having awoke with the fright, discovered that he had not been asleep above ten minutes.

III. Dreams consisting of the revival of old associations respecting things which had entirely passed out of the mind, and which seemed to have been forgotten. It is often impossible to trace the manner in which these dreams arise; and some of the facts connected with them scarcely appear referable to any principle with which we are at present acquainted. The following example occurred to a particular friend of mine, and may be relied upon in its most minute particulars:—

The gentleman was at the time connected with one of the principal banks in Glasgow, and was at his place at the teller's table, where money is paid, when a person entered demanding payment of a sum of six pounds. There were several people waiting, who were, in turn, entitled to be attended before him; but he was extremely impatient, and rather noisy; and, being besides a remarkable stammerer, he became so annoying, that another gentleman requested my friend to pay him his money and get rid of him. He did so, accordingly, but with an expression of impatience at being obliged to attend to him before his turn, and thought no more of the transaction. At the end of the year, which was eight or nine months after, the books of the bank could not be made to balance, the deficiency being exactly six pounds. Several days and nights had been spent in endeavoring to discover the error, but without success; when, at last, my friend returned home, much fatigued, and went to bed. He dreamed of being at his place in the bank, and the whole transaction with the stammerer, as now detailed, passed before him in all its particulars. He awoke under a full impression that the dream was to lead him to a discovery of what he was so anxiously in search of; and, on examination, soon discovered that the sum paid to this person in the manner now mentioned, had been neglected to be inserted in the book of interests, and that it exactly accounted for the error in the balance.

Revival of forgotten associations. Case of the teller of a bank.

This case, upon a little consideration, will appear to be exceedingly remarkable, because the impression recalled in this singular manner was one of which there was no consciousness at the time when it occurred; and, consequently, we cannot suppose that any association took place which could have assisted in recalling it. For the fact upon which the importance of the case rested was, not his having paid the money, but having neglected to insert the payment. Now of this there was no impression made upon the mind at the time, and we can scarcely conceive on what principle it could be recalled. The deficiency being six pounds, we may, indeed, suppose the gentleman endeavoring to recollect whether there could have been a payment of this sum made in any irregular manner which could have led to an omission, or an error; but in the transactions of an extensive bank, in a great commercial city, a payment of six pounds, at the distance of eight or nine months, could have made but a very faint impression; and upon the whole, the case presents, perhaps, one of the most remarkable mental phenomena connected with this curious subject. The following is of the same nature, though much less extraordinary, from the shortness of the interval; and it may perhaps be considered as a simple act of memory, though, for the same reason as in the former case, we cannot trace any association which could have recalled the circumstance:—A gentleman who was appointed to an office in one of the principal banks in Edinburgh found, on balancing his first day's transactions, that the money under his charge was deficient by ten pounds. After many fruitless attempts to discover the cause of the error, he went home, not a little annoyed by the result of his first experiment in banking. In the night he dreamed that he was at his place in the bank, and that a gentleman who was personally known to him presented a draught for ten pounds. On awaking, he recollected the dream, and also recollected that the gentleman who appeared in it had actually received ten pounds. On going to the bank, he found that he had neglected to enter the payment, and that the gentleman's order had by accident fallen among some pieces of

---

Remarkable circumstance in this case? Another similar example.

paper, which had been thrown on the floor to be swept away.

I have formerly referred to some remarkable cases in which languages long forgotten were recovered during a state of delirium. Something very analogous seems to occur in dreaming, of which I have received the following example from an able and intelligent friend. In his youth he was very fond of the Greek language, and made considerable progress in it; but afterwards, being actively engaged in other pursuits, he so entirely forgot it that he cannot even read the words. But he has often dreamed of reading Greek works which he had been accustomed to use at college, and with a most vivid impression of fully understanding them.

A further, and most interesting illustration of the class of dreams referred to under this head, is found in an anecdote lately published by the distinguished author of the Waverly novels, and considered by him as authentic:—" Mr. R. of Bowland, a gentleman of landed property in the vale of Gala, was prosecuted for a very considerable sum, the accumulated arrears of teind, (or tithe,) for which he was said to be indebted to a noble family, the titulars, (lay impropriators of the tithes.) Mr. R. was strongly impressed with the belief that his father had, by a form of process peculiar to the law of Scotland, purchased these lands from the titular, and therefore that the present prosecution was groundless. But after an industrious search among his father's papers, an investigation of the public records, and a careful inquiry among all persons who had transacted law-business for his father, no evidence could be recovered to support his defence. The period was now near at hand when he conceived the loss of his lawsuit to be inevitable, and he had formed his determination to ride to Edinburgh next day, and make the best bargain he could in the way of compromise. He went to bed with this resolution, and with all the circumstances of the case floating upon his mind, had a dream to the following purpose:—His father, who had been many years dead, appeared to him, he thought, and asked him why he was disturbed in his mind. In dreams

Knowledge of languages revived in dreams. Example. Anecdote related by Walter Scott. Narrate all the circumstances.

men are not surprised at such apparitions. Mr. R. thought that he informed his father of the cause of his distress, adding that the payment of a considerable sum of money was the more unpleasant to him, because he had a strong consciousness that it was not due, though he was unable to recover any evidence in support of his belief. 'You are right, my son,' replied the paternal shade; 'I did acquire right to these teinds, for payment of which you are now prosecuted. The papers relating to the transaction are in the hands of Mr. ——, a writer (or attorney) who is now retired from professional business, and resides at Inveresk, near Edinburgh. He was a person whom I employed on that occasion for a particular reason, but who never, on any other occasion, transacted business on my account. It is very possible,' pursued the vision, 'that Mr. —— may have forgotten a matter which is now of a very old date; but you may call it to his recollection by this token, that when I came to pay his account, there was difficulty in getting change for a Portugal piece of gold, and that we were forced to drink out the balance at a tavern.'

"Mr. R. awoke in the morning, with all the words of his vision imprinted on his mind, and thought it worth while to ride across the country to Inveresk, instead of going straight to Edinburgh. When he came there he waited on the gentleman mentioned in the dream, a very old man; without saying any thing of the vision, he inquired whether he remembered having conducted such a matter for his deceased father. The old gentleman could not at first bring the circumstance to his recollection; but, on mention of the Portugal piece of gold, the whole returned upon his memory; he made an immediate search for the papers, and recovered them,—so that Mr. R. carried to Edinburgh the documents necessary to gain the cause which he was on the verge of losing."

There is every reason to believe that this very interesting case is referable to the principle lately mentioned: that the gentleman had heard the circumstances from his father, but had entirely forgotten them, until the frequent and intense application of his mind to the subject with which they were connected at length gave rise to a train of associa

---

Principle illustrated by this case? Explanation of it?

tion which recalled them in the dream. To the same principle are referable the two following anecdotes, which I have received as entirely authentic. A gentleman of the law in Edinburgh had mislaid an important paper, relating to some affairs on which a public meeting was soon to be held. He had been making most anxious search for it for many days; but the evening of the day preceding that on which the meeting was to be held had arrived, without his being able to discover it. He went to bed under great anxiety and disappointment, and dreamed that the paper was in a box appropriated to the papers of a particular family, with which it was in no way connected: it was accordingly found there in the morning.—Another individual, connected with a public office, had mislaid a paper of such importance, that he was threatened with the loss of his situation if he did not produce it. After a long but unsuccessful search, under intense anxiety, he also dreamed of discovering the paper in a particular place, and found it there accordingly.

IV. A class of dreams which presents an interesting subject of observation includes those in which a strong propensity of character, or a strong mental emotion, is imbodied into a dream, and by some natural coincidence is fulfilled. A murderer mentioned by Mr. Combe had dreamed of committing murder some years before the event took place. But more remarkable still are those instances, many of them authentic, in which a dream has given notice of an event which was occurring at the time, or occurred soon after. The following story has been long mentioned in Edinburgh, and there seems no reason to doubt its authenticity:—A clergyman had come to this city from a short distance in the country, and was sleeping at an inn, when he dreamed of seeing a fire, and one of his children in the midst of it. He awoke with the impression, and instantly left town on his return home. When he arrived within sight of his house, he found it on fire, and got there in time to assist in saving one of his children, who, in the alarm and confusion, had been left in a situation of danger. With-

---

Case of the Edinburgh lawyer. Dreams resulting from some strong propensity of character. Case mentioned by Mr. Combe? Case of the clergyman?

out calling in question the possibility of supernatural communication in such cases, this striking occurrence, of which I believe there is little reason to doubt the truth, may perhaps be accounted for on simple and natural principles. Let us suppose, that the gentleman had a servant who had shown great carelessness in regard to fire, and had often given rise in his mind to a strong apprehension that he might set fire to the house. His anxiety might be increased by being from home, and the same circumstance might make the servant still more careless. Let us farther suppose that the gentleman, before going to bed, had, in addition to this anxiety, suddenly recollected that there was on that day, in the neighborhood of his house, some fair or periodical merry-making, from which the servant was very likely to return home in a state of intoxication. It was most natural that these impressions should be imbodied into a dream of his house being on fire, and that the same circumstances might lead to the dream being fulfilled.

A gentleman in Edinburgh was affected with aneurism of the popliteal artery, for which he was under the care of two eminent surgeons, and the day was fixed for the operation. About two days before the time appointed for it, the wife of the patient dreamed that a change had taken place in the disease, in consequence of which the operation would not be required. On examining the tumor in the morning, the gentleman was astonished to find that the pulsation had entirely ceased; and, in short, this turned out to be a spontaneous cure. To persons not professional it may be right to mention that the cure of popliteal aneurism without an operation is a very uncommon occurrence, not happening in one out of numerous instances, and never to be looked upon as probable in any individual case. It is likely, however, that the lady had heard of the possibility of such a termination, and that her anxiety had very naturally imbodied this into a dream; the fulfilment of it at the very time when the event took place is certainly a very remarkable coincidence. The following anecdotes also I am enabled to give as entirely authentic. A lady dreamed that an aged female relative had been murdered by a black servant, and the dream occurred more than once. She was then so im

Explanation of it? The Edinburgh patient. Narrate the circumstances.

pressed by it that she went to the house of the lady to whom it related, and prevailed apon a gentleman to watch in an adjoining room during the following night. About three o'clock in the morning, the gentleman, hearing footsteps on the stairs, left his place of concealment, and met the servant carrying up a quantity of coals. Being questioned as to where he was going, he replied, in a confused and hurried manner, that he was going to mend his mistress' fire,—which, at three o'clock in the morning, in the middle of summer, was evidently impossible ; and, on further investigation, a strong knife was found concealed beneath the coals. Another lady dreamed that a boy, her nephew, had been drowned along with some young companions with whom he had engaged to go on a sailing excursion in the Frith of Forth. She sent for him in the morning, and, with much difficulty, prevailed upon him to give up his engagement; his companions went and were all drowned. A gentleman dreamed that the devil carried him down to the bottom of a coal-pit, where he threatened to burn him, unless he would agree to give himself up to his service. This he refused to do, and a warm altercation followed. He was at last allowed to depart, upon condition of sending down an individual whom the devil named, a worthless character well known in the neighborhood. A few days after, this person was found drowned, and under circumstances which gave every reason to believe that his death had been voluntary. A lady in Edinburgh had sent her watch to be repaired: a long time elapsed without her being able to recover it, and, after many excuses, she began to suspect that something was wrong. She now dreamed that the watchmaker's boy, by whom the watch was sent, had dropped it in the street, and injured it in such a manner that it could not be repaired. She then went to the master, and, without any allusion to her dream, put the question to him directly; when he confessed that it was true.

Such coincidences derive their wonderful character from standing alone and apart from those numerous instances in which such dreams take place without any fulfilment. An instance of a very singular kind is mentioned by Mr. Joseph

---

Dream of a murder. Danger of drowning apparently foretold by a dream. Other cases? The lady and her watch.

Taylor, and is given by him as an undoubted fact. A young man who was at an academy a hundred miles from home dreamed that he went to his father's house in the night, tried the front-door, but found it locked; got in by a back-door, and finding nobody out of bed, went directly to the bedroom of his parents. He then said to his mother, whom he found awake, "Mother, I am going a long journey, and am come to bid you good-bye." On this she answered, under much agitation, "Oh, dear son, thou art dead!" He instantly awoke, and thought no more of his dream, until, a few days after, he received a letter from his father inquiring very anxiously after his health, in consequence of a frightful dream his mother had on the same night in which the dream now mentioned occurred to him. She dreamed that she heard some one attempt to open the front-door, then go to the back-door, and at last come into her bedroom. She then saw it was her son, who came to the side of her bed, and said, "Mother, I am going a long journey, and am come to bid you good-bye;" on which she exclaimed, "Oh, dear son, thou art dead!" But nothing unusual happened to any of the parties. The singular dream must have originated in some strong mental impression which had been made on both the individuals about the same time; and to have traced the source of it would have been a matter of great interest.

On a similar principle, we are to account for some of the stories of second sight:—a gentleman sitting by the fire on a stormy night, and anxious about some of his domestics who are at sea in a boat, drops asleep for a few seconds, dreams very naturally of drowning men, and starts up with an exclamation that his boat is lost. If the boat returns in safety, the vision is no more thought of. If it is lost, as is very likely to happen, the story passes for second sight; and it is, in fact, one of the anecdotes that are given as the most authentic instances of it.

It is unnecessary to multiply examples of the fulfilment of dreams on the principles which have now been mentioned; but I am induced to add the following, as it is certainly of a very interesting kind, and as I am enabled to give it as

---

Case of the academy student? Relate the circumstances. Explanation. Second sight, how explained.

entirely authentic in all its particulars. A most respectable clergyman in a country parish of Scotland, made a collection at his church for an object of public benevolence, in which he felt very deeply interested. The amount of the collection, which was received in ladles carried through the church, fell greatly short of his expectation; and, during the evening of the day, he frequently alluded to this with expressions of much disappointment. In the following night he dreamed that three one-pound notes had been left in one of the ladles, having been so compressed that they had stuck in the corner when the ladle was emptied. He was so impressed by the vision, that at an early hour in the morning he went to the church, found the ladle which he had seen in his dream, and drew from one of the corners of it three one-pound notes. This interesting case is perhaps capable of explanation upon simple principles. It appears, that on the evening preceding the day of the collection the clergyman had been amusing himself by calculating what sum his congregation would probably contribute, and that in doing so he had calculated on a certain number of families, who would not give him less than a pound each. Let us then suppose that a particular ladle, which he knew to have been presented to three of these families, had been emptied in his presence, and found to contain no pound notes His first feeling would be that of disappointment; but, in afterward thinking of the subject, and connecting it with his former calculation, the possibility of the ladle not having been fully emptied might dart across his mind. This impression, which perhaps he did not himself recollect, might then be imbodied into the dream, which, by a natural coincidence, was fulfilled.

The four classes which have now been mentioned appear to include the principal varieties of dreams; and it is often a matter of great interest to trace the manner in which the particular associations arise. Cases of dreams are indeed on record, which are not referable to any of the principles which have been mentioned, and which do not admit of explanation on any principles which we are able to trace.

The clergyman and the charitable collection. Relate the whole case. Do these classes include all? Other cases on record?

Many of these histories, there is every reason to believe, derive their marvellous character from embellishment and exaggeration; and in some instances which have been related to me in the most confident manner, I have found this to be the case after a little investigation. Others, however, do not admit of this explanation, and we are compelled to receive them as facts which we can in no degree account for. Of this kind I shall only add the following example; and I shall do so without any attempt at explanation, and without any other comment than that its accuracy may be relied on in all its particulars. Two ladies, sisters, had been for several days in attendance upon their brother, who was ill of a common sore throat, severe and protracted, but not considered as attended with danger. At the same time, one of them had borrowed a watch from a female friend, in consequence of her own being under repair;—this watch was one to which particular value was attached on account of some family associations, and some anxiety was expressed that it might not meet with any injury. The sisters were sleeping together in a room communicating with that of their brother, when the elder of them awoke in a state of great agitation, and having roused the other, told her that she had had a frightful dream. "I dreamed," said she, "that Mary's watch stopped; and that, when I told you of the circumstance, you replied, much worse than that has happened, for ——'s breath has stopped also,"—naming their brother who was ill. To quiet her agitation, the younger sister immediately got up, and found the brother sleeping quietly, and the watch, which had been carefully put by in a drawer, going correctly. The following night the very same dream occurred, followed by similar agitation, which was again composed in the same manner,—the brother being again found in a quiet sleep, and the watch going well. On the following morning, soon after the family had breakfasted, one of the sisters was sitting by her brother, while the other was writing a note in the adjoining room. When her note was ready for being sealed, she was proceeding to take out, for this purpose, the watch alluded to, which had been put by in her

---

Their credibility. Are some unaccountable? Example; the two ladies. Relate the whole story

writing-desk,—she was astonished to find it had stopped. At the same instant she heard a scream of intense distress from her sister in the other room,—their brother, who had still been considered as going on favorably, had been seized with a sudded fit of suffocation, and had just breathed his last

There are various other circumstances relating to the philosophy of dreams, which may be mentioned very briefly. It has been alleged that we never dream of objects which we have not seen. On this I cannot decide; but we certainly dream of things in combinations in which they never occurred to us. Our dreams appear to be very much influenced by the intensity of our conceptions, and, in this respect, there is great variety in regard to the objects of the different senses. Our most vivid conceptions are certainly of objects of sight; and they appear to be much less distinct in regard to tastes, smells, and even sounds. Accordingly, I think dreams are chiefly occupied with objects of sight; and I am not sure that we dream of tastes, or smells, or even of sounds, except when a sound actually takes place, as in several instances which have been mentioned. This, indeed, only applies to simple sounds, for we certainly dream of persons speaking to us, and of understanding what they say; but I am not sure that this is necessarily accompanied with a conception of sound. I am informed by a friend, who is a keen sportsman, that he often dreams of being on shooting excursions;—that he starts his game, and points his gun, but never succeeds in firing it. It sometimes seems to miss fire, but in general there appears to be something wrong with the lock, so that it cannot be moved. A gentleman, mentioned by Dr. Darwin, had been for thirty years so deaf that he could be conversed with only in writing, or by forming letters with the fingers. He assured Dr. Darwin, that he never dreamed of persons conversing with him, except by the fingers or in writing, and that he never had the impression of hearing them speak. Two persons who had long been blind also

---

Other principles relating to the philosophy of dreams. Dreams occupied principally with what objects? Why? Case of the sportsman. Point illustrated by it? The deaf gentleman's dreams

informed him, that they never dreamed of visible objects since the loss of their sight. Mr. Bew, however, in the Manchester Memoirs, mentions a blind gentleman who dreamed of the figure, though he could not distinguish the varieties, of the human countenance; and Smellie mentions of Dr. Blacklock, who lost his sight at the age of a few months, that in his dreams he had a distinct impression of a sense which he did not possess when awake. He described his impression by saying that when awake there were three ways by which he could distinguish persons, namely,—by hearing them speak, by feeling the head and shoulders, and by attending to the sound and manner of their breathing. In his dreams, however, he had a vivid impression of objects in a manner distinct from any of these modes. He imagined that he was united to them, by a kind of distant contact, which was effected by threads or strings passing from their bodies to his own.

On a similar principle, probably, we may explain the fact that dreams refer chiefly to persons or events which we have actually seen, though they are put into new combinations; and that we more rarely dream of objects of simple memory unless they have been strongly associated with some object of conception. Thus we seldom dream of events or characters in ancient history. Dr. Beattie, indeed, mentions having dreamed of crossing the Alps with Hannibal; but such dreams, I think, are very rare. It would be curious to observe their occurrence, and to trace the train that leads to them.

It appears, then, that the mental operations which take place in dreaming consist chiefly of old conceptions and old associations, following one another according to some principle of succession over which we have no control. But there are facts on record which show mental operations in dreams of a much more intellectual character. Many people have been conscious of something like composition in dreams. Dr. Gregory mentions that thoughts which sometimes occurred to him in dreams, and even the particular expressions in which they were conveyed, appeared to

---

The blind man's dreams. To what persons and things do our dreams chiefly refer? Exception; Dr. Beattie's dream. Inference from these cases. Composition in dreams? Dr. Gregory.

him afterward when awake so just in point of reasoning and illustration, and so good in point of language, that he has used them in his college lectures, and in his written lucubrations. Condorcet related of himself, that when engaged in some profound and obscure calculations, he was often obliged to leave them in an incomplete state, and retire to rest; and that the remaining steps, and the conclusion of his calculations, had more than once presented themselves in his dreams. Dr. Franklin also informed Cabanis that the bearings and issue of political events, which had puzzled him when awake, were not unfrequently unfolded to him in his dreams. A gentleman of Edinburgh, whose name is deeply associated with the literature of his country, had been one day much amused by reading a very witty epigram by Piron on the French Academy. In a dream the following night he composed a parody or imitation of it, much at the expense of a learned society in Edinburgh, and some individuals of this city. A gentleman had been reading an account of cruelties practised upon some Christians in Turkey by the mutilation of their noses and ears. In a dream the following night he witnessed the execution of a punishment of this kind, and heard a Turk who was standing by address the sufferer in some doggerel rhymes, which he distinctly recollected and repeated in the morning. Another gentleman invented a French verb in a dream. He thought he was in a very close sort of penthouse with such a number of persons that they were threatened with suffocation, as there appeared no way of letting in air. In this state he called out, "*il faut detoiter.*" There is no such word, but it was evidently formed from *toit*, the roof of a building.

The following anecdote has been preserved in a family of rank in Scotland, the descendants of a distinguished lawyer of the last age:—This eminent person had been consulted respecting a case of great importance and much difficulty; and he had been studying it with intense anxiety and attention. After several days had been occupied in this manner, he was observed by his wife to rise from his bed in the night and go to a writing-desk which stood

Condorcet. Franklin. A literary gentleman of Edinburgh. Other cases. Anecdote of the Scotch lawyer.

in the bedroom. He then sat down and wrote a long paper, which he put carefully by in the desk, and returned to bed. The following morning he told his wife that he had a most interesting dream;—that he had dreamed of delivering a clear and luminous opinion respecting a case which had exceedingly perplexed him; and that he would give any thing to recover the train of thought which had passed before him in his dream. She then directed him to the writing-desk, where he found the opinion clearly and fully written out, and which was afterward found to be perfectly correct.

There can be no doubt that many dreams take place which are not remembered, as appears from the fact of a person talking in his sleep so as to be distinctly understood without remembering any thing of the impression that gave rise to it. It is probable, also, that the dreams which are most distinctly remembered, are those which occur during imperfect sleep, or when the sleep begins to be broken by an approach towards waking. Another very peculiar state has perhaps occurred to most people, in which there is a distressing dream, and at the same time an impression that it probably is only a dream. This appears to take place in a still more imperfect state of sleep, in which there is the immediate approach to waking, and to the exercise of the reasoning powers. But there are some very singular facts on record of this kind of reasoning being applied to dreams for the purpose of dissipating them. Dr. Beattie mentions of himself, that in a dream he once found himself standing in a very peculiar situation on the parapet of a bridge. Recollecting, he says, that he never was given to pranks of this nature, he began to fancy that it might be a dream, and determined to throw himself headlong, in the belief that this would restore his senses, which accordingly took place. In the same manner Dr. Reid cured himself of a tendency to frightful dreams, with which he had been annoyed from his early years. He endeavored to fix strongly on his mind the impression that all such dangers in dreams are but imaginary; and determined, whenever in a dream he found himself on the brink of a precipice, to throw himself

---

Forgotten dreams. What dreams probably most distinctly remembered? Peculiar state of mind in dreams Dr. Beattie's case Dr. Reid.

over, and so dissipate the vision. By persevering in this method he so removed the propensity that for forty years he was never sensible of dreaming, though he was very attentive in his observation on the subject.

Some persons are never conscious of dreaming; and a gentleman, mentioned by Locke, was not sensible of dreaming till he had a fever at the age of twenty-six or twenty-seven.

A leading peculiarity in the phenomena of dreaming, is the loss of power over the succession of our thoughts. We have seen that there are some exceptions to this, but the fact applies to by far the greater number of dreams, and some curious phenomena appear to be referable to it. Of this kind are probably some of those singular instances of imaginary difficulties occurring in dreams on subjects on which none could be felt in the waking state. It is not uncommon for a clergyman to dream that he is going to preach, and cannot find his text; or for a clergyman of the Church of England, that he cannot find the place in the prayer-book. This, I think, can only be explained by supposing that in the chain of ideas passing through the mind, the church and prayer-book had come up, but had then led off into some other train, and not into that of actually going on with the service; while, at the same time, there arose in the mind a kind of impression that, under these circumstances, it ought to have been gone on with.

The remarkable analogy between dreaming and insanity has already been referred to; and I shall only add the following illustration:—Dr. Gregory mentions a maniac who had been for some time under his care, and entirely recovered. For a week after his recovery he was harassed during his dreams by the same rapid and tumultuous thoughts, and the same violent passions by which he had been agitated during his insanity.

The slight outline which has now been given of dreaming, may serve to show that the subject is not only curious but important. It appears to be worthy of careful investi-

---

Persons unconscious of dreams. Power over the succession of thoughts lost in dreams. Common troubles. Analogy between dreaming and insanity? Example illustrating it

gation, and there is much reason to believe that an extensive collection of authentic facts, carefully analyzed, would unfold principles of very great interest in reference to the philosophy of the mental powers.

II. SOMNAMBULISM.

Somnambulism appears to differ from dreaming chiefly in the degree in which the bodily functions are affected. The mind is fixed in the same manner as in dreaming upon its own impressions as possessing a real and present existence in external things; but the bodily organs are more under the control of the will, so that the individual acts under the influence of his erroneous conceptions, and holds conversation in regard to them. He is also, to a certain degree, susceptible of impressions from without through his organs of sense; not, however, so as to correct his erroneous impressions, but rather to be mixed up with them. A variety of remarkable phenomena arise out of these peculiarities, which will be illustrated by a slight outline of this singular affection.

The first degree of somnambulism generally shows itself by a propensity to talk during sleep; the person giving a full and connected account of what passes before him in dreams, and often revealing his own secrets or those of his friends. Walking during sleep is the next degree, and that from which the affection derives its name. The phenomena connected with this form are familiar to every one. The individual gets out of bed; dresses himself; if not prevented, goes out of doors, walks frequently over dangerous places in safety; sometimes escapes by a window, and gets to the roof of a house; after a considerable interval, returns and goes to bed; and all that has passed conveys to his mind merely the impression of a dream. A young nobleman, mentioned by Horstius, living in the citadel of Bres lau, was observed by his brother, who occupied the same room, to rise in his sleep, wrap himself in a cloak, and escape by a window to the roof of the building. He there

Difference between somnambulism and dreaming. State of the senses? First degree of somnambulism? Next degree? Instance of it?

tore in pieces a magpie's nest, wrapped the young birds in his cloak, returned to his apartment, and went to bed. In the morning he mentioned the circumstances as having occurred in a dream, and could not be persuaded that there had been any thing more than a dream, till he was shown the magpies in his cloak. Dr. Prichard mentions a man who rose in his sleep, dressed himself, saddled his horse, and rode to the place of a market which he was in the habit of attending once every week; and Martinet mentions a man who was accustomed to rise in his sleep and pursue his business as a saddler. There are many instances on record of persons composing during the state of somnambulism; as of boys rising in their sleep and finishing their tasks which they had left incomplete. A gentleman at one of the English universities had been very intent during the day in the composition of some verses which he had not been able to complete: during the following night he rose in his sleep and finished his composition; then expressed great exultation, and returned to bed.

In these common cases the affection occurs during ordinary sleep; but a condition very analogous is met with, coming on in the daytime in paroxysms, during which the person is affected in the same manner as in the state of somnambulism, particularly with an insensibility to external impressions: this presents some singular phenomena. These attacks in some cases come on without any warning; in others, they are preceded by a noise or a sense of confusion in the head. The individuals then become more or less abstracted, and are either unconscious of any external impression, or very confused in their notions of external things. They are frequently able to talk in an intelligible and consistent manner, but always in reference to the impression which is present in their own minds. They in some cases repeat long pieces of poetry, often more correct ly than they can do in their waking state, and not unfrequently things which they could not repeat in their state of health, or of which they were supposed to be entirely ignorant. In other cases, they hold conversation with imaginary beings, or relate circumstances or conversations

---

Other examples? Case of the English scholar. Attacks in the daytime. Various effects produced.

which occurred at remote periods, and which they were supposed to have forgotten. Some have been known to sing in a style far superior to any thing they could do in their waking state; and there are some well-authenticated instances of persons in this condition expressing themselves correctly in languages with which they were imperfectly acquainted. I had lately under my care a young lady who is liable to an affection of this kind, which comes on repeatedly during the day, and continues from ten minutes to an hour at a time. Without any warning, her body becomes motionless, her eyes open, fixed, and entirely insensible; and she becomes totally unconscious of any external impression. She has been frequently seized while playing on the piano, and has continued to play over and over a part of a tune with perfect correctness, but without advancing beyond a certain point. On one occasion, she was seized after she had begun to play from the book a piece of music which was new to her. During the paroxysm, she continued the part which she had played, and repeated it five or six times with perfect correctness; but, on coming out of the attack, she could not play it without the book. During the paroxysms the individuals are, in some instances, totally insensible to any thing that is said to them; but in others they are capable of holding conversation with another person with a tolerable degree of consistency, though they are influenced to a certain degree by their mental visions, and are very confused in their notions of external things. In many cases, again, they are capable of going on with the manual occupations in which they had been engaged before the attack. This occurred remarkably in a watchmaker's apprentice mentioned by Martinet. The paroxysms in him appeared once in fourteen days, and commenced with a feeling of heat extending from the epigastrium to the head. This was followed by confusion of thought, and this by complete insensibility; his eyes were open, but fixed and vacant, and he was totally insensible to any thing that was said to him, or to any external impression. But he continued his usual employment, and was always much astonished, on his recovery, to find the change

---

The author's patient. Insensibility during the paroxysms. The watchmaker's apprentice. Point illustrated by this case?

that had taken place in his work since the commencement of the paroxysm. This case afterward passed into epi lepsy.

Some remarkable phenomena are presented by this sin gular affection, especially in regard to exercises of memory and the manner in which old associations are recalled into the mind; also in the distinct manner in which the individu als sometimes express themselves on subjects with which they had formerly shown but an imperfect acquaintance In some of the French cases of epidemic " extase," this has been magnified into speaking unknown languages, predicting future events, and describing occurrences of which the persons could not have possessed any knowledge. These stories seem in some cases to resolve themselves merely into embellishment of what really occurred, but in others there can be no doubt of connivance and imposture. Some facts however appear to be authentic, and are sufficiently remarkable. Two females, mentioned by Bertrand, expressed themselves during the paroxysm very distinctly in Latin. They afterward admitted that they had some acquaintance with the language, though it was imperfect. An ignorant servant-girl, mentioned by Dr. Dewar, during paroxysms of this kind, showed an astonishing knowledge of geography and astronomy; and expressed herself in her own language in a manner which, though often ludicrous, showed an understanding of the subject. The alternations of the seasons, for example, she explained by saying that the earth was set *a-gee.* It was afterward discovered that her notions on these subjects had been derived from overhearing a tutor giving instructions to the young people of the family. A woman who was some time ago in the infirmary of Edinburgh, on account of an affection of this kind, during the paroxysms mimicked the manner of the physicians, and repeated correctly some of their prescriptions in the Latin language.

Another very singular phenomenon, presented by some instances of this affection, is what has been called, rather incorrectly, a state of double consciousness. It consists in

Phenomena in regard to the memory. French cases? Explanation of them. Case of two females. The servant-girl. Explanation of these cases?

the individual recollecting, during a paroxysm, circumstances which occurred in a former attack, though there was no remembrance of them during the interval. This, as well as various other phenomena connected with the affection, is strikingly illustrated in a case described by Dr. Dyce of Aberdeen, in the Edinburgh Philosophical Transactions. The patient was a servant-girl, and the affection began with fits of somnolency, which came upon her suddenly during the day, and from which she could, at first, be roused by shaking, or by being taken out into the open air. She soon began to talk a great deal during the attacks, regarding things which seemed to be passing before her as a dream; and she was not at this time sensible of any thing that was said to her. On one occasion she repeated distinctly the baptismal service of the Church of England, and concluded with an extemporary prayer. In her subsequent paroxysms she began to understand what was said to her, and to answer with a considerable degree of consistency, though the answers were generally to a certain degree influenced by her hallucinations. She also became capable of following her usual employments during the paroxysm; at one time she laid out the table correctly for breakfast, and repeatedly dressed herself and the children of the family, her eyes remaining shut the whole time. The remarkable circumstance was now discovered that during the paroxysm she had a distinct recollection of what took place in former paroxysms, though she had no remembrance of it during the intervals. At one time she was taken to church while under the attack, and there behaved with propriety, evidently attending to the preacher; and she was at one time so much affected as to shed tears. In the interval she had no recollection of having been at church; but in the next paroxysm she gave a most distinct account of the sermon, and mentioned particularly the part of it by which she had been so much affected.

This woman described the paroxysms as coming on with a cloudiness before her eyes and a noise in the head. During the attack her eyelids were generally half-shut; her eyes sometimes resembled those of a person affected

---

Double consciousness? Case described by Dr. Dyce. Relate the circumstances. Symptoms preceding and attending the attack?

with amaurosis, that is, with a dilated and insensible state of the pupil, but sometimes they were quite natural. She had a dull vacant look; but, when excited, knew what was said to her, though she often mistook the person who was speaking; and it was observed, that she seemed to discern objects best which were faintly illuminated. The paroxysms generally continued about an hour, but she could often be roused out of them; she then yawned and stretched herself, like a person awaking out of sleep, and instantly knew those about her. At one time, during the attack, she read distinctly a portion of a book which was presented to her; and she often sung, both sacred and common pieces, incomparably better, Dr. Dyce affirms, than she could do in the waking state. The affection continued to recur for about six months, and ceased when a particular change took place in her constitution.

Another very remarkable modification of this affection is referred to by Mr. Combe, as described by major Elliot, professor of mathematics in the United States' Military Academy at West Point. The patient was a young lady of cultivated mind, and the affection began with an attack of somnolency, which was protracted several hours beyond the usual time. When she came out of it, she was found to have lost every kind of acquired knowledge. She immediately began to apply herself to the first elements of education, and was making considerable progress, when, after several months, she was seized with a second fit of somnolency. She was now at once restored to all the knowledge which she possessed before the first attack, but without the least recollection of any thing that had taken place during the interval. After another interval she had a third attack of somnolency, which left her in the same state as after the first. In this manner she suffered these alternate conditions for a period of four years, with the very remarkable circumstance that during the one state she retained all her original knowledge; but during the other, that only which she had acquired since the first attack. During the healthy interval, for example, she was remarkable for the beauty of her penmanship, but during the paroxysm wrote a poor awkward hand. Persons introduced to her during the

---

Result of this case. Case at West Point? Her hand-writing?

paroxysms she recognised only in a subsequent paroxysm, but not in the interval; and persons whom she had seen for the first time during the healthy interval she did not recognise during the attack.

In reference to this very curious subject, the author is induced to add a fact which has been recently communicated to him. A young woman of the lower rank, aged nineteen, became insane about two years ago; but was gentle, and applied herself eagerly to various occupations. Before her insanity she had been only learning to read, and to form a few letters; but during her insanity she taught herself to write perfectly, though all attempts of others to teach her failed, as she could not attend to any person who tried to do so. She has intervals of reason, which have frequently continued three weeks, sometimes longer. During these she can neither read nor write; but immediately on the return of her insanity she recovers her power of writing, and can read perfectly.

Of the remarkable condition of the mental faculties, exemplified in these cases, it is impossible to give any explanation. Something very analogous to it occurs in other affections, though in a smaller degree. Dr. Prichard mentions a lady who was liable to sudden attacks of delirium, which, after continuing for various periods, went off as suddenly, leaving her at once perfectly rational. The attack was often so sudden that it commenced while she was engaged in interesting conversation, and on such occasions it happened, that on her recovery from the state of delirium, she instantly recurred to the conversation she had been engaged in at the time of the attack, though she had never referred to it during the continuance of the affection. To such a degree was this carried, that she would even complete an unfinished sentence. During the subsequent paroxysm, again, she would pursue the train of ideas which had occupied her mind in the former. Mr. Combe also mentions a porter, who in a state of intoxication left a parcel at a wrong house, and when sober could not recollect what he had done with it. But the next time he got drunk, he recollected where he had left it, and went and recovered it.

Her acquaintances? The insane girl. Possibility of an explanation of these cases? Analogous case mentioned by Dr. Prichard. The intoxicated porter.

III. INSANITY.

Reason we have considered to be that exercise of mind by which we compare facts with each other, and mental impressions with external things. By means of it we are enabled to judge of the relations of facts, and of the agreement between our impressions and the actual state of things in the external world. We have seen also that peculiar power which is possessed by the mind in a healthy state,—of arresting or changing the train of its thoughts at pleasure,—of fixing the attention upon one, or transferring it to another,—of changing the train into something which is analogous to it, or of dismissing it altogether. This power is, to a greater or less degree, lost in insanity; and the result is one of two conditions. Either the mind is entirely under the influence of a single impression, without the power of varying or dismissing it, and comparing it with other impressions; or it is left at the mercy of a chain of impressions which have been set in motion, and which succeed one another according to some principle of connection over which the individual has no control. In both cases the mental impression is believed to have a real and present existence in the external world; and this false belief is not corrected by the actual state of things as they present themselves to the senses, or by any facts or considerations which can be communicated by other sentient beings. Of the cause of this remarkable deviation from the healthy state of the mental functions we know nothing. We may trace its connection with concomitant circumstances in the bodily functions, and we may investigate certain effects which result from it; but the nature of the change and the manner in which it is produced are among those points in the arrangements of the Almighty Creator which entirely elude our researches.

It appears, then, that there is a remarkable analogy between the mental phenomena in insanity and in dreaming; and that the leading peculiarities of both these conditions are referable to two heads:—

Reason; its definition? Power over the succession of thoughts. Effects of insanity? Cause? Analogy between insanity and dreaming.

1. The impressions which arise in the mind are believed to be real and present existences, and this belief is not corrected by comparing the conception with the actual state of things in the external world.

2. The chain of ideas or images which arise follow one another according to certain associations over which the individual has no control; he cannot, as in a healthy state, vary the series or stop it at his will.

In the numerous forms of insanity, we shall see these characters exhibited in various degrees; but we shall be able to trace their influence in one degree or another through all the modifications; and, in the higher states, or what we call perfect mania, we see them exemplified in the same complete manner as in dreaming. The maniac fancies himself a king possessed of boundless power, and surrounded by every form of earthly splendor; and, with all his bodily senses in their perfect exercise, this hallucination is in no degree corrected by the sight of his bed of straw and all the horrors of his cell.

From this state of perfect mania the malady is traced through numerous gradations to forms which exhibit slight deviations from the state of a sound mind. But they al. show, in one degree or another, the same leading characters, namely, that some impression has taken possession of the mind, and influences the conduct in a manner in which it would not affect a sound understanding; and that this is not corrected by facts and considerations which are calculated immediately to relieve the erroneous impression. The lower degrees of this condition we call eccentricity· and, in common language, we often talk of a man being crazed upon a particular subject. This consists in giving to an impression or a fancy undue and extravagant importance, without taking into account other facts and considerations which ought to be viewed in connection with it. The man of this character acts with promptitude upon a single idea, and seems to perceive nothing that interferes with it· he forms plans, and sees only important advantages which would arise from the accomplishment of them, without perceiving difficulties or objections. The impression itself

---

Two leading peculiarities? When most completely exemplified? Leading characters the same in all stages. Lower stage, what? Nature of eccentricity

may be correct, but an importance is attached to it disproportioned to its true tendency; or consequences are deduced from, and actions founded upon it, which would not be warranted in the estimate of a sound understanding. It is often difficult to draw the line between certain degrees of this condition and insanity; and, in fact, they very often pass into each other. This will be illustrated by the following example :—

A clergyman in Scotland, after showing various extravagances of conduct, was brought before a jury to be cognosced; that is, by a form of Scotch law to be declared incapable of managing his own affairs, and placed under the care of trustees. Among the acts of extravagance alleged against him was, that he had burnt his library. When he was asked by the jury what account he could give of this part of his conduct, he replied in the following terms :— "In the early part of my life I had imbibed a liking for a most unprofitable study, namely, controversial divinity. On reviewing my library, I found a great part of it to consist of books of this description, and I was so anxious that my family should not be led to follow the same pursuit, that I determined to burn the whole." He gave answers equally plausible to questions which were put to him respecting other parts of his conduct; and the result was that the jury found no sufficient ground for cognoscing him; but in the course of a fortnight from that time he was in a state of decided mania.

It is, therefore, incorrect to say of insanity, as has been said, that the maniac reasons correctly upon unsound data. His data may be unsound, that is, they may consist of a mental image which is purely visionary, as in the state of perfect mania lately referred to; but this is by no means necessary to constitute the disease; for his premises may be sound, though he distorts them in the results which he deduces from them. This was remarkably the case in the clergyman now mentioned. His premises were sound and consistent, namely, his opinion of the unprofitable nature of the study of controversial divinity, and his anxiety that his family should not prosecute it. His insanity consisted in

Case of the clergyman. His defence before the jury. Erroneous theory of insanity. Illustrated by the preceding case.

the rapid and partial view which he took of the means for accomplishing his purpose,—burning his whole library. Had he sold his library or that part of it which consisted of controversial divinity, the measure would have been in correct relation to the object which he had in view; and if we suppose that in going over his library he had met with some books of an immoral tendency, to have burnt these to prevent them from falling into the hands of any individual would have been the act both of a wise and virtuous man. But to burn his whole library to prevent his family from studying controversial divinity, was the suggestion of insanity,—distorting entirely the true relation of things, and carrying an impression, in itself correct, into consequences which it in no degree warranted.

A remarkable peculiarity in many cases of insanity is, a great activity of mind, and rapidity of conception,—a tendency to seize rapidly upon incidental or partial relations of things,—and often a fertility of imagination which changes the character of the mind, sometimes without remarkably distorting it. The memory, in such cases, is entire, and even appears more ready than in health; and old associations are called up with a rapidity quite unknown to the individual in his sound state of mind. A gentleman, mentioned by Dr. Willis, who was liable to periodical attacks of insanity, said that he expected the paroxysms with impatience, because he enjoyed during them a high degree of pleasure. "Every thing appeared easy to me. No obstacles presented themselves, either in theory or practice. My memory acquired all of a sudden a singular degree of perfection. Long passages of Latin authors occurred to my mind. In general I have great difficulty in finding rhythmical terminations, but then I could write verses with as great facility as prose." "I have often," says Pinel, "stopped at the chamber door of a literary gentleman who, during his paroxysms, appears to soar above the mediocrity of intellect that was familiar to him, solely to admire his newly acquired powers of eloquence. He declaimed upon the subject of the revolution with all the force, the dignity and the purity of language that this very interesting subject

---

Examination of his reasoning. Remarkable effects of insanity in some cases. Case mentioned by Dr. Willis? By Pinel?

could admit of. At other times he was a man of very ordinary abilities."

It is this activity of thought and readiness of association that gives to maniacs of a particular class an appearance of great ingenuity and acuteness. Hence they have been said to reason acutely upon false premises; and one author has even alleged that a maniac of a particular kind would make an excellent logician. But to say that a maniac reasons either soundly or acutely is an abuse of terms. He reasons plausibly and ingeniously; that is, he catches rapidly incidental and partial relations; and from the rapidity with which they are seized upon, it may sometimes be difficult at first to detect their fallacy. He might have made a skilful logician of the schools, whose ingenuity consisted in verbal disputes and frivolous distinctions; but he never can be considered as exercising that sound logic, the aim of which is to trace the real relations of things, and the object of which is truth.

The peculiar character of insanity, in all its modifications appears to be that a certain impression has fixed itself upon the mind in such a manner as to exclude all others; or to exclude them from that influence which they ought to have on the mind in its estimate of the relations of things. This impression may be entirely visionary and unfounded; or it may be in itself true, but distorted in the applications which the unsound mind makes of it, and the consequences which are deduced from it. Thus a man of wealth fancies himself a beggar, and in danger of dying of hunger. Another takes up the same impression who has, in fact, sustained some considerable loss. In the one, the impression is entirely visionary, like that which might occur in a dream; in the other, it is a real and true impression, carried to consequences which it does not warrant.

There is great variety in the degree to which the mind is influenced by the erroneous impression. In some cases it is such as entirely excludes all others, even those immediately arising from the evidence of the senses, as in the state of perfect mania formerly referred to. In many others,

Results of this in many cases. The reasoning of a maniac. Peculiar character of insanity? Examples. Changes of character effected by it.

though in a less degree than this, it is such as to change the whole character. The particular manner in which this more immediately appears will depend, of course, upon the nature of the erroneous impression. A person formerly most correct in his conduct and habits may become obscene and blasphemous; accustomed occupations become odious to him; the nearest and most beloved friends become objects of his aversion and abhorrence. Much interesting matter of observation often arises out of these peculiarities, and it is no less interesting to observe during convalescence the gradual return to former habits and attachments. A young lady, mentioned by Dr. Rush, who had been for some time confined in a lunatic asylum, had shown for several weeks every mark of a sound mind except one,—she hated her father. At length, she one day acknowledged with pleasure the return of her filial attachment, and was soon after discharged, entirely recovered. Even when the erroneous impression is confined to a single subject, it is remarkable how it absorbs the attention, to the exclusion of other feelings of a most intense and powerful kind. I knew a person of wealth who had fallen into a temporary state of melancholic hallucination, in connection with a transaction in business which he regretted having made, but of which the real effect was of a trifling nature. While in this situation, the most severe distress occurred in his family, by the death of one of them under painful circumstances, without his being affected by it in the slightest degree.

The uniformity of the impressions of maniacs is indeed so remarkable that it has been proposed by Pinel as a test for distinguishing real from feigned insanity. He has seen melancholics confined in the Bicetre for twelve, fifteen, twenty, and even thirty years; and through the whole of that period their hallucination has been limited to one subject. Others, after a course of years, have changed from one hallucination to another. A man, mentioned by him, was for eight years constantly haunted with the idea of being poisoned: he then changed his hallucination, became sovereign of the world and extremely happy, and thus continued for four years.

The sudden revival of old impressions, after having been

Dr Rush's patient. Uniformity of the impressions of maniacs.

long entirely suspended by mental hallucinations, presents some of the most singular phenomena connected with this subject. Dr. Prichard mentions an interesting case of this kind from the American Journal of Science. A man had been employed for a day with a beetle and wedges in splitting pieces of wood for erecting a fence. At night, before going home, he put the beetle and wedges into the hollow of an old tree, and directed his sons, who had been at work in an adjoining field, to accempany him next morning to assist in making the fence. In the night he became maniacal, and continued in a state of insanity for several years, during which time his mind was not occupied with any of the subjects with which he had been conversant when in health. After several years his reason returned suddenly, and the first question he asked was whether his sons had brought home the beetle and wedges. They, being afraid of entering upon any explanation, only said that they could not find them; on which he arose from his bed, went to the field where he had been at work so many years before, and found where he had left them the wedges and the iron rings of the beetle, the wooden part being entirely mouldered away. A lady, mentioned in the same journal, had been intensely engaged for some time in a piece of needle-work. Before she had completed it, she became insane, and continued in that state for seven years, after which her reason returned suddenly. One of the first questions she asked related to her needle-work, though she had never alluded to it, so far as was recollected, during her illness. I have formerly alluded to the remarkable case of a lady who was liable to periodical paroxysms of delirium, which often attacked her so suddenly, that in conversation she would stop in the middle of a story, or even of a sentence, and branch off into the subject of her hallucination. On the return of her reason, she would resume the conversation in which she was engaged at the time of the attack, beginning exactly where she had left off, though she had never alluded to it during the delirium; and on the next attack of delirium she would resume the subject of hallucination with which she had been occupied at the conclusion of the

---

Revival of old impressions Story of the beetle and wedges. The piece of needle-work. Other cases.

former paroxysm. In some cases there is a total loss of the impression of time respecting the period occupied by the attack, which on the partial recovery of the patient shows itself by singular fancies. A man, mentioned by Haslam, maintained that he had seen the seed sown in a particular field, and on passing it again three or four days after saw the reapers at work cutting down the corn. The interval of which he had thus lost entirely the impression, had been spent in a state of furious insanity; from this he had in so far recovered as, by a mere act of observation and memory, to form this notion, but not so far as, by an act of comparison or judgment, to perceive its absurdity.

Among the most singular phenomena connected with insanity we must reckon those cases in which the hallucination is confined to a single point, while on every other subject the patient speaks and acts like a rational man: and he often shows the most astonishing power of avoiding the subject of his disordered impression, when circumstances make it advisable for him to do so. A man, mentioned by Pinel, who had been for some time confined in the Bicetre, was on the visitation of a commissary ordered to be discharged as perfectly sane, after a long conversation in which he had conducted himself with the greatest propriety. The officer prepared the *procès vèrbal* for his discharge, and gave it him to put his name to it, when he subscribed himself Jesus Christ, and then indulged in all the reveries connected with that delusion. Lord Erskine gives a very remarkable history of a man who indicted Dr. Munro for confining him without cause in a mad house. He underwent a most rigid examination by the counsel of the defendant without discovering any appearance of insanity, until a gentleman came into court who desired a question to be put to him respecting a princess with whom he had corresponded in cherry-juice. He immediately talked about the princess in the most insane manner, and the cause was at an end. But this having taken place in Westminster, he commenced another action in the city of London, and on this occasion no effort could induce him to expose his insanity; so that

---

Case mentioned by Haslam? Derangement on a single point. The prisoner in the Bicetre. Case given by Lord Erskine.

the cause was dismissed only by bringing against him the evidence taken at Westminster. On another occasion Lord Erskine examined a gentleman who had indicted his brother for confining him as a maniac, and the examination had gone on for great part of a day without discovering any trace of insanity. Dr. Sims then came into court, and informed the counsel that the gentleman considered himself as the Savior of the world. A single observation addressed to him in this character showed his insanity, and put an end to the cause. Many similar cases are on record. Several years ago a gentleman in Edinburgh who was brought before a jury to be cognosced, defeated every attempt of the opposite counsel to discover any trace of insanity, until a gentleman came into court who ought to have been present at the beginning of the case, but had been accidentally detained. He immediately addressed the patient by asking him what were his latest accounts from the planet Saturn, and speedily elicited proofs of his insanity.

Of the nature and cause of that remarkable condition of the mental faculties which gives rise to the phenomena of insanity, we know nothing. We can only observe the facts, and endeavor to trace among them some general principle of connection: and even in this there is great difficulty, chiefly from the want of observations particularly directed to this object. There would be much interesting subject of inquiry in tracing the origin of the particular chain of ideas which arise in individual cases of insanity; and likewise the manner in which similar impressions are modified in different cases, either by circumstances in the natural disposition of the individual, or by the state of his bodily functions at the time. From what has been observed, it seems probable that in both these respects there is preserved a remarkable analogy to dreaming. The particular hallucinations may be chiefly referred to the following heads:—

I. Propensities of character, which had been kept under restraint by reason or by external circumstances, or old habits which had been subdued or restrained, developing themselves without control, and leading the mind into trains of fancies

---

Other similar cases. Cause of insanity? Our knowledge on the subject confined to what? Classes of hallucinations? Old habits or propensities.

arising out of them. Thus a man of an aspiring, ambitious character may imagine himself a king, or great personage; while in a man of a timid, suspicious disposition, the mind may fix upon some supposed injury, or loss either of property or reputation.

II. Old associations recalled into the mind, and mixed up perhaps with more recent occurrences, in the same manner as we often see in dreaming. A lady mentioned by Dr. Gooch, who became insane in consequence of an alarm from a house on fire in her neighborhood, imagined that she was the Virgin Mary, and had a luminous halo around her head.

III. Visions of the imagination which have formerly been indulged in, of that kind which we call waking dreams, or castle-building, recurring to the mind in this condition, and now believed to have a real existence. I have been able to trace this source of the hallucination. In one case, for example, it turned upon an office to which the individual imagined he had been appointed; and it was impossible to persuade him to the contrary, or even that the office was not vacant. He afterward acknowledged that his fancy had at various times been fixed upon that appointment, though there were no circumstances that warranted him in entertaining any expectation of it. In a man mentioned by Dr. Morison, the hallucination turned upon circumstances which had been mentioned when his fortune was told by a Gipsey.

IV. Bodily feelings giving rise to trains of associations, in the same extravagant manner as in dreaming. A man, mentioned by Dr. Rush, imagined that he had a Caffre in his stomach, who had got into it at the cape of Good Hope, and had occasioned him a constant uneasiness ever since. In such a case, it is probable that there had been some fixed or frequent uneasy feeling at the stomach, and that about the commencement of his complaint he had been strongly impressed by some transaction in which a Caffre was concerned.

Old associations. Visions of imagination. Case? Bodily feelings. Dr. Rush's patient.

V. There seems reason to believe that the hallucinations of the insane are often influenced by a certain sense of the new and singular state in which their mental powers really are, and a certain feeling, though confused and ill-defined, of the loss of that power over their mental processes which they possessed when in health. To a feeling of this kind I am disposed to refer the impression so common among the insane of being under the influence of some supernatural power. They sometimes represent it as the working of an evil spirit, and sometimes as witchcraft. Very often they describe it as a mysterious and undue influence which some individual has obtained over them, and this influence they often represent as being carried on by means of electricity, galvanism, or magnetism. This impression being once established of a mysterious agency, or a mysterious change in the state and feelings of the individual, various other incidental associations may be brought into connection with it, according as particular circumstances have made a deep impression on the mind. A man mentioned by Pinel, who had become insane during the French revolution, imagined that he had been guillotined; that the judges had changed their mind after the sentence was executed, and had ordered his head to be put on again; and that the persons intrusted with this duty had made a mistake, and put a wrong head upon him. Another individual, mentioned by Dr. Conolly, imagined that he had been hanged, and brought to life by means of galvanism; and that the whole of his life had not been restored to him.

Out of the same undefined feeling of mental processes very different from those of their healthy state probably arises another common impression, namely, of intercourse with spiritual beings, visions, and revelations. The particular character of these, perhaps, arises out of some previous processes of the mind, or strong propensity of the character; and the notion of a supernatural revelation may proceed from a certain feeling of the new and peculiar manner in which the impression is fixed upon the mind. A priest, mentioned by Pinel, imagined that he had a commission from the Virgin Mary to murder a certain individual, who

---

Influence of a sense of their state on the insane. Cases mentioned? Ideas of communication with supernatural beings. Story of the priest?

was accused of infidelity. It is probable that the patient in this case had been naturally of a violent and irascible disposition; that he had come in contact with this person, and had been annoyed and irritated by infidel sentiments uttered by him; and that a strong feeling in regard to him had thus been excited in his mind, which, in his insane state, was formed into this vision.

When the mental impression is of a depressing character, that modification of the disease is produced which is called melancholia. It seems to differ from mania merely in the subject of hallucination, and accordingly we find the two modifications pass into each other, the same patient being at one time in a state of melancholic depression, and at another of maniacal excitement. It is, however, more common for the melancholic to continue in the state of depression, and generally in reference to one subject; and the difference between him and the exalted maniac does not appear to depend upon the occasional cause. For we sometimes find persons who have become deranged in connection with overwhelming calamities, show no depression, nor even a recollection of their distresses, but the highest state of exalted mania. The difference appears to depend chiefly upon constitutional peculiarities of character

The most striking peculiarity of melancholia is the prevailing propensity to suicide; and there are facts connected with this subject which remarkably illustrate what may be called the philosophy of insanity. When the melancholic hallucination has fully taken possession of the mind, it becomes the sole object of attention, without the power of varying the impression, or of directing the thoughts to any facts or considerations calculated to remove or palliate it. The evil seems overwhelming and irremediable, admitting neither of palliation, consolation, nor hope. For the process of mind calculated to diminish such an impression, or even to produce the hope of a palliation of the evil, is precisely that exercise of mind which, in this singular condition, is lost or suspended; namely, a power of changing the subject of thought, of transferring the attention to other facts

---

Melancholy. How distinguished from mania? Most striking peculiarity of melancholy? Overwhelming influence of the melancholy feelings.

and considerations, and of comparing the mental impression with these, and with the actual state of external things. Under such a conviction of overwhelming and hopeless misery, the feeling naturally arises of life being a burden and this is succeeded by a determination to quit it. When such an association has once been formed, it also fixes itself upon the mind, and fails to be corrected by those considerations which ought to remove it. That it is in this manner the impression arises, and not from any process analogous to the determination of a sound mind, appears, among other circumstances, from the singular manner in which it is often dissipated; namely, by the accidental production of some new impression, not calculated in any degree to influence the subject of thought, but simply to give a momentary direction of the mind to some other feeling. Thus a man, mentioned by Pinel, had left his house in the night with the determined resolution of drowning himself, when he was attacked by robbers. He did his best to escape from them, and, having done so, returned home, the resolution of suicide being entirely dissipated. A woman, mentioned, I believe, by Dr. Burrows, had her resolution changed in the same manner, by something falling on her head after she had gone out for a similar purpose.

A very singular modification occurs in some of these cases. With the earnest desire of death, there is combined an impression of the criminality of suicide; but this, instead of correcting the hallucination, only leads to another and most extraordinary mode of effecting the purpose; namely, by committing murder, and so dying by the hand of justice. Several instances are on record in which this remarkable mental process was distinctly traced and avowed; and in which there was no mixture of malice against the individuals who were murdered. On the contrary, they were generally children; and in one of the cases, the maniac distinctly avowed his resolution to commit murder, with a view of dying by a sentence of law, and at the same time his determination that his victim should be a child, as he should thus avoid the additional guilt of sending a person out of the world in a state of unrepented sin. The mental process in

---

Why they cannot be removed? Case mentioned by Pinel? **Singular modification of the disease?** Instances?

such a case presents a most interesting subject of reflection It appears to be purely a process of association, without the power of reasoning. I should suppose that there had been at a former period, during a comparatively healthy state of the mental faculties, a repeated contemplation of suicide, which had been always checked by an immediate conviction of its dreadful criminality. In this manner, a strong connection had been formed, which, when the idea of suicide afterward came into the mind during the state of insanity, led to the impression of its heinousness, not by a process of reasoning, but by simple association. The subsequent steps are the distorted reasonings of insanity, mixed with some previous impression of the safe condition of children dying in infancy. This explanation, I think, is strongly countenanced by the consideration, that had the idea of the criminality of suicide been in any degree a process of reasoning, a corresponding conviction of the guilt of murder must have followed it. I find, however, one case which is at variance with this hypothesis. The reasoning of that unfortunate individual was, that if he committed murder and died by the hand of justice, there would be time for making his peace with the Almighty between the crime and his execution, which would not be the case if he should die by suicide. This was a species of reasoning, but it was purely the reasoning of insanity.

Attempts have been made to refer insanity to disease of bodily organs, but hitherto without much success. In some instances we are able to trace a connection of this kind; but in a large proportion we can trace no bodily disease. On this subject, as well as various other points connected with the phenomena of insanity, extensive and careful observation will be required before we are entitled to advance to any conclusions. In regard to what have been called the moral causes of insanity, also, I suspect there has been a good deal of fallacy, arising from considering as a moral cause what was really a part of the disease. Thus we find so many cases of insanity referred to erroneous views of religion, so many to love, so many to ambition, &c. But

---

Explanation. Exception Erroneous theory of insanity. Can *any* connection b traced? Common fallacy?

perhaps it may be doubted whether that which was in these cases considered as the cause, was not rather, in many instances, a part of the hallucination. This, I think, applies in a peculiar manner to the important subject of religion, which, by a common but very loose mode of speaking, is often mentioned as a frequent cause of insanity. When there is a constitutional tendency to insanity, or to melancholy, one of its leading modifications, every subject is distorted to which the mind can be directed, and none more frequently or more remarkably than the great questions of religious belief. But this is the effect, not the cause; and the frequency of this kind of hallucination, and the various forms which it assumes, may be ascribed to the subject being one to which the minds of all men are so naturally directed in one degree or another, and of which no man living can entirely divest himself. Even when the mind does give way under a great moral cause, such as overwhelming misfortunes, we often find that the hallucination does not refer to them, but to something entirely distinct: striking examples of this are mentioned by Pinel.

Insanity is, in a large proportion of cases, to be traced to hereditary predisposition; and this is often so strong that no prominent moral cause is necessary for the production of the disease, and probably no moral treatment would have any effect in preventing it. We must, however, suppose, that where a tendency to insanity exists, there may be, in many cases, circumstances in mental habits or mental discipline calculated either to favor or to counteract the tendency. Insanity frequently commences with a state in which particular impressions fix themselves upon the mind in a manner entirely disproportioned to their true relations; and in which these false impressions fail to be corrected by the judgment comparing them with other impressions, or with external things. In so far as mental habits may be supposed to favor or promote such a condition, this may be likely to result from allowing the mind to wander away from the proper duties of life, or to luxuriate amid scenes of the imagination; and permitting mental emotions, of whatever kind, to be excited in a manner disproportioned to the

---

Is religious melancholy the cause or effect of insanity? Hereditary predisposition Influence of mental habits in promoting it?

true relations of the objects which give rise to them; in short, from allowing the mind to ramble among imaginary events, or to be led away by slight and casual relations, instead of steadily exercising the judgment in the investigation of truth. We might refer to the same head habits of distorting events, and of founding upon them conclusions which they do not warrant. These, and other propensities and habits of a similar kind, constitute what is called an ill-regulated mind. Opposed to it is that habit of cool and sound exercise of the understanding by which events are contemplated in their true relations and consequences, and mental emotions arise out of them such as they are really calculated to produce. Every one must be familiar with the difference which exists among different individuals in this respect; and even in the same individual at different times. We trace the influence of the principle in the impression which is made by events coming upon us suddenly and unexpectedly; and the manner in which the emotion is gradually brought to its proper bearings, as the mind accommodates itself to the event, by contemplating it in its true relations. In such a mental process as this, we observe the most remarkable diversities among various individuals. In some, the mind rapidly contemplates the event in all its relations, and speedily arrives at the precise impression or emotion which it is in truth fitted to produce. In others, this is done more slowly, perhaps more imperfectly, and probably not without the aid of suggestions from other minds; while, in some, the first impression is so strong and so permanent, and resists in such a manner those considerations which might remove or moderate it, that we find difficulty in drawing the line between it and that kind of false impression which constitutes the lower degree of insanity. Habits of mental application must also exert a great influence; and we certainly remark a striking difference between those who are accustomed merely to works of imagination and taste, and those whose minds have been rigidly exercised to habits of calm and severe inquiry. A fact is mentioned by Dr. Conolly which if it shall be confirmed by farther observation, would lead to some most im-

---

Habits which tend to avert it? Diversities among individuals. Influence of habits of mental application? Dr. Conolly's testimony?

portant reflections. He states that it appears from the registers of the Bicetre, that maniacs of the more educated classes consist almost entirely of priests, artists, painters, sculptors, poets, and musicians; while no instance, it is said, occurs of the disease in naturalists, physicians, geometricians, or chemists.

The higher degrees of insanity are in general so distinctly defined in their characters as to leave no room for doubt in deciding upon the nature of the affection. But it is otherwise in regard to many of the lower modifications; and great discretion is often required in judging whether the conduct of an individual, in particular instances, is to be considered as indicative of insanity. This arises from the principle, which must never be lost sight of, that in such cases we are not to decide simply from the facts themselves, but by their relation to other circumstances, and to the previous habits and character of the individual. There are many peculiarities and eccentricities of character which do not constitute insanity; and the same peculiarities may afford reason for suspecting insanity in one person and not in another; namely, when in the former they have appeared suddenly, and are much opposed to his previous uniform character; while, to the latter, they have been long known to be habitual and natural. Thus, acts of thoughtless prodigality and extravagance may, in one person, be considered entirely in accordance with his uniform character; while the same acts, committed by a person formerly distinguished by sedate and prudent conduct, may give good ground for suspecting insanity, and in fact constitute a form in which the affection very often appears. In ordinary cases of insanity, a man's conduct is to be tried by a comparison with the average conduct of other men; but, in many of the cases now referred to, he must be compared with his former self.

Another caution is to be kept in mind, respecting the mental impressions of the individual in these slight or suspected cases of insanity; that an impression which gives reason for suspecting insanity in one case, because we know

---

Higher degrees of insanity well marked. Lower degrees. Necessity of caution. Mental peculiarities which are sometimes mistaken for insanity. Another caution?

it to be entirely unfounded and imaginary, may allow of no such conclusion in another, in which it has some reasonable or plausible foundation. Insane persons indeed often relate stories which hang together so plausibly and consistently, that we cannot say whether we are to consider them as indicative of insanity, until we have ascertained whether they have any foundation, or are entirely imaginary. In one instance which was referred to in the discussions respecting a late remarkable case, the principal fact alleged against the individual was, his having taken up a suspicion of the fidelity of his wife. But it turned out to be a very general opinion among his neighbors that the impression was well-founded. The same principle applies to the antipathies against intimate friends which are often so remarkable in the insane. They may be of such a nature as decidedly to mark the hallucination of insanity,—as when a person expresses a dislike to a child, formerly beloved, on the ground that he is not really his child, but an evil spirit which has assumed his form. This is clearly insanity; but if the antipathy be against a friend or relative, without any such reason assigned for it, we require to keep in view the inquiry, whether the impression be the result of hallucination, or whether the relative has really given any ground for it. In all slight or doubtful cases, much discretion should be used in putting an individual under restraint, and still more in immediately subjecting him to confinement in an asylum for lunatics. But there is one modification in which all such delicacy must be dispensed with, namely, in those melancholic cases which have shown any tendency to suicide. Whenever this propensity has appeared, no time is to be lost in taking the most effectual precautions; and the most painful consequences have very often resulted, in cases of this description, from misplaced delicacy and delay.

The subject of hallucination in insanity we have seen may be either entirely imaginary and groundless, or may be a real event viewed in false relations, and carried to false consequences. This view of the subject bears upon an important practical point which has been much agitated, name-

---

Stories related by the insane. Some impressions conclusive proof of insanity. Tendency to suicide. Subjects of hallucination twofold.

ly, the liability of maniacs to punishment; and which has been ably and ingeniously argued by Lord Erskine in his defence of Hatfield, who fired at his majesty King George III. The principle contended for by this eminent person is that when a maniac commits a crime under the influence of an impression which is entirely visionary, and purely the hallucination of insanity, he is not the object of punishment; but that, though he may have shown insanity in other things, he is liable to punishment if the impression under which he acted was true, and the human passion arising out of it was directed to its proper object. He illustrates this principle by contrasting the case of Hatfield with that of Lord Ferrers. Hatfield had taken a fancy that the end of the world was at hand, and that the death of his majesty was in some way connected with important events which were about to take place. Lord Ferrers, after showing various indications of insanity, murdered a man against whom he was known to harbor deep-rooted resentment, on account of real transactions in which that individual had rendered himself obnoxious to him. The former, therefore, is considered as an example of the pure hallucination of insanity, the latter as one of human passion founded on real events and directed to its proper object. Hatfield, accordingly, was acquitted, but Lord Ferrers was convicted of murder and executed. The contrast between the two cases is sufficiently striking; but it may be questioned whether it will bear all that Lord Erskine has founded upon it. There can be no doubt of the first of his propositions, that a person acting under the pure hallucination of insanity, in regard to impressions which are entirely unfounded, is not the object of punishment. But the converse does not seem to follow; namely, that the man becomes an object of punishment merely because the impression was founded in fact, and because there was a human passion directed to its proper object. For it is among the characters of insanity not only to call up impressions which are entirely visionary, but also to distort and exaggerate those which are true, and to carry them to consequences which they do not warrant in the estimation of a sound mind. A person, for instance,

---

Important practical point? Argument of Lord Erskine? His positions? His illustration of it? Relate the case. Author's view of this subject?

who has suffered a loss in business which does not affect his circumstances in any important degree, may imagine, under the influence of hallucination, that he is a ruined man, and that his family is reduced to beggary. Now, were a wealthy man under the influence of such hallucination to commit an outrage on a person who had defrauded him of a trifling sum, the case would afford the character mentioned by Lord Erskine, namely, human passion founded upon real events, and directed to its proper object: but no one, probably, would doubt for a moment that the process was as much the result of insanity as if the impression had been entirely visionary. In this hypothetical case, indeed, the injury, though real, is slight; but it does not appear that the principle is necessarily affected by the injury being great, or more in relation to the result which it leads to according to the usual course of human passion. It would appear probable, therefore, that in deciding a doubtful case, a jury ought to be guided, not merely by the circumstances of the case itself, but by the evidence of insanity in other things. This, accordingly, appears to have been the rule on which a jury acted in another important case mentioned by Lord Erskine, in which an unfortunate female, under the influence of insanity, murdered a man who had seduced and deserted her. Here was a real injury of the highest description, and human passion founded upon it and directed to its proper object; but the jury, on proof of derangement in other things, acquitted the prisoner, who accordingly soon passed into a state of "undoubted and deplorable insanity." In the case of Lord Ferrers, also, it would appear that the decision proceeded, not so much upon the principle of human passion directed to its proper object, as upon an impression that his lordship's previous conduct had been indicative of uncontrolled violence of temper, rather than actual insanity.

Some of the points which have been briefly alluded to seem to bear on the practical part of this important subject,—the moral treatment of insanity. Without entering on any lengthened discussion, some leading principles may be referred to the following heads:—

Illustration of it? Lord Erskine's reasoning examined. Considerations which should influence a jury? Case of the female murderer. Practical part of this subject

I. It will be generally admitted that every attempt to reason with a maniac is not only fruitless, but rather tends to fix more deeply his erroneous impression. An important rule in the moral management of the insane will therefore probably be, to avoid every allusion to the subject of their hallucination, to remove from them every thing calculated by association to lead to it, and to remove them from scenes and persons likely to recall or keep up the erroneous impression. Hence, probably, in a great measure arises the remarkable benefit of removing the insane from their usual residence, friends, and attendants, and placing them in new scenes, and entirely under the care of strangers. The actual effect of this measure is familiar to every one who is in any degree conversant with the management of the insane. That the measure may have its full effect, it appears to be of importance that the patient should not, for a considerable time, be visited by any friend or acquaintance; but should be separated from every thing connected with his late erroneous associations. The danger also is well known which attends premature return to home and common associates;—immediate relapse having often followed this, in cases which had been going on for some time in the most favorable manner.

II. Occupation. This is referable to two kinds, namely, bodily and mental. The higher states of mania in general admit of no occupation; but, on the contrary, often require coercion. A degree below this may admit of bodily occupation; and when this can be accomplished in such a manner as fully to occupy the attention and produce fatigue there is reason to believe that much benefit may result from it. Dr. Gregory used to mention a farmer in the north of Scotland who had acquired uncommon celebrity in the treatment of the insane; and his method consisted chiefly in having them constantly employed in the most severe bodily labor. As soon, also, as the situation of the patient will admit of it, mental occupation must be considered as of the utmost importance: it should not consist merely of desulto-

Principles of the moral treatment of the insane. Reasoning fruitless. Removing them from the scenes to which they have been accustomed. Occupation The Scotch farmer.

ry employment or amusement, but should probably be regulated by two principles:—1. Occupations calculated to lead the mind gradually into a connected series of thought. When the mental condition of the patient is such as to make it practicable, nothing answers so well as a course of history, the leading events being distinctly written out in the form of a table, with the dates. Thus the attention is fixed in an easy and connected manner; and in cases which admit of such occupation being continued the effect is often astonishing. 2. Endeavoring to discover the patient's former habits and favorite pursuits, at a period previous to the hallucination, and unconnected with it; and using means for leading his attention to these. I have already alluded to the complete suspension of all former pursuits and attachments which often takes place in insanity, and to a return of them as being frequently the most marked and satisfactory symptom of convalescence. This is, in such cases, to be considered as a sign, not a cause of the improvement; but there seems every reason to believe that the principle might be acted upon with advantage in the moral treatment of certain forms of insanity. On a similar principle, it is probable that in many cases much benefit might result from moral management calculated to revive associations of a pleasing kind, in regard to circumstances anterior to the occurrence of the malady.

III. Careful classification of the insane, so that the mild and peaceful melancholic may not be harassed by the ravings of the maniac. The importance of this is obvious; but of still greater importance it will probably be, to watch the first dawnings of reason, and instantly to remove the patient from all associates by whom his mind might be again bewildered. The following case, mentioned by Pinel, is certainly an extreme one, but much important reflection arises out of it in reference both to this and the preceding topic: A musician confined in the Bicetre, as one of the first symptoms of returning reason, made some slight allusions to his favorite instrument. It was immediately procured for him; he occupied himself with music for several hours

---

Mental occupation; when expedient? How to be regulated. Classification of the insane. Case of the musician

every day, and his convalescence seemed to be advancing rapidly. But he was then unfortunately allowed to come frequently into contact with a furious maniac, by meeting him in the gardens. The musician's mind was unhinged; his violin was destroyed; and he fell back into a state of insanity which was considered as confirmed and hopeless.

Cases of decided insanity in general admit of little moral treatment, until the force of the disease has been broken in some considerable degree. But among the numerous modifications which come under the view of the physician, there are various forms in which, by judicious moral management, a great deal is to be accomplished. Some of these affections are of a temporary nature, and have so little influence on a man's general conduct in life, that they are perhaps not known beyond his own family, or confidential friends. In some of these cases the individual is sensible of the singular change which has taken place in the state of his mental powers, and laments the distortion of his feelings and affections. He complains, perhaps, that he has lost his usual interest in his family, and his usual affection for them; and that he seems to be deprived of every feeling of which he was formerly susceptible. The truth is, that the mind has become so occupied by the erroneous impression as to be inaccessible to any other, and incapable of applying to any pursuit, or following out a train of thought.

A most interesting affection of this class often comes under the observation of the physician, consisting of deep but erroneous views of religion, generally accompanied with disturbed sleep and considerable derangement of the system, and producing a state of mind closely bordering upon insanity. It occurs most commonly in young persons of acute and susceptible feelings, and requires the most delicate and cautious management. Two modes of treatment are frequently adopted in regard to it, both equally erroneous. The one consists in hurrying the individual into the distraction of company, or a rapid journey; the other, in urging religious discussions, and books of profound divinity. Both are equally injudicious, especially the latter; for every attempt to discuss the important subject to which the

---

Moral treatment in decided cases. Interesting form of insanity? Its character? Common modes of treatment? Their effects?

distorted impression refers only serves to fix the hallucination more deeply. The mode of treatment which I have always found most beneficial consists of regular exercise, with attention to the general health; and in enforcing a course of reading of a nature likely to fix the mind, and carry it forward in a connected train. Light reading or mere amusement will not answer the purpose. A regular course of history, as formerly mentioned, appears to succeed best, and fixing the attention by writing out the dates and leading events in the form of a table. When the mind has been thus gradually exercised for some time in a connected train of thought, it is often astonishing to observe how it will return to the subject which had entirely overpowered it, with a complete dissipation of former erroneous impressions. A frequent complaint at the commencement of such an exercise is that the person finds it impossible to fix the attention, or to recollect the subject of even a few sentences: this is part of the disease, and by perseverance gradually disappears. This experiment I have had occasion to make many times, and it has always appeared to me one of extreme interest. I do not say that it has uniformly succeeded, for the affection frequently passes into confirmed insanity; but it has succeeded in a sufficient number of instances to give every encouragement for a careful repetition of it. The same observations and the same mode of treatment apply to the other forms of partial hallucination. The plan is, of course, to be assisted by regular exercise, and attention to the general health, which is usually much impaired. The affections are particularly connected in a very intimate manner with a disordered state of the stomach and bowels, and with derangements in the female constitution. Means adapted to these become, therefore, an essential part of the management.

There has been considerable discussion respecting the distinction between insanity and idiocy. It has been said that the insane reason justly on false premises; and that idiots reason falsely on sound premises. This does not seem to be well founded. It would appear that a maniac may reason either upon false or true premises; but that in

Proper mode of treatment? Difficulty, and remedy for it. Distinction between insanity and idiocy?

either case his reasoning is influenced by distorted views of the relations of things. The idiot, on the other hand, does not reason at all; that is, though he may remember the facts he does not trace their relations. Idiocy appears to consist, in a greater or less degree, in a simply impaired or weakened state of the mental powers; but this is not insanity. On the contrary, we have seen that, in the insane, certain mental powers may be in the highest state of activity,—the memory recalling things long gone by,—the imagination forming brilliant associations,—every faculty in the highest activity except the power of tracing correct relations. I have already referred to a gentleman mentioned by Pinel, who possessed during the paroxysm a brilliancy of conception and readiness of memory which were not natural to him. Another, mentioned by the same writer, who was infatuated with the chimera of perpetual motion, constructed pieces of mechanism which were the result of the most profound combinations, at the time when he was so mad that he believed his head to have been changed. A female, mentioned, I believe, by Dr. Rush, sang with great beauty and sweetness, which she could not do when she was sane; and a musician played, when insane, much better than when he was well.

In that remarkable obliteration of the mental faculties, on the other hand, which we call idiocy, fatuity, or dimentia, there is none of the distortion of insanity. It is a simple torpor of the faculties, in the higher degrees amounting to total insensibility to every impression; and some remarkable facts are connected with the manner in which it arises without bodily disease. A man, mentioned by Dr. Rush, was so violently affected by some losses in trade that he was deprived almost instantly of all his mental faculties. He did not take notice of any thing, not even expressing a desire for food, but merely taking it when it was put into his mouth. A servant dressed him in the morning, and conducted him to a seat in his parlor, where he remained the whole day, with his body bent forward, and his eyes fixed on the floor. In this state he continued nearly five years, and then recovered completely and rather suddenly.

The idiot? State of the faculties in insanity? Remarkable instances. State of the faculties in idiocy? Case mentioned by Dr. Rush.

The account which he afterward gave of his condition during this period was, that his mind was entirely lost; and that it was only about two months before his final recovery that he began to have sensations and thoughts of any kind. These at first served only to convey fears and apprehensions, especially in the night-time. Of perfect idiocy produced in the same manner by a moral cause an affecting example is given by Pinel:—Two young men, brothers, were carried off by the conscription, and, in the first action in which they were engaged, one of them was shot dead by the side of the other. The survivor was instantly struck with perfect idiocy. He was taken home to his father's house, where another brother was so affected by the sight of him, that he was seized in the same manner; and in this state of perfect idiocy they were both received into the Bicetre. I have formerly referred to various examples of this condition supervening on bodily disease. In some of them the affection was permanent; in others it was entirely recovered from.

The most striking illustration of the various shades of idiocy is derived from the modifications of intellectual condition observed in the cretins of the Vallais. These singular beings are usually divided into three classes, which receive the name of cretins, semi-cretins, and cretins of the third degree. The first of these classes, or perfect cretins, are in point of intellect scarcely removed above mere animal life. Many of them cannot speak, and are only so far sensible of the common calls of nature as to go, when excited by hunger, to places where they have been accustomed to receive their food. The rest of their time is spent either in basking in the sun or sitting by the fire, without any trace of intelligence. The next class, or semi-cretins, show a higher degree of intelligence; they remember common events, understand what is said to them, and express themselves in an intelligent manner on the most common subjects. They are taught to repeat prayers, but scarcely appear to annex any meaning to the words which they employ; and they cannot be taught to read or write, or

---

His own account of his condition? Idiocy produced by a moral cause: the brothers. The cretins of the Vallais. Classes of them. First class? Their condition? Second class? Their condition?

even to number their fingers. The cretins of the third degree learn to read and write, though with very little understanding of what they read, except on the most common topics. But they are acutely alive to their own interest, and extremely litigious. They are without prudence or discretion in the direction of their affairs, and the regulation of their conduct; yet obstinate, and unwilling to be advised. Their memory is good as to what they have seen or heard, and they learn to imitate what they have observed in various arts, as machinery, painting, sculpture, and architecture; but it is mere imitation without invention. Some of them learn music in the same manner; and others attempt poetry of the lowest kind, distinguished by mere rhyme. It is said that none of them can be taught arithmetic, but I do not know whether this has been ascertained to be invariably true; there is no doubt that it is a very general peculiarity.

The imbecile in other situations show characters very analogous to these. Their memory is often remarkably retentive; but it appears to be merely a power of retaining facts or words in the order and connection in which they have been presented to them, without the capacity of tracing relations, and forming new associations. In this manner, they sometimes acquire languages, and even procure a name for a kind of scholarship; and they learn to imitate in various arts, but without invention. Their deficiency appears to be in the powers of abstracting, recombining, and tracing relations; consequently they are deficient in judgment, for which these processes are necessary. The maniac, on the other hand, seizes relations acutely, rapidly, and often ingeniously, but not soundly. They are only incidental relations, to which he is led by some train of association existing in his own mind; but they occupy his attention in such a manner that he does not admit the consideration of other relations, or compare them with those which have fixed themselves upon his mind.

The states of idiocy and insanity, therefore, are clearly distinguished in the more complete examples of both; but many instances occur in which they pass into each other,

---

Third class? Describe them. The imbecile. Their memory? In what deficient? The maniac compared with them? Distinction between idiocy and insanity?

and where it is difficult to say to which of the affections the case is to be referred. I believe they may also be, to a certain extent, combined; or that there may be a certain diminution of the mental powers existing along with that distortion which constitutes insanity. They likewise alternate with one another,—maniacal paroxysms often leaving the patient, in the intervals, in a state of idiocy. A very interesting modification of another kind is mentioned by Pinel: Five young men were received into the Bicetre, whose intellectual faculties appeared to be really obliterated; and they continued in this state for periods of from three to upwards of twelve months. They were then seized with paroxysms of considerable violence, which continued from fifteen to twenty-five days, after which they all entirely recovered.

Idiocy can seldom be the subject either of medical or moral treatment; but the peculiar characters of it often become the object of attention in courts of law, in relation to the competency of imbecile persons to manage their own affairs; and much difficulty often occurs in tracing the line between competency and incompetency. Several years ago a case occurred in Edinburgh, which excited much discussion, and shows, in a striking manner, some of the peculiarities of this condition of the mental faculties:—A gentleman of considerable property having died intestate, his heir-at-law was a younger brother, who had always been reckoned very deficient in intellect; and, consequently, his relatives now brought an action into the court of session, for the purpose of finding him incompetent, and obtaining the authority of the court for putting him under trustees. In the investigation of this case, various respectable persons deponed that they had long known the individual, and considered him as decidedly imbecile in his understanding, and incapable of managing his affairs. On the other hand, most respectable evidence was produced, that he had been, when at school, an excellent scholar in the languages, and had repeatedly acted as a private tutor to boys; that he was remarkably attentive to his own interest, and very strict in

---

Sometimes connected. Remarkable case of five young men? Treatment for idiocy? Difficult question in regard to them? Case in Edinburgh. Evidence on both sides?

making a bargain; that he had been proposed as a candidate for holy orders, and, on his first examination in the languages, had acquitted himself well; but that, in the subsequent trials, in which the candidate is required to deliver a discourse, he had been found incompetent. The court of session, after long pleadings, decided that this individual was incapable of managing his affairs. The case was then appealed to the house of lords, where, after farther protracted proceedings, this decision was affirmed. I was well acquainted with this person, and was decidedly of opinion that he was imbecile in his intellects. At my suggestion the following experiment was made in the course of the investigation. A small sum of money was given him, with directions to spend it, and present an account of his disbursement, with the addition of the various articles. He soon got rid of the money, but was found totally incapable of this very simple process of arithmetic, though the sum did not exceed a few shillings. This individual, then, it would appear, possessed the simple state of memory, which enabled him to acquire languages; but was deficient in the capacity of combining, reflecting, or comparing. His total inability to perform the most simple process of arithmetic was a prominent character in the case, analogous to what I have already stated in regard to the cretins. In doubtful cases of the kind, I think this might be employed as a negative test with advantage; for it probably will not be doubted that a person who is incapable of such a process is incompetent to manage his affairs.

It is a singular fact that the imbecile are, in general, extremely attentive to their own interest, and perhaps most commonly cautious in their proceedings. Ruinous extravagance, absurd schemes, and quixotic ideas of liberality and magnificence are more allied to insanity; the former may become the dupes of others, but it is the latter who are most likely to involve and ruin themselves.

Before leaving the subject of Insanity, there is a point of great interest which may be briefly referred to. It bears, in a very striking manner, upon what may be called the pathology of the mental powers; but I presume not to touch

Decision? Appeal and final decision. Experiment with him? Its result? Singular fact in regard to the imbecile?

upon it except in the slightest manner. In the language of common life, we sometimes speak of a moral insanity, in which a man rushes headlong through a course of vice and crime, regardless of every moral restraint, of every social tie, and of all consequences, whether more immediate or future. Yet, if we take the most melancholy instance of this kind that can be furnished by the history of human depravity, the individual may still be recognised, in regard to all physical relations, as a man of a sound mind; and he may be as well qualified as other men for the details of business, or even the investigations of science. He is correct in his judgment of all the physical relations of things; but, in regard to their moral relations, every correct feeling appears to be obliterated. If a man, then, may thus be correct in his judgment of all physical relations, while he is lost to every moral relation, we have strong ground for believing that there is in his constitution a power distinct from reason, but which holds the same sway over his moral powers that reason does among his intellectual; and that the influence of this power may be weakened or lost, while reason remains unimpaired. This is the moral principle, or the power of conscience. It has been supposed by some to be a modification of reason, but the considerations now referred to appear to favor the opinion of their being distinct. That this power should so completely lose its sway while reason remains unimpaired, is a point in the moral constitution of man which it does not belong to the physician to investigate. The fact is unquestionable; the solution is to be sought for in the records of eternal truth.

IV. SPECTRAL ILLUSIONS.

The theory of spectral illusions is closely connected with that of the affections treated of in the preceding parts of this section; and I shall conclude this subject with a very brief notice of some of the most authentic facts relating to them, under the following heads:—

I. False perceptions, or impressions made upon the senses

Moral insanity Its character? Moral principle. Spectral illusions· classes. False perceptions only, in which the mind does not participate. Of this class there are several modifications, which have been referred to under the subject of perception. I add in this place the following additional examples :—A gentleman of high mental endowments, now upwards of eighty years of age, of a spare habit, and enjoying uninterrupted health, has been for eleven years liable to almost daily visitations from spectral figures. They in general present human countenances; the head and upper parts of the body are distinctly defined; the lower parts are, for the most part, lost in a kind of cloud. The figures are various, but he recognises the same countenances repeated from time to time, particularly, of late years, that of an elderly woman, with a peculiarly arch and playful expression, and a dazzling brilliancy of eye, who seems just ready to speak to him. They appear also in various dresses, such as that of the age of Louis XIV.; the costume of ancient Rome; that of the modern Turks and Greeks; but more frequently of late, as in the case of the female now mentioned, in an old-fashioned Scottish plaid of Tartan, drawn up and brought forward over the head, and then crossed below the chin, as the plaid was worn by aged women in his younger days. He can seldom recognise among the spectres any figure or countenance which he remembers to have seen; but his own face has occasionally been presented to him, gradually undergoing the change from youth to manhood, and from manhood to old age. The figures appear at various times of the day, both night and morning; they continue before him for some time, and he sees them almost equally well with his eyes open or shut, in full daylight or in darkness. They are almost always of a pleasant character, and he seems to court their presence as a source of amusement to him. He finds that he can banish them by drawing his hand across his eyes, or by shutting and opening his eyelids once or twice for a second or two; but on these occasions they often appear again soon after. The figures are sometimes of the size of life, and sometimes in miniature; but they are always defined and finished with the clearness and minuteness of the finest painting. They sometimes ap-

Examples. Form and appearance of the figures? Costume? Times of their appearing? His command over them? Their size?

pear as if at a considerable distance, and gradually ap proach until they seem almost to touch his face; at other times they float from side to side, or disappear in ascending or descending. In general, the countenance of the spectre is presented to him; but on some occasions he sees the back of the head, both of males and females, exhibiting various fashions of wigs and head-dresses, particularly the flowing, full-bottomed wig of a former age. At the time when these visions began to appear to him, he was in the habit of taking little or no wine, and this has been his common practice ever since; but he finds that any addition to his usual quantity of wine increases the number and vivacity of the visions. Of the effect of bodily illness he can give no account, except that once, when he had a cold and took a few drops of laudanum, the room appeared entirely filled with peculiarly brilliant objects, gold and silver ornaments, and precious gems; but the spectral visions were either not seen or less distinct. Another gentleman, who died some time ago at the age of eighty, for several years before his death never sat down to table at his meals without the impression of sitting down with a large party dressed in the fashion of fifty years back. This gentleman was blind of one eye, and the sight of the other was very imperfect; on this account he wore over it a green shade, and he had often before him the image of his own countenance, as if it were reflected from the inner surface of the shade. A very remarkable modification of this class of illusions has been communicated to me by Dr. Dewar of Stirling. It occurred in a lady who was quite blind, her eyes being also disorganized and sunk. She never walked out without seeing a little old woman with a red cloak and a crutch, who seemed to walk before her. She had no illusions when within doors.

II. Real dreams, though the person was not at the time sensible of having slept, nor consequently of having dreamed. A person, under the influence of some strong mental impression, drops asleep for a few seconds, perhaps without being sensible of it; some scene or person connected

---

Effect of wine? Effect of illness? Another case? Case of the blind lady? **Real dreams.**

with the impression appears in a dream, and he starts up under the conviction that it was a spectral appearance. I have formerly proposed a conjecture by which some of the most authentic stories of second sight may be referred to this principle; others seem to be referable to the principles to be mentioned under the next head. Several cases mentioned by Dr. Hibbert are also clearly of the nature of dreams. The analogy between dreaming and spectral illusions is also beautifully illustrated by an anecdote which I received lately from the gentleman to whom it occurred, an eminent medical friend. Having sat up late one evening, under considerable anxiety about one of his children, who was ill, he fell asleep in his chair, and had a frightful dream, in which the prominent figure was an immense baboon. He awoke with the fright, got up instantly, and walked to a table which was in the middle of the room. He was then quite awake and quite conscious of the articles around him; but close by the wall, in the end of the apartment, he distinctly saw the baboon making the same horrible grimaces which he had seen in his dream; and the spectre continued visible for about half a minute.

III. Intense mental conceptions so strongly impressed upon the mind as for the moment to be believed to have a real existence. This takes place when, along with the mental emotion, the individual is placed in circumstances in which external impressions are very slight; as solitude, faint light, and quiescence of body. It is a state closely bordering upon dreaming, though the vision occurs while the person is in the waking state. The following example is mentioned by Dr. Hibbert:—A gentleman was told of the sudden death of an old and intimate friend, and was deeply affected by it. The impression, though partially banished by the business of the day, was renewed from time to time by conversing on the subject with his family and other friends. After supper, he went by himself to walk in a small court behind his house, which was bounded by extensive gardens. The sky was clear, and the night serene; and no light was falling upon the court from any of the windows. As he

---

Second sight. Cases. Example; dream of the baboon. Intense mental conceptions. Under what circumstances most frequent? Case of the apparition

walked down stairs, he was not thinking of any thing connected with his deceased friend; but when he had proceeded at a slow pace about half-way across the court, the figure of his friend started up before him in a most distinct manner at the opposite angle of the court. "He was not in his usual dress, but in a coat of a different color, which he had for some months left off wearing. I could even remark a figured vest which he had also worn about the same time; also a colored silk handkerchief around his neck, in which I had used to see him in a morning; and my powers of vision seemed to become more keen as I gazed on the phantom before me." The narrator then mentions the indescribable feeling which shot through his frame; but he soon recovered himself, and walked briskly up to the spot, keeping his eyes intently fixed upon the spectre. As he approached the spot it vanished, not by sinking into the earth, but seeming to melt insensibly into air.

A similar example is related by a most intelligent writer in the Christian Observer for October, 1829:—"An intimate friend of my early years, and most happy in his domestic arrangements, lost his wife under the most painful circumstances, suddenly, just after she had apparently escaped from the dangers of an untoward confinement with her first child. A few weeks after this melancholy event, while travelling during the night on horseback, and in all probability thinking over his sorrows, and contrasting his present cheerless prospects with the joys which so lately gilded the hours of his happy home, the form of his lost relative appeared to be presented to him at a little distance in advance. He stopped his horse, and contemplated the vision with great trepidation, till in a few seconds it vanished away. Within a few days of this appearance, while he was sitting in his solitary parlor late at night, reading by the light of a shaded taper, the door, he thought, opened, and the form of his deceased partner entered, assured him of her complete happiness, and enjoined him to follow her footsteps." This second appearance was probably a dream; the first is distinctly referable to the principles stated in the preceding observations.

Effect on the observer? Case described in the Christian Observer. First appearance? Second appearance? Explanation of the two?

An interesting case referable to this head is described by Sir Walter Scott, in his late work on Demonology and Witchcraft: "Not long after the death of a late illustrious poet, who had filled, while living, a great station in the eye of the public, a literary friend, to whom the deceased had been well known, was engaged during the darkening twilight of an autumn evening in perusing one of the publications which professed to detail the habits and opinions of the distinguished individual who was now no more. As the reader had enjoyed the intimacy of the deceased to a considerable degree he was deeply interested in the publication, which contained some particulars relating to himself and other friends. A visiter was sitting in the apartment, who was also engaged in reading. Their sitting-room opened into an entrance-hall rather fantastically fitted up with articles of armor, skins of wild animals, and the like. It was when laying down his book, and passing into this hall, through which the moon was beginning to shine, that the individual of whom I speak saw right before him, and in a standing posture, the exact representation of his departed friend, whose recollection had been so strongly brought to his imagination. He stopped for a single moment, so as to notice the wonderful accuracy with which fancy had impressed upon the bodily eye the peculiarities of dress and posture of the illustrious poet. Sensible, however, of the delusion, he felt no sentiment save that of wonder at the extraordinary accuracy of the resemblance, and stepped onwards towards the figure, which resolved itself, as he approached, into the various materials of which it was composed. These were merely a screen occupied by great-coats, shawls, plaids, and such other articles as usually are found in a country entrance-hall."

On this part of the subject I shall only add the following example, which I have received from Dr. Andrew Combe: A gentleman, a friend of his, has in his house a number of phrenological casts, among which is particularly conspicuous a bust of Curran. A servant-girl belonging to the family, after undergoing great fatigue, awoke early one morning, and beheld at the foot of her bed the apparition of Curran

---

Case desc ibed by Walter Scott. Narrate the circumstances. Apparition of Curran

ran. He had the same pale and cadaverous aspect as in the bust, but he was now dressed in a sailor's jacket, and his face was decorated with an immense pair of whiskers. In a state of extreme terror she awoke her fellow-servant and asked whether she did not see the spectre. She, however, saw nothing, and endeavored to rally her out of her alarm; but the other persisted in the reality of the apparition, which continued visible for several minutes. The gentleman, it appears, keeps a pleasure yacht, the seamen belonging to which are frequently in the house. This, perhaps, was the origin of the sailor's dress in which the spectre appeared; and the immense whiskers had also probably been borrowed from one of these occasional visiters.

To the same principle we are probably to refer the stories of the apparitions of murdered persons haunting the murderer, until he was driven to give himself up to justice; many examples of this kind are on record. Similar effects have resulted in other situations from intense mental excitement. A gentleman, mentioned by Dr. Conolly, when in great danger of being wrecked in a boat on the Eddystone rocks, said he actually saw his family at the moment. In similar circumstances of extreme and immediate danger, others have described the history of their past lives being represented to them in such a vivid manner, that at a single glance the whole was before them, without the power of banishing the impression. To this head we are also to refer some of the stories of second sight: namely, by supposing that they consisted of spectral illusions arising out of strong mental impression, and by some natural coincidence fulfilled in the same manner as we have seen in regard to dreams. Many of these anecdotes are evidently embellished and exaggerated; but the following I have received from a most respectable clergyman, as being to his personal knowledge strictly true: In one of the Western Isles of Scotland, a congregation was assembled on a Sunday morning, and in immediate expectation of the appearance of the clergyman, when a man started up, uttered a scream, and stood looking to the pulpit with a countenance expressive

---

Its dress? Explanation? Explanation of apparitions of murdered persons? Effect of strong mental excitement in other cases? Stories of second sight. Authentic narrative of second sight?

of terror. As soon as he could be prevailed on to speak, he exclaimed, "Do you not see the minister in the pulpit, dressed in a shroud?" A few minutes after this occurrence the clergyman appeared in his place, and conducted the service, apparently in his usual health; but in a day or two after was taken ill and died before the following Sunday.

The effect of opium is well known in giving an impression of reality to the visions of conception or imagination; several striking examples of this will be found in the Confessions of an Opium-Eater. These are in general allied, or actually amount to the delusions of delirium, but they are sometimes entirely of a different nature. My respected friend, the late Dr. Gregory, was accustomed to relate a remarkable instance which occurred to himself. He had gone to the north country by sea to visit a lady, a near relation, in whom he felt deeply interested, and who was in an advanced state of consumption. In returning from the visit, he had taken a moderate dose of laudanum, with the view of preventing sea-sickness, and was lying on a couch in the cabin, when the figure of the lady appeared before him in so distinct a manner, that her actual presence could not have been more vivid. He was quite awake, and fully sensible that it was a phantasm produced by the opiate, along with his intense mental feeling, but he was unable by any effort to banish the vision.

Some time ago I attended a gentleman affected with a painful local disease, requiring the use of large opiates, but which often failed in producing sleep. In one watchful night there passed before him a long and regular exhibition of characters and transactions connected with certain occurrences which had been the subject of much conversation in Edinburgh some time before. The characters succeeded each other with all the regularity and vividness of a theatrical exhibition; he heard their conversation and long speeches that were occasionally made, some of which were in rhyme; and he distinctly remembered, and repeated next day, long passages from these poetical effusions. He was quite awake, and quite sensible that the whole was a phantasm, and he remarked that when he opened his eyes the

---

Effect of opium? Case of Dr. Gregory? Case observed by the author?

vision vanished, but instantly reappeared whenever he closed them.

IV. Erroneous impressions, connected with bodily disease, generally disease in the brain. The illusions, in these cases, arise in a manner strictly analogous to dreaming, and consist of some former circumstances recalled into the mind, and believed for the time to have a real and present existence. The diseases in connection with which they arise are generally of an apoplectic or inflammatory character, sometimes epileptic; and they are very frequent in the affection called delirium tremens, which is produced by a continued use of intoxicating liquors. Dr. Gregory used to mention in his lectures a gentleman liable to epileptic fits, in whom the paroxysm was generally preceded by the appearance of an old woman in a red cloak, who seemed to come up to him, and strike him on the head with her crutch; at that instant he fell down in the fit. It is probable that there was in this case a sudden attack of headache, connected with the accession of the paroxysm, and that this led to the vision in the same manner as bodily feelings give rise to dreams. One of the most singular cases on record of spectral illusions referable to this class, is that of Nicolai, a bookseller in Berlin, as described by himself, and quoted by Dr. Ferriar:—By strong mental emotions he seems to have been thrown into a state bordering upon mania; and, while in this condition, was haunted constantly, while awake, for several months, by figures of men, women, animals, and birds. A similar case is mentioned by Dr. Alderston:—A man who kept a dram-shop saw a soldier endeavoring to force himself into his house in a menacing manner; and, in rushing forward to prevent him, he was astonished to find it a phantom. He had afterward a succession of visions of persons long dead, and others who were living. This man was cured by bleeding and purgatives: and the source of his first vision was traced to a quarrel which he had some time before with a drunken soldier. A gentleman from America, who is also men-

* Effects of disease. Common character of the diseased? Example. Explanation Case of Nicolai? The keeper of the dram-shop. His cure?

tioned by Dr. Alderston, was seized with severe headache and complained of troublesome dreams; and, at the same time, had distinct visions of his wife and family, whom he had left in America. In the state of delirium tremens such visions are common, and assume a variety of forms. I have known a patient describe distinctly a dance of fairies going on in the floor of the apartment, and give a most minute account of their figures and dresses.

Similar phantasms occur, in various forms, in febrile diseases. A lady whom I attended some years ago on account of an inflammatory affection of the chest, awoke her husband one night, at the commencement of her disorder, and begged him to get up instantly. She said she had distinctly seen a man enter the apartment, pass the foot of her bed, and go into a closet which entered from the opposite side of the room. She was quite awake, and fully convinced of the reality of the appearance; and, even after the closet was examined, it was found almost impossible to convince her that it was a delusion. There are numerous examples of this kind on record. The writer in the Christian Observer, lately referred to, mentions a lady who, during a severe illness, repeatedly saw her father, who resided at the distance of many hundred miles, come to her bedside, and, withdrawing the curtain, address her in his usual voice and manner. A farmer, mentioned by the same writer, in returning from a market, was deeply affected by a most extraordinary brilliant light, which he thought he saw upon the road, and by an appearance in the light, which he supposed to be our Savior. He was greatly alarmed, and spurring his horse, galloped home; remained agitated during the evening; was seized with typhus fever, then prevailing in the neighborhood, and died in about ten days. It was afterward ascertained that on the morning of the day of the supposed vision, before he left home, he had complained of headache and languor; and there can be no doubt that the spectral appearance was connected with the commencement of the fever. Entirely analogous to this but still more striking in its circumstances, is a case which I have received from an eminent medical friend; and the

---

The American. Cases in febrile diseases The author's patient. Case described in the Christian Observer? The apparition? Explanation of it?

subject of it was a near relation of his own, a lady about fifty. On returning one evening from a party, she went into a dark room to lay aside some part of her dress, when she saw distinctly before her the figure of death, as a skeleton, with his arm uplifted, and a dart in hand. He instantly aimed a blow at her with the dart, which seemed to strike her on the left side. The same night she was seized with fever, accompanied by symptoms of inflammation in the left side; but recovered after a severe illness. So strongly was the vision impressed upon her mind, that even for some time after her recovery she could not pass the door of the room in which it occurred without discovering agitation; declaring that it was there she met with her illness.

A highly intelligent friend whom I attended several years ago, in a mild but very protracted fever, without delirium, had frequent interviews with a spectral visiter, who presented the appearance of an old gray-headed man, of a most benignant aspect. His visits were always conducted exactly in the same manner: he entered the room by a door which was on the left hand side of the bed, passed the end of the bed, and seated himself on a chair on the right hand side: he then fixed his eyes upon the patient with an expression of intense interest and pity, but never spoke; continued distinctly visible for some seconds, and then seemed to vanish into air. His visits were sometimes repeated daily for several days, but sometimes he missed a day: and the appearance continued for several weeks. The same gentleman on another occasion, when in perfect health, sitting in his parlor in the evening, saw distinctly in the corner of the room a female figure in a kneeling posture, who continued visible for several seconds.

In a lady, whose case is mentioned in the Edinburgh Journal of Science for April, 1830, there was an illusion affecting both sight and hearing. She repeatedly heard her husband's voice calling to her by name, as if from an adjoining room; and on one occasion saw his figure most distinctly, standing before the fire in the drawing-room, when he had left the house half an hour before. She went

---

The apparition of a skeleton. Effect upon the mind? The spectral visiter? Circumstances of his visits? Double illusion. Circumstances of the case?

and sat down within two feet of the figure, supposing it to be her husband, and was greatly astonished that he did not answer when she spoke to him. The figure continued visible for several minutes, then moved towards a window at the farther end of the room, and there disappeared. A few days after this appearance, she saw the figure of a cat lying on the hearth-rug; and, on another occasion, while adjusting her hair before a mirror, late at night, she saw the countenance of a friend, dressed in a shroud, reflected from the mirror, as if looking over her shoulder. This lady had been for some time in bad health, being affected with pectoral complaints, and much nervous debility. A remarkable feature of this case was the illusion of hearing; and of this I have received another example from a medical friend in England. A clergyman, aged fifty-six, accustomed to full living, was suddenly seized with vomiting, vertigo, and ringing in his ears, and continued in rather an alarming condition for several days. During this time, he had the sound in his ears of tunes most distinctly played, and in accurate succession. This patient had, at the same time, a very remarkable condition of vision, such as I have not heard of in any other case. All objects appeared to him inverted. This peculiarity continued three days, and then ceased gradually;—the objects by degrees changing their position, first to the horizontal, and then to the erect.

V. To these sources of spectral illusions we are to add, though not connected with our present subject, those which originate in pure misconception; the imagination working up into a spectral illusion something which is really a very trivial occurrence. Of this class is an anecdote, mentioned by Dr. Hibbert, of a whole ship's company being thrown into the utmost state of consternation by the apparition of a cook who had died a few days before. He was distinctly seen walking ahead of the ship, with a peculiar gait, by which he was distinguished when alive, from having one of his legs shorter than the other. On steering the ship towards the object, it was found to be a piece of floating wreck A story referable to the same principle is related by Dr.

Various apparitions. The case of the clergyman? His vision? Misconception Anecdote of the ship's company?

Ferriar:—A gentleman travelling in the Highlands of Scotland was conducted to a bedroom which was reported to be haunted by the spirit of a man who had there committed suicide. In the night he awoke under the influence of a frightful dream, and found himself sitting up in bed with a pistol grasped in his right hand. On looking round the room he now discovered, by the moonlight, a corpse dressed in a shroud reared against the wall, close by the window; the features of the body, and every part of the funeral apparel, being perceived distinctly. On recovering from the first impulse of terror, so far as to investigate the source of the phantom, it was found to be produced by the moonbeams forming a long bright image through the broken window.

Two esteemed friends of mine, while travelling in the Highlands, had occasion to sleep in separate beds in one apartment. One of them, having awoke in the night, saw by the moonlight a skeleton hanging from the head of his friend's bed; every part of it being perceived in the most distinct manner. He instantly got up to investigate the source of the illusion, and found it to be produced by the moonbeams falling upon the drapery of the bed, which had been thrown back, in some unusual manner, on account of the heat of the weather. He returned to bed and soon fell asleep. But having awoke again some time after, the skeleton was still so distinctly before him, that he could not sleep without again getting up to trace the origin of the phantom. Determined not to be disturbed a third time, he now brought down the curtain into its usual state, and the skeleton appeared no more.

The traveller in the Highlands. The apparition? Explanation of it?

PART IV.

VIEW OF THE QUALITIES AND ACQUIREMENTS WHICH CONSTITUTE A WELL REGULATED MIND.

In concluding this outline of facts regarding the intellectual powers and the investigation of truth, we may take a slight review of what those qualities are which constitute a well regulated mind, and which ought to be aimed at by those who desire either their own mental culture, or that of others who are under their care. The more important considerations may be briefly recapitulated in the following manner :—

I. The cultivation of a habit of steady and continuous attention ; or of properly directing the mind to any subject which is before it, so as fully to contemplate its elements and relations. This is necessary for the due exercise of every other mental process, and is the foundation of all improvement of character, both intellectual and moral. We shall afterward have occasion to remark, how often sophistical opinions and various distortions of character may be traced to errors in this first act of the mind, or to a misdirection and want of due regulation of the attention. There is, indeed, every reason to believe that the diversities in the power of judging, in different individuals, are much less than we are apt to imagine ; and that the remarkable differences observed in the act of judging are rather to be ascribed to the manner in which the mind is previously directed to the facts on which the judgment is afterward to be exercised. It is related of Sir Isaac Newton that when he was questioned respecting the mental qualities which formed the peculiarity of his character, he referred it entirely to the power which he had acquired of continuous attention.

Subject of Part IV? First quality? Its importance. Evils resulting from a want of it? To what two causes may differences in acts of judging be ascribed? Which most commonly the true cause? Newton's remark?

The following directions and cautions will very much assist the pupil in acquiring this intellectual habit.

1. Attempt but one thing at a time, and devote your whole attention exclusively to it. Many young persons continually violate this principle. They will try to study a lesson, and listen to an interesting conversation at the same time, hoping to secure simultaneously the advantage of the one and the pleasure of the other. But, in fact, the pleasure of the conversation is destroyed by the uneasy and distracting feeling which the circumstances occasion, and the attention to the book is of the most superficial and useless character; so that both objects are lost. In the same manner, a pupil engaged in some mathematical calculations will station himself at a window, where he may look down on some busy scene, the animating influences of which, he imagines, may cheer his labors; whereas, in fact, in such a case, he can neither enjoy the prospect nor perform his work.

2. Another most common way by which habits of inattention and wandering of mind are formed and fixed, is, not attempting exactly to do two things, but attempting one with the mind all the time perplexed with doubt whether it ought not to be doing another. This is a very common source of injury. The most ruinous consequences to the intellectual habits of the young, especially, often result from it; for they seldom have much plan or system in the arrangement of their time. He who acts from the impulse of the moment, must be always exposed to this difficulty; for this impulse will continually fluctuate and vary. He will take up one book, and after reading a page will think another would be more interesting, and changing from one to the other will lose all the benefit of both. Or he will be employed in studying a lesson, with his mind all the time distracted with the question which he continually stops to consider, whether he shall not give up his lesson and read a story, or he will read the story with a secret conviction that he ought to be studying a lesson. There cannot be practices more destructive to present enjoyment, or more ruinous to the habits of the mind.

3. Another most common cause of careless and superficial habits of attention is, undertaking what is not fairly within the powers of the individual. If a reader cannot fully understand and appreciate the work which he has undertaken, he insensibly acquires the habit of running over it with his eye, while his mind is really occupied with something else. He receives perhaps a few ideas, he catches a little of the train of thought, but he enters not into the spirit of the work at all. Thousands and thousands of books are read in this way, the reader taking merely what lies upon the surface, and having no idea that there is any thing below. This too is destructive to all correct habits of attention.

By these three precautions, viz. carefully confining the attention to the single object which for the time being is before it,—regulating the selection of objects by some systematic principle, so that while we

---

First principle? Common modes of violating it. Consequences? Second principle Common ways of violating it? Consequences. Third principle. Consequences of violating it? Recapitulation of the three principles?

are pursuing one study no other neglected duty can come in to claim our attention—and never undertaking what is not fairly within the reach of our powers,—we may soon acquire habits of continuous and steady attention, at least in the study of books. But in order to form correct habits of attention in the highest sense, it is not enough for the individual to practise on books. He must practise on men and things. That is, he must not only, when engaged in reading, attend to his books, but when out in society, and surrounded by persons, and by the various objects of life, he must attend to them. That mind is as badly disciplined which loses itself in a revery when surrounded by society, as the one which continually wanders in search of amusement when its possessor is endavoring to confine it to books. In a word, give the whole attention with a vigor and earnestness to the object, *whatever it may be,* which, for the time being, is properly before you.

Faithful practice on these principles will soon give the pupil this first quality of a well regulated mind.

II. Nearly connected with the former, and of equal importance, is a careful regulation and control of the succession of our thoughts. This remarkable faculty is very much under the influence of cultivation, and on the power so acquired depends the important habit of regular and connected thinking. It is primarily a voluntary act; and in the exercise of it in different individuals there are the most remarkable differences. In some the thoughts are allowed to wander at large without any regulation, or are devoted only to frivolous and transient objects; while others habitually exercise over them a stern control, directing them to subjects of real importance, and prosecuting these in a regular and connected manner. This important habit gains strength by exercise, and nothing, certainly, has a greater influence in giving tone and consistency to the whole character. It may not, indeed, be going too far to assert that our condition, in the scale both of moral and intellectual beings, is in a great measure determined by the control which we have acquired over the succession of our thoughts, and by the subjects on which they are habitually exercised.

The regulation of the thoughts is, therefore, a high concern, in the man who devotes his attention to it as a study of supreme importance, the first great source of astonishment will be the manner in which his thoughts have been

---

To what applicable besides the study of books? General principle? Second quality? How far voluntary? Differences of character in this respect. Consequences depending?

occupied in many an hour and many a day that has passed over him. The leading objects to which the thoughts may be directed, are referable to three classes. (1.) The ordinary engagements of life, or matters of business, with which every man is occupied in one degree or another; including concerns of domestic arrangement, personal comfort, and necessary recreation. Each of these deserves a certain degree of attention, but this requires to be strictly guided by its real and relative importance; and it is entirely unworthy of a sound and regulated mind to have the attention solely or chiefly occupied with matters of personal comfort, or of trivial importance, calculated merely to afford amusement for the passing hour. (2.) Visions of the imagination built up by the mind itself when it has nothing better to occupy it. The mind cannot be idle, and when it is not occupied by subjects of a useful kind, it will find a resource in those which are frivolous or hurtful,—in mere visions, waking dreams, or fictions, in which the mind wanders from scene to scene, unrestrained by reason, probability or truth. No habit can be more opposed to a healthy condition of the mental powers; and none ought to be more carefully guarded against by every one who would cultivate the high acquirement of a well regulated mind. (3.) Entirely opposed to the latter of these modes, and distinct also in a great measure from the former, is the habit of following out a connected chain of thoughts on subjects of importance and of truth, whenever the mind is disengaged from the proper and necessary attention to the ordinary transactions of life. The particular subjects to which the thoughts are directed in cultivating this habit, will vary in different individuals; but the consideration of the relative value of them does not belong to our present subject. The purpose of these observations is simply to impress the value of that regulation of the thoughts by which they can always find an occupation of interest and importance distinct from the ordinary transactions of life, or the mere pursuit of frivolous engagements; and also totally distinct from that destructive habit by which the mind is allowed to run to waste amid visions and fictions unworthy of a waking man.

Classification of the objects of thought? First class? Its proper importance? Second class? Influence of this habit? Third class. Influence of this habit?

In acquiring this second quality of a well regulated mind, there are several ways in which the pupil may practise. It will of course be understood that this head refers to the employment of the thoughts when they are at liberty, as when the individual is walking, or sitting alone, or engaged in those employments which do not necessarily occupy the mind. The following are some of the methods by which the mind can be in such cases usefully employed.

1. Reviewing, and fixing in the memory, what has been read, or learned in any other way. You have been engaged, we will imagine, in a book of travels; now you can call up to mind the scenes described there. Commence the journey with the traveller in imagination, anew, and go regularly forward, calling up to mind as fully as possible all the adventures and incidents which the book described. The same may be done with any other work.

2. Pursuing a connected train of thought on some useful subject selected for this purpose. You take, for instance, for your subject, "Common instances of Insincerity," and making a logical division of it, you consider one head at a time, regularly examining it in all its bearings and relations, as if you were going to write a treatise upon the subject. You first think, perhaps, of insincere professions for the sake of *civility*,—call to mind as many cases as you can, and arrange and classify them. In the next place you take cases of false appear ances assumed from *vanity*, and pursue this in the same way. Thus the whole subject may be explored, and reduced to order and system in your own mind. The subjects which may in this way be examined are innumerable.

3. Systematic and attentive *observation*. In this case, the thoughts are not engaged in reviewing past attainments, or in exploring a subject of reflection, but in examining with interest and care visible objects around. If riding through a new country he may study its geographical features, or the pursuits and occupations of its inhabitants If taking an evening walk, he can examine with care the plants or flowers he sees, or, by conversation with the various individuals he may meet with, increase his knowledge of human character and action. He may thus draw off his thoughts from the field of mere reflection, and apply them, with active interest, to the objects or the scene through which he moves. He may, if he chooses to regulate in some degree these studies, select some class of objects to examine, or some point towards which his observations shall tend. For example, when rambling in the fields, he may employ himself in finding as many *proofs of contrivance* as he can in the works of nature, and to this point direct all his inquiries and observations on his walk, whether he looks at an insect or a plant, or the form and structure of a hill.

Such are the various ways by which solitary thought may be regulated. Reviewing past studies; reflecting systematically on some new

---

Ways in which the thoughts may be employed. First mode. Example? Second mode? Example? Third mode? Examples? Recapitulation?

subject; and the scientific and active examination of nature. It must not be understood, however, that the writer recommends that every hour of reflection or solitude should be rigidly devoted to such purposes. There must be *recreation*, which such exercises will not afford; for thought, guided by these principles, will be *study*, and in the case of the young, it will be study of the severest kind. It is, however, an effort which must be often made, or the mind will never acquire the full command of its powers.

III. The cultivation of an active, inquiring state of mind which seeks for information from every source that comes within its reach, whether in reading, conversation, or personal observation. With this state of mental activity ought to be closely connected attention to the authenticity of facts so received; avoiding the two extremes of credulity and scepticism.

IV. The habit of correct association; that is, connecting facts in the mind according to their true relations, and to the manner in which they tend to illustrate each other. This, as we have formerly seen, is one of the principal means of improving the memory; particularly of the kind of memory which is an essential quality of a cultivated mind; namely, that which is founded not upon incidental connections, but on true and important relations. Nearly allied to this is the habit of reflection, or of tracing carefully the relations of facts, and the conclusions and principles which arise out of them. It is in this manner, as was formerly mentioned, that the philosophical mind often traces remarkable relations, and deduces important conclusions; while to the common understanding the facts appear to be very remote, or entirely unconnected.

It is very important that the pupil should understand distinctly and precisely what is meant by this "*correct association.*" Let us suppose a case. It may perhaps seem rather trivial, but no other one will fully illustrate the case. Suppose you are riding in the stage with a sea captain, who wears a white hat. The conversation turns on the subject of the form of ships. You tell him you should suppose that they would make their way more easily through the water if they were made narrow across the bows or forward part, and gradually increas

---

Recreation sometimes necessary. Third quality? Fourth quality? Correct association? The kind of memory essential to a cultivated mind? Tracing the relations of facts? Example to illustrate the two modes of association?

ing towards the stern, so as to force open the water like a wedge. He tells you that this is found by experience to be a bad construction, for on this plan the friction of the water is great along the whole side, whereas by making the ship broad near the bows, and gradually tapering towards the stern, it opens a sufficient passage through the water at once, and the friction along the sides is relieved. In other words, that it is more important to avoid friction along the sides, than resistance at the bows. He tells you also that the Creator has formed fishes, and all animals who are intended to move in water, on this principle.

Now after hearing such a conversation as this, a person of well disciplined mind will pause a moment, and connect these facts with his other knowledge on the same subjects—that is, the construction of ships,—the resistance of fluids,—and the admirable mechanism of the Creator's works. And he will establish this connection so firmly, that when at a future time any of these subjects come up in conversation, this information will come up too; and thus all his knowledge on such subjects, from whatever sources derived, will form one connected and harmonious whole. On the other hand, the person whose mind is undisciplined and unregulated, will perhaps have this knowledge associated in his mind with no other idea than that he was riding in a stage when he heard it, or that his informant wore a white hat. Perhaps he would not think of the subject again, until he meets, some weeks after, a gentleman in the street, wearing a white hat, the sight of which may remind him of his fellow-traveller, and the conversation about the construction of ships. Thousands of individuals have their ideas grounded on such principles as these.

Such is the difference between correct scientific association, and that which is merely accidental and trivial. And a moment's reflection will show the reader the immense superiority of the former, for all the purposes for which knowledge is to be used. We must of course learn facts and principles at various times, and under every possible variety of circumstances. But though they cannot in all cases be acquired in order, they may be put in order as soon as they are acquired. Every truth, as soon as it is possessed, must be carried *to its proper place* in the intellectual store-house, or else all will soon be inextricable confusion.

V. A careful selection of the subjects to which the mind ought to be directed. These are, in some respects, different in different persons, according to their situations in life but there are certain objects of attention which are peculiarly adapted to each individual, and there are some which are equally interesting to all. In regard to the latter, an appropriate degree of attention is the part of every wise

---

Facts stated by the captain? Proper mode of associating and remembering these facts? Improper mode? Importance of correct habits of association. Fifth quality? Selection of subjects. Principles which should guide.

man; in regard to the former, a proper selection is the foundation of excellence. One individual may waste his powers in that desultory application of them which leads to an imperfect acquaintance with a variety of subjects; while another allows his life to steal over him in listless inactivity, or application to trifling pursuits. It is equally melancholy to see high powers devoted to unworthy objects; such as the contests of party on matters involving no important principle, or the subtleties of sophistical controversy. For rising to eminence in any intellectual pursuit, there is not a rule of more essential importance than that of doing one thing at a time; avoiding distracting and desultory occupations; and keeping a leading object habitually before the mind, as one in which it can at all times find an interesting resource when necessary avocations allow the thoughts to recur to it. A subject which is cultivated in this manner, not by regular periods of study merely, but as an habitual object of thought, rises up and expands before the mind in a manner which is altogether astonishing. If along with this habit there be cultivated the practice of constantly writing such views as arise, we perhaps describe that state of mental discipline by which talents of a very moderate order may be applied in a conspicuous and useful manner to any subject to which they are devoted. Such writing need not be made at first with any great attention to method, but merely put aside for future consideration; and in this manner the different departments of a subject will develop and arrange themselves as they advance in a manner equally pleasing and wonderful.

VI. A due regulation and proper control of the imagination; that is, restricting its range to objects which harmonize with truth, and are adapted to the real state of things with which the individual is or may be connected. We have seen how much the character is influenced by this exercise of the mind; that it may be turned to purposes of the greatest moment, both in the pursuits of science and in the cultivation of benevolence and virtue; but that, on the

Frequent waste of intellectual powers. Essential principle? Effects of it? Writing? Sixth quality? The imagination, how to be regulated?

other hand, it may be so employed as to debase both the moral and intellectual character.

VII. The cultivation of calm and correct judgment—applicable alike to the formation of opinions, and the regulation of conduct. This is founded, as we have seen, upon the habit of directing the attention distinctly and steadily to all the facts and considerations bearing upon a subject and it consists in contemplating them in their true relations, and assigning to each the degree of importance of which it is worthy. This mental habit tends to guard us against forming conclusions either with listless inattention to the views by which we ought to be influenced, or with attention directed to some of these, while we neglect others of equal or greater importance. It is, therefore, opposed to the influence of prejudice and passion,—to the formation of sophistical opinions,—to party spirit,—and to every propensity which leads to the adoption of principles on any other ground than calm and candid examination, guided by sincere desire to discover the truth. In the purely physical sciences, distorted opinions are seldom met with, or make little impression, because they are brought to the test of experiment, and thus their fallacy is exposed. But it is otherwise in those departments which do not admit of this remedy. Sophisms and partial deductions are, accordingly, met with in medicine, political economy, and metaphysics; and too often in the still higher subjects of morals and religion. In the economy of the human mind, it is indeed impossible to observe a more remarkable phenomenon than the manner in which a man who, in the ordinary affairs of life, shows the general characters of a sound understanding, can thus resign himself to the influence of an opinion founded upon partial examination. He brings ingeniously to the support of his dogma every fact and argument that an possibly be turned to its defence; and explains away or overlooks every thing that tends to a different conclusion; while he appears anxious to convince others, and really seems to have persuaded himself, that he is engaged in an honest investigation of truth. This propensity gains

Seventh quality? Correct judgment. Founded on what? Effects of it? Opposed to what? In what sciences is most caution required? Common case of error on this point?

strength by indulgence, and the mind, which has yielded to its influence, advances from one pretended discovery to another,—mistaking its own fancies for the sound conclusions of the understanding, until it either settles down into some monstrous sophism, or perhaps concludes by doubting of every thing.

The manner in which the most extravagant opinions ar maintained by persons who give way to this abuse of their powers of reasoning, is scarcely more remarkable than the facility with which they often find zealous proselytes. It is, indeed, difficult to trace the principles by which various individuals are influenced in thus surrendering their assent, with little examination, often on subjects of the highest importance. In some it would appear to arise from the mere pleasure of mental excitement; in others, from the love of singularity, and the desire of appearing wiser than their neighbors; while, in not a few, the will evidently takes the lead in the mental process, and opinions are seized upon with avidity, and embraced as truth, which recommend themselves to previously existing inclinations of the heart. But whatever may be the explanation, the influence of the principle is most extensive; and sentiments of the most opposite kinds may often be traced to the facility with which the human mind receives opinions which have been presented to it by some extrinsic influence. This influence may be of various kinds. It may be the power of party, or the persuasion of a plausible and persevering individual; it may be the supposed infallibility of a particular system, it may be the mere empire of fashion, or the pretensions of a false philosophy. The particular result, also, may differ, according as one or other of these causes may be in operation. But the intellectual condition is the same; and the distortion of character which arises out of it, whether bigotry. superstition, or scepticism, may be traced to a similar process; namely, to an influence which directs the mind upon some other principle than a candid investigation of truth. In a similar manner we may perhaps account for the facts, that the lowest superstition and the most daring

Consequences? Influence of such powers on other minds? Causes of this? Various forms of it? Various ill effects? Two opposite errors to which it leads?

scepticism frequently pass into each other; and that the most remarkable examples of both are often met with in the same situations, namely, those in which the human mind is restrained from free and candid inquiry. On the other hand, it would appear that the universal toleration, and full liberty of conscience, which characterize a free and enlightened country, are calculated to preserve from the two extremes of superstition and scepticism. In other situations, it is striking to remark how often those who revolt from the errors of a false faith take refuge in infidelity.

The mental qualities which have been referred to in the preceding observations, constituting an active, attentive, and reflecting mind, should be carefully cultivated by all who desire their own mental improvement. The man who has cultivated them with adequate care, habitually exercises a process of mind which is equally a source of improvement and of refined enjoyment. Does a subject occur to him, either in conversation or reflection, in which he feels that his knowledge is deficient, he commences, without delay, an eager pursuit of the necessary information. In prosecuting any inquiry, whether by reading or observation, his attention is acutely alive to the authenticity of facts, the validity of arguments, the accuracy of processes of investigation, principles which are illustrated by the facts and conclusions deduced from them, the character of observers, the style of writers; and thus, all the circumstances which come before him are made acutely and individually the objects of attention and reflection. Such a man acquires a confidence in his own powers and resources to which those are strangers who have not cultivated this kind of mental discipline. The intellectual condition arising out of it is applicable alike to every situation in which a man can be placed, whether the affairs of ordinary life, the pursuits of science, or those higher inquiries and relations which concern him as a moral being.

In the affairs of ordinary life, this mental habit constitutes what we call an intelligent thinking man, whose attention is alive to all that is passing before him, who thinks acutely

Remedy? Effects of cultivating these qualities? On the individual's own character? On his success in life? Character formed by these habits in ordinary life?

and eagerly on his own conduct and that of others, and is constantly deriving useful information and subjects of reflection from occurrences which, by the listless mind, are passed by and forgotten. This habit is not necessarily connected with acquired knowledge, or with what is commonly called intellectual cultivation; but is often met with, in a high degree, in persons whose direct attainments are of a very limited kind. It is the foundation of caution and prudence in the affairs of life, and may perhaps be considered as the basis of that quality, of more value to its possessor than any of the sciences, which is commonly called sound good sense. It is the origin, also, of what we call presence of mind, or a readiness in adapting resources to circumstances. A man of this character, in whatever emergency he happens to be placed, forms a prompt, clear, and defined judgment of whatever conduct or expedient the situation requires, and acts with promptitude upon his decision. In both these respects he differs equally from the listless inactivity of one description of men, and the rash, hasty, and inconsiderate conduct of another. He differs not less from characters of a third class, who, though they may be correct in their judgment of what ought to be done, arrive at their decision or act upon it too slowly for the circumstances, and consequently are said, according to a common proverb, to be wise behind time. The listless and torpid character, indeed, may occasionally be excited by emergencies to a degree of mental activity which is not natural to him; and this is, in many instances, the source of a readiness of conception and a promptitude in action which the individual does not exhibit in ordinary circumstances.

In the pursuits of science these mental qualities constitute observing and inventive genius, two conditions of mind which lie at the foundation of all philosophical eminence. By *observing genius* I mean that habit of mind by which the philosopher not only acquires truths relating to any subjects, but arranges and generalizes them in such a manner

---

Is extensive knowledge essential to it? Results of it; caution and prudence. Presence of mind. Conduct in emergencies? Three classes of men, in respect to energy of action? Character formed by these habits in scientific pursuits. Observing genius,—what?

as to show how they yield conclusions which escape the mere collector of facts. He likewise analyzes phenomena, and thus traces important relations among facts which, to the common mind, appear very remote and dissimilar. I have formerly illustrated this by the manner in which Newton traced a relation between the fall of an apple from a tree, and those great principles which regulate the movements of the heavenly bodies. By *inventive genius*, again, I mean that active, inquiring state of mind, which not only deduces, in this manner, principles from facts when they are before it, but which grasps after principles by eager anticipation, and then makes its own conjectures the guides to observation or experiment. This habit of mind is peculiarly adapted to the experimental sciences; and in these, indeed, it may be considered as the source of the most important discoveries. It leads a man not only to observe and connect the facts, but to go in search of them, and to draw them, as it were, out of that concealment in which they escape the ordinary observer. In doing so, he takes for his guides certain conjectures or assumptions which have arisen out of his own intense contemplation of the subject. These may be as often false as true; but if found false, they are instantly abandoned; and by such a course of active inquiry he at length arrives at the development of truth. From him are to be expected discoveries which elude the observation, not of the vulgar alone, but even of the philosopher who, without cultivating this habit of invention, is satisfied with tracing the relations of facts as they happen to be brought before him by the slower course of testimony or occasional observation. The man who only amuses himself with conjectures, and rests satisfied in them without proof, is the mere visionary or speculatist, who injures every subject to which his speculations are directed.

In the concerns which relate to man as a moral being, this active, inquiring, and reflecting habit of mind is not less applicable than in matters of minor interest. The man who cultivates it directs his attention intensely and eagerly to the great truths which belong to his moral condition, seeks to estimate distinctly his relation to them, and to feel

---

Example? Newton. Inventive genius,—what? His guides? Proper use of theories? Character formed by these habits in respect to moral progress?

their influence upon his moral principles. This constitutes the distinction between the individual who merely professes a particular creed, and him who examines it till he makes it a matter of understanding and conviction, and then takes its principles as the rule of his emotions, and the guide of his conduct. Such a man also contemplates in the same manner his relations to other men; questions himself rigidly regarding the duties which belong to his situation, and his own observance of them. He contemplates others with a kind of personal interest, enters into their wants and feelings, and participates in their distresses. In all his relations, whether of justice, benevolence, or friendship, he acts not from mere incidental impulse, but upon clear and steady principles. In this course of action many may go along with him when the requirements of the individual case are pointed out and impressed upon them; but that in which the mass of mankind are wanting, is the state of mental activity which easily contemplates its various duties and relations, and thus finds its way to the line of conduct appropriate to the importance of each of them.

VIII. For a well regulated understanding, and particularly for the application of it to inquiries of the highest import, there is indispensably necessary a sound condition of the moral feelings. This important subject belongs properly to another department of mental science; but we have seen its extensive influence on the due exercise of the intellectual powers; and it is impossible to lose sight of the place which it holds in the general harmony of the mental functions required for constituting that condition, of greater value than any earthly good, which is strictly to be called a well regulated mind. This high attainment consists not in any cultivation, however great, of the intellectual powers; but requires also a corresponding and harmonious culture of the benevolent affections and moral feelings; a due regulation of the passions, emotions, and desires; and a full recognisance of the supreme authority of conscience over the whole intellectual and moral system. Cold and contracted, indeed, is that view of man which regards his un

---

Important distinction in regard to the adoption of moral and religious principle? Proper views of one's own duties? Of the interests of others? Of the relations of life? Eighth quality? Importance of it? What implied in it?

derstanding alone; and barren is that system, however wide its range, which rests in the mere attainment of truth. The highest state of man consists in his purity as a moral being; and in the habitual culture and full operation of those principles by which he looks forth to other scenes and other times. Among these are desires and longings which nought in earthly science can satisfy; which soar beyond the sphere of sensible things, and find no object worthy of their capacities until, in humble adoration, they rest in the contemplation of God. Truths then burst upon the mind which seem to rise before it in a progressive series, each presenting characters of new and mightier import. The most aspiring understanding, awed by the view, feels the inadequacy of its utmost powers; yet the mind of the humble inquirer gains strength as it advances. There is now felt, in a peculiar manner, the influence of that healthy condition of the moral feelings which leads a man not to be afraid of the truth. For, on this subject, we are never to lose sight of the remarkable principle of our nature formerly referred to, by which a man comes to reason himself into the belief of what he wishes to be true; and shuts his mind against, or even arrives at an actual disbelief of, truths which he fears to encounter. It is striking, also, to remark how closely the philosophy of human nature harmonizes with the declarations of the sacred writings; where this condition of mind is traced to its true source, in the corruption of the moral feelings, and is likewise shown to involve a high degree of guilt, in that rejection of truth which is its natural consequence: "This is the condemnation, that light is come into the world, and men loved darkness rather than light, because their deeds were evil. For every one that doeth evil hateth the light, neither cometh to the light, lest his deeds should be reproved. But he that doeth truth cometh to the light, that his deeds may be made manifest, that they are wrought in God."

This condition of mind presents a subject of intense interest to every one who would study his own mental condition, either as an intellectual or a moral being. In each in-

The highest state of man? Influence of lofty moral aims? Correspondence between the philosophy of human nature and the declarations of Scripture? Passage quoted?

dividual instance, it may be traced to a particular course of thought and of conduct, by which the mind went gradually more and more astray from truth and from virtue. In this progress, each single step was felt to be a voluntary act; but the influence of the whole, after a certain period, is to distort the judgment, and deaden the moral feelings on the great questions of truth and rectitude. Of this remarkable phenomenon in the economy of man, the explanation is beyond the reach of our faculties; but the facts are unquestionable, and the practical lesson to be derived from them is of deep and serious import. The first volition by which the mind consciously wanders from truth, or the moral feelings go astray from virtue, may impart a morbid influence which shall perpetuate itself and gain strength in future volitions, until the result shall be to poison the whole intellectual and moral system. Thus, in the wondrous scheme of sequences which has been established in the economy of the human heart, one volition may impart a character to the future man,—the first downward step may be fatal.

Every candid observer of human nature must feel this statement to be consistent with truth; and, by a simple and legitimate step of reasoning, a principle of the greatest interest seems to arise out of it. When this loss of harmony among the mental faculties has attained a certain degree, we do not perceive any power in the mind itself capable of correcting the disorder which has been introduced into the moral system. Either, therefore, the evil is irremediable and hopeless, or we must look for an influence from without the mind, which may afford an adequate remedy. We are thus led to discover the adaptation and the probability of the provisions of the Christian revelation, where an influence is indeed disclosed to us capable of restoring the harmony which has been destroyed, and of raising man anew to the sound and healthy condition of a moral being. We cannot perceive any improbability, that the Being who originally framed the wondrous fabric, may thus hold intercourse with it, and provide a remedy for its moral disorders; and thus a statement, such as human reason never could

---

Gradual progress away from virtue. Its influence upon moral sensibility? Consequences of a first step? Condition hopeless at last without foreign aid. From what quarter aid is to be sought. Presumption in favor of the gospel.

have anticipated, comes to us invested with every element of credibility and of truth.

The sound exercise of the understanding, therefore, is closely connected with the important habit of looking within; or of rigidly investigating our intellectual and moral condition. This leads us to inquire what opinions we have formed, and upon what grounds we have formed them what have been our leading pursuits, whether these have been guided by a sound consideration of their real value, or whether important objects of attention have been lightly passed over, or entirely neglected. It leads us further to contemplate our moral condition, our desires, attachments, and antipathies; the government of the imagination, and the regimen of the heart; what is the habitual current of our thoughts; and whether we exercise over them that control which indicates alike intellectual vigor and moral purity. It leads us to review our conduct, with its principles and motives, and to compare the whole with the great standards of truth and rectitude. This investigation is the part of every wise man. Without it, an individual may make the greatest attainments in science, may learn to measure the earth, and to trace the course of the stars, while he is entirely wanting in that higher department, the knowledge of himself.

On these important subjects, I would more particularly address myself to that interesting class for whom this work is more particularly intended, the younger members of the medical profession. The considerations which have been submitted to them, while they appear to carry the authority of truth, are applicable at once to their scientific investigations, and to those great inquiries, equally interesting to men of every degree, which relate to the principles of moral and religious belief. On these subjects, a sound condition of mind will lead them to think and judge for themselves with a care and seriousness adapted to the solemn import of the inquiry, and without being influenced by the dogmas of those who, with little examination, presume to decide with confidence on matters of eternal moment. Of the modifications of that distortion of character which has com

---

Self-examination necessary. What implied in it? Opinions and pursuits. Feelings. Conduct. Address to young students.

monly received the name of cant, the cant of hypocrisy has been said to be the worst; but there is another which may fairly be placed by its side, and that is the cant of infidelity, the affectation of scoffing at sacred things by men who have never examined the subject, or never with an attention in any degree adequate to its momentous importance. A well regulated mind must at once perceive that this is alike unworthy of sound sense and sound philosophy. If we require the authority of names, we need only to be reminded, that truths which received the cordial assent of Boyle and Newton, of Haller and Boerhaave, are at least deserving of grave and deliberate examination. But we may dismiss such an appeal as this; for nothing more is wanted to challenge the utmost seriousness of every candid inquirer, than the solemn nature of the inquiry itself. The medical observer, in an especial manner, has facts at all times before him, which are in the highest degree calculated to fix his deep and serious attention. In the structure and economy of the human body he has proofs, such as no other branch of natural science can furnish, of the power and wisdom of the Eternal One. Let him resign his mind to the influence of these proofs, and learn to rise in humble adoration to the Almighty Being of whom they witness; and, familiar as he is with human suffering and death, let him learn to estimate the value of those truths which have power to heal the broken heart, and to cheer the bed of death with the prospect of immortality.

Infidelity. Distinguished advocates of Christianity? Higher evidence of it? Conclusion?

PROFESSOR COFFIN'S WORKS.

COFFIN'S ECLIPSES.

Solar and Lunar Eclipses, Familiarly Illustrated and Explained, with the Method of Calculating them according to the Theory of Astronomy, as taught in the New England Colleges.

COFFIN'S CONIC SECTIONS.

Elements of Conic Sections and Analytical Geometry.

These works, by Prof. James H. Coffin, of Lafayette College, Pa., have received the highest recommendations from qualified authority. Of the second named, (Conic Sections, &c.) Prof. Loomis, (College of New Jersey,) Prof. Sadler, Prof. Mason, and other distinguished gentlemen, unite in approval.

BY LYMAN PRESTON.

PRESTON'S DISTRICT SCHOOL BOOK-KEEPING,

Affording an interesting and profitable exercise for youth, being especially designed for Classes in our Common Schools.

PRESTON'S BOOK-KEEPING BY SINGLE ENTRY.

Adapted to the use of Retailers, Farmers, Mechanics, and Common Schools.

PRESTON'S TREATISE ON BOOK-KEEPING;

A common-sense guide to a common-sense mind. In two parts—the first the Single Entry method, the second being arranged more particularly for the instruction of young men who contemplate the pursuit of mercantile business, showing the method of keeping accounts by Double Entry, and embracing a variety of useful forms. This is the most popular work upon the subject, and is in very extensive use throughout the country.

ADAMS'S ARITHMETICAL SERIES.

ADAMS'S PRIMARY ARITHMETIC,

Or Mental Operationsin Numbers, an Introduction to Adams's New Arithmetic, revised edition. An excellent work for young learners.

ADAMS'S NEW ARITHMETIC. Revised edition.

By Daniel Adams, M.D. A new edition of this superior work, with various improvements and additions, as the wants of the times demand. A Key is published separately.

ADAMS'S MENSURATION, MECHANICAL POWERS, AND MACHINERY.

This admirable work is designed as a sequel to the Arithmetic.

ADAMS'S BOOK-KEEPING.

A Treatise on Book-keeping by Single Entry, accompanied by blanks for the use of learners.

ABBOTT'S SERIES.

ABBOTT'S READERS.

The Mount Vernon Reader for Junior Classes. 18mo.
The Mount Vernon Reader for Middle Classes. 18mo.
The Mount Vernon Reader for Senior Classes. 12mo.

ABBOTT'S FIRST ARITHMETIC.

The Mount Vernon Arithmetic. Part First: Elementary.
The Mount Vernon Arithmetic. Part Second: Fractions.

ABBOTT'S ABERCROMBIE'S PHILOSOPHY.

Inquiries concerning the Intellectual Powers and the Investigation of Truth. By John Abercrombie, M.D. F.R.S. Edited, with additions, by Jacob Abbott.

The Philosophy of the Moral Feelings. By John Abercrombie. Edited by Jacob Abbott.

ABBOTT'S DRAWING CARDS.

In three Sets, 40 Cards to each.

WHELPLEY'S COMPEND OF HISTORY.

With Questions by Joseph Emerson. 12mo.

BADLAM'S WRITING BOOKS.

The Common School Writing Books. A New Series of Nine Numbers. By Otis G. Badlam.

ADDICK'S ELEMENTS OF THE FRENCH LANGUAGE.

An excellent elementary work.

GIRARD'S ELEMENTS OF THE SPANISH LANGUAGE.

A practical work to Teach, to Speak, and Write Spanish. By J. F. Girard.

KIRKHAM'S GRAMMAR.

English Grammar in Familiar Lectures, for the Use of Schools By Samuel Kirkham. The work is very extensively used.

DAY'S MATHEMATICS.

A Treatise for Students, by President Day, of Yale College.

THE GOVERNMENTAL INSTRUCTOR.

A Brief and Comprehensive View of the Government of the United States, and of the State Governments, in easy lessons, for the use of Schools. By J. B. Shurtleff.

THE OXFORD DRAWING-BOOK.

Containing Progressive Lessons on Sketching, Drawing and Coloring Landscape Scenery, Animals and the Human Figure. With 100 Lithographic Drawings. 4to.

JOHN RUBENS SMITH'S DRAWING-BOOK.

The Rudiments of the Art explained in Easy Progressive Les sons, embracing Drawing and Shading. With numerous Copper-plate Engravings.

STUDIES IN FLOWER PAINTING.

By Jas. Andrews. Colored plates.

DYMOND'S ESSAYS.

On the Principles of Morality, and the Private and Political Rights and Obligations of Mankind. By J. Dymond.

KEMPIS.

The Imitation of Christ. By Thomas à Kempis. Translated by John Payne, with Introductory Essay by Thomas Chalmers.

ÆSOP'S FABLES.

A New Version, by Rev. Thomas James. Illustrated by James Tenniel. The best edition published in the country.

OUR COUSINS IN OHIO.

By Mary Howitt. From the Diary of an American Mother. 18mo.

GABRIEL.

A Story of Wichnor Wood. By Mary Howitt,

THE AMERICAN SCHOOL PRIMER.

Illustrated. 46 pp., 12mo.

THE CHILD'S PRIMER.

Illustrated. 36 pp., 18mo.

JOHN WOOLMAN'S JOURNAL.

DAVID SANDS' JOURNAL.

THE NEW TESTAMENT

8vo. Large print.

ENGLISH LANGUAGE.

LOVELL'S ELOCUTIONARY WORKS.

THE UNITED STATES SPEAKER. A copious selection of exercises in Elocution, from the most approved writers. By JOHN E. LOVELL. 12mo......$1 00

NEW SCHOOL DIALOGUES; or Dramatic Selections, for the use of Schools and Families. By JOHN E. LOVELL. 12mo..................................$1 00

ABBOTT'S READERS.

THE MOUNT VERNON READER FOR JUNIOR CLASSES. 18mo..$ 19
THE MOUNT VERNON READER FOR MIDDLE CLASSES. 18mo.. 31
THE MOUNT VERNON READER FOR SENIOR CLASSES. 12mo... 63

These works are prepared by the Rev. JACOB ABBOTT, with especial reference to their moral effect upon the pupil. The distinguished reputation of the author, and his long experience as a teacher, are the best warrant of their value.

KIRKHAM'S ENGLISH GRAMMAR.

AN ENGLISH GRAMMAR FOR THE USE OF SCHOOLS. By SAMUEL KIRKHAM. 12mo.. 50

Kirkham's English Grammar is well known to the community; and, notwithstanding the host of rival treatises, still holds its place as a valuable text-book. Its sale is as large as that of any work of its size. The present edition is carefully revised, with additions by a practical teacher.

MILLS'S OUTLINES OF RHETORIC.

OUTLINES OF RHETORIC AND BELLES-LETTRES. By A. MILLS, A.M. 12mo.. 63

The author has based this work upon that of Blair, and by his judicious arrangement of his materials, has effected the desired end, to make the study interesting as well as useful to scholars.

HISTORY.

WHELPLEY'S COMPEND OF UNIVERSAL HISTORY, from the earliest times, with additions and corrections. By JOSEPH and SAMUEL EMERSON. 12mo..$ 88

An interesting and valuable compendium of historical knowledge.

GOVERNMENT.

SHURTLEFF'S GOVERNMENTAL INSTRUCTOR. A brief and comprehensive view of the Government of the United States and of the State Governments. For schools and general use. By J. B. SHURTLEFF. Revised edition. 12mo.. 50

Very valuable information, in a cheap form, for every citizen.

www.ingramcontent.com/pod-product-compliance
Lightning Source LLC
LaVergne TN
LVHW010216110826
845151LV00004B/1100

9781425526986